GW01161406

EARLY AMERICA IN MINIATURES: The 18th Century

By MARIE WOODRUFF

Photography by Charles E. Woodruff

STERLING PUBLISHING CO., INC. NEW YORK

Oak Tree Press Co., Ltd. London & Sydney

OTHER BOOKS OF INTEREST

Appliqué and Reverse Appliqué
Balsa Wood Modelling
Bargello Stitchery
Corn-Husk Crafts
Creating from Remnants
Creative Lace-Making with Thread & Yarn
Decoupage: Simple & Sophisticated
Family Book of Crafts
Family Book of Hobbies
Giant Book of Crafts
How to Make Things Out of Paper
Lacquer & Crackle
Needlepoint Simplified
Papier Mâché Crafts
Practical Encyclopedia of Crafts
Sewing Without a Pattern
Three-Dimensional Decoupage
Whittling and Wood Carving

For my daughter Kimberlee

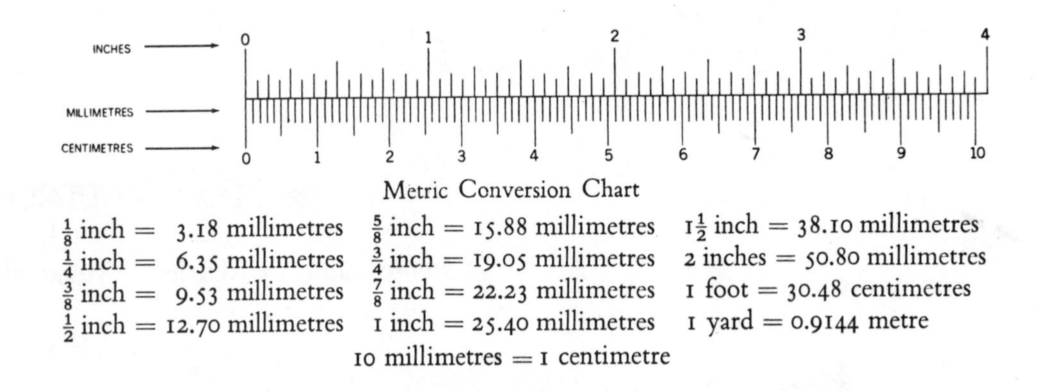

Metric Conversion Chart

$\frac{1}{8}$ inch = 3.18 millimetres	$\frac{5}{8}$ inch = 15.88 millimetres	$1\frac{1}{2}$ inch = 38.10 millimetres
$\frac{1}{4}$ inch = 6.35 millimetres	$\frac{3}{4}$ inch = 19.05 millimetres	2 inches = 50.80 millimetres
$\frac{3}{8}$ inch = 9.53 millimetres	$\frac{7}{8}$ inch = 22.23 millimetres	1 foot = 30.48 centimetres
$\frac{1}{2}$ inch = 12.70 millimetres	1 inch = 25.40 millimetres	1 yard = 0.9144 metre

10 millimetres = 1 centimetre

419 Park Avenue South, New York, N.Y. 10016
Distributed in Australia and New Zealand by Oak Tree Press Co., Ltd.,
P.O. Box J34, Brickfield Hill, Sydney 2000, N.S.W.
Distributed in the United Kingdom and elsewhere in the British Commonwealth
by Ward Lock Ltd., 116 Baker Street, London W 1
Manufactured in the United States of America

Library of Congress Catalog Card No.: 76-19797
Sterling ISBN 0-8069-5370-5 Trade Oak Tree 7061-2510-X
5371-3 Library

Contents

(Color Section Follows Page 64)

Foreword

In planning for my daughter's first Christmas, I thought it would be nice to give her a dollhouse, a really grand one with which she could play, and of which she would be proud for many years, and perhaps even pass on to her daughter some day. I shopped and shopped, but found that grand dollhouses were just not available in stores. I settled on a rugged, plastic, baby-proof dollhouse, but my mind lingered on where and how I could get my daughter that fine, elegant dollhouse.

I, therefore, began research on dollhouses, only to find that a dollhouse of the quality in which I was interested would require specially skilled craftsmen who would need several months, even years, to construct the house and its furnishings. A cabinet-type dollhouse seemed to be the most practical and economical type. But the collecting of furniture and accessories presented yet another problem.

The cost of dollhouse furniture and accessories is sometimes that of their full-scale counterparts, and in some cases even more! As a practice project, I papier-mâchéd for my daughter, Kimberlee, a white "brick" International Christmas Castle and presented it to her for her second Christmas, so that she would have a home for her collection of dolls of the world. The castle has a huge turreted balcony to house the dolls themselves, and is complete with drawbridge, electricity, "piped in" music, working tower clock, and four towers that can be lighted as lamps. It has only one room: a royal drawing room whose furnishings cost a lot several years ago. Since I had planned a nine-room colonial doll mansion, I concluded that making my own furniture and accessories would be the best answer.

Again, I found through research that there are hundreds of books written about collecting dollhouses, furnishings, and accessories throughout the entire world, but I could find almost nothing on how-to-do-it-yourself in the realm in which I was interested—the traditional one-inch to one-foot scale wood furnishings, reasonably authentic in detail—for I was not interested in anything made out of cardboard or merely suggestive of its full-scale counterpart.

There was only one way I could achieve my goal. Thus, I continued researching, now on American architecture and furnishings. I decided on an 18th century dollhouse in commemoration of America's Bicentennial.

Next, I measured all of my full-scale furnishings so that I could scale down the dollhouse miniatures to the traditional one-inch to one-foot scale. When I completed all my research,

The charming 18th century outfit worn by the owner of the Woodruff Dollhouse was modified slightly from the Simplicity Pattern #6299. Notice how well scaled the dollhouse is to its owner's size!

I designed and drew all the patterns for the furniture and accessories, and traced the patterns onto $\frac{3}{16}$-inch wood for power sawing. A few pieces were traced onto $\frac{1}{8}$-inch and $\frac{1}{4}$-inch plywood. Then the fun work began.

My husband designed and constructed the basic cabinet dollhouse itself and the circular "flying" staircase, and did all the power sawing of the furniture, while I assembled the pieces, glued, sanded, stained, sanded again, shellacked, and upholstered the furniture, decorated the dollhouse, and crafted the accessories. By Kimberlee's fourth birthday, we had enough of the Woodruff Dollhouse together to officially present it to her. My husband and I gave an 18th century birthday party for Kimberlee and 17 of her friends for whom I made mob caps and cavalier hats in true spirit of colonial America. Kimberlee wore a complete 18th century ensemble that I had made for her. Her lavishly decorated birthday cake, designed and baked by Mrs. Sandy Cameron of Palos Verdes Estates, California, was topped with a six-inch-tall doll whose costume was a replica of Kimberlee's birthday ensemble. It was this doll that spearheaded the idea to design and to make period costumes for the dolls of the house as well. Most dollhouses are uninhabited. If they are peopled, the dolls are dressed very dowdily in commercially made costumes and are somehow insignificant to the "setting." Research indicated that it is difficult to clothe six-inch dolls without glueing the clothes or sewing them right onto the dolls themselves. I did not find this so at all, probably because I designed very simple patterns that any novice could follow, and varied the styles by using lace and other accessories. The vests on the men actually button with real, miniature buttons!

An entire summer was spent on designing and making chandeliers, drapes, accessories, and rugs, as well as designing and making costumes for 18 dolls.

Furnishing and decorating the Woodruff Dollhouse will never really be finished. It will be a lifetime family project of fun just like furnishing and decorating our real house.

* * *

The purpose of this book is to aid you in making an elegant and grand dollhouse on which you need not spend an exorbitant amount of money.

The book is not a history on or a guide to collecting dollhouse miniatures, but rather a step-by-step guidebook of patterns, ideas, and suggestions to help you build a dollhouse, and to make and to personalize authentic period furniture and accessories in true scale. There are also simple, easy-to-follow patterns for all the dolls' costumes and their accessories.

It is simple to buy miniatures of which there are thousands available. Some of them are of good quality; others are only fair. All are expensive! Good quality miniatures have increased approximately 50 per cent in price in the last few years. Miniatures are big business, and they are a good investment. Think how much more valuable a one-of-a-kind piece of furniture upholstered in a remnant from your daughter's first birthday dress will be a few years from now, not only in terms of monetary worth, but sentimental value. Think what your dollhouse will be worth when your little girl is ready to pass it on to her daughter! Of course, a generation from now, there will surely be changes made in the dollhouse, for, like furnishing your own home, even after the dollhouse is completely equipped, you may want to add an accessory here and there, or reupholster a chair, or supplement the wardrobe. And, even though you may want to follow the patterns in this book per se, the choice of stain or fabric or color or decoration is still yours, in which case the miniature then becomes a special creation quite unlike any other.

One of the prerequisites to starting a dollhouse project is to be aware of the value of discards. Building your own dollhouse is excellent conservation practice. A bottle cap, for instance, has many possibilities. For example, you can make—for virtually nothing—a fine, copper pot that you would have to otherwise buy by using a shallow bottle cap and a tiny strip of stiff cardboard for the handle, and then spraying the entire project with copper-colored enamel. A bottle cap enamelled and embellished with hand-painted decorations or decoupaged ornaments takes on an imported porcelain look that would cost quite a bit to buy. A bottle cap and coat hanger wire for the handle sprayed flat black makes an authentic-looking cooking pot for the fireplace. A bottle cap covered with pretty Con-Tact paper, gift wrapping paper or some colorful fabric and ribbon makes a convincing hat box (see page 132 for other uses for the bottle cap). There are literally hundreds of everyday discards—from scraps of fabric to inexpensive junk jewelry—that are discussed in this book to help you imaginatively craft beautiful, authentic period furnishings for your dollhouse.

Finally, a dollhouse project is a wonderful family activity. Souvenirs from family trips and vacations are fun to collect. Also, everyone can do something, whether it is power sawing, building, handicrafting and decorating, or simply contributing fabrics or shopping for furnishings. Even the children for whom the dollhouse is built can help; Kimberlee helped knead, out of baker's clay (see page 32), the miniature loaves of bread which are expensive to buy! She also helped select fabrics for the dolls' costumes, and toys for the child's bedroom.

I wrote this book to help you and your family get as much of a thrill assembling and furnishing your heirloom dollhouse as we did.

Marie Woodruff

Introduction

The Woodruff Dollhouse described in this book was designed in commemoration of the United States Bicentennial. All the furnishings, as well as the accessories and decorations, are authentic to that historical period. Thus, all the patterns for the furniture here are for 18th century (or earlier) styles.

You do not need to imitate every aspect of this house in creating yours. You can—in fact, you should—choose an historical time period you are interested in. You can then adapt the furniture patterns here to suit your needs, or you can mix some of the colonial and antique styles presented here with the décor of your choice. The vogue in home decorating today is mix-and-match—this holds true for your dollhouse as well. Do not feel restricted by the specific ideas here, but use the ingenious and creative ideas to construct the dollhouse of your dreams.

If you do decide upon creating an 18th century dollhouse, it is helpful for you to understand something of 18th century American homes and the way of life of the people who lived in them.

A Glance at the Homes of 18th Century America

The 18th century in America was an era of settlement, colonial development, independence, nationalism, and democracy. Most of all, it was a time of achievement, wealth, and elegance, particularly after the end of the hard-fought battle for independence.

The typical house in Colonial America was adapted from the Italian Palladian style, first evident during the 16th century. Colonial America copied the basic Palladian style, but called it Georgian. Even though the Palladian-Georgian home was architecturally symmetrical, the Georgian style in the United States did not have four geometrically identical sides as did the true Palladian style in Europe. The homes were usually built of wood; better homes utilized stone or brick.

The typical house consisted of a grand central hall, which extended through the entire house, flanked on each side by two spacious rooms to which were sometimes attached one- or two-storey dependencies. The grand staircase led from the central hall on the ground floor to the central hall on the next floor. Three-storey homes were not uncommon.

The Home Interior

Increasing success and prosperity enabled the colonists to lavishly furnish and decorate their expensive mansions. Imported books on architecture and interior decoration from abroad had a tremendous impact on the lives of the affluent colonists. England was the major source of interior decorating information, but France, Italy, and the Orient also contributed a variety of interesting ideas.

Lighting and heating were crude by 20th century standards, but certainly much more romantic. Candles were the chief source of light, although later in the century, Benjamin Franklin invented the wick-tube oil lamp, from which evolved lamps made of hurricane glass and ornate porcelain. The oil lamp provided better light less expensively than the candlewick. Silver, brass, pewter, and crystal chandeliers were perfected in design, grandiosity, and elegance during the colonial times. Wall candle sconces and romantic candle holders were numerous throughout the house.

Wood and coal were the only sources of heat; therefore, almost every room was equipped with either a fireplace, a Franklin stove (invented by Benjamin Franklin), or a pot-bellied stove. Fireplaces were especially popular. They were beautifully designed and richly decorated with mantels and over-mantels, and were usually set as the focal point of the room. Invariably, the fireplace wall was the most richly adorned wall in the room, almost as if in tribute to the fireplace.

Water was drawn from a well and brought into the house for all domestic use. The water pitcher and basin served as the 18th century's water faucet and sink. Chamber pots kept under the bed were essentially the 18th century's small portable toilets.

Because a wide variety of woods was plentiful, walls were generally richly dado (that is, with the lower part decorated differently, such as with wood panels, than the upper part) or full-wall panelled, or painted over in white, grey, green, or teal blue. Popular woods were teakwood, walnut, mahogany, pine, and oak. Silk and damask fabrics, mural paintings, imported wallpapers, and tapestries were becoming popular replacements for the white-washed plaster walls. Queen Anne framed mirrors, silhouette paintings, spoon racks, embroidered samplers, candle sconces, portrait paintings, and on-the-wall clocks were among the important wall decorations. Projecting dentiled cornices, and shell and acanthus leaf wood carving for the walls, pediments, and cabinets all distinguished the Georgian décor.

Ceilings were decoratively plaster-ornamented, beamed, or just left plain and painted. Some ceilings had rosette mouldings from which chandeliers were hung.

Floors were generally pine wood plank; better floors were made from teakwood, cherry, or beech parquetry. Imported Aubusson and Oriental rugs, and domestically made oval-braid, hooked, needlepoint, and embroidered rugs adorned the highly polished, stained floors.

Windows were adorned with draperies of imported silks, damasks, and linens, trimmed with fringes and laces, and corniced with valances, the swag and cascade being the most popular styles. Matching fabric from the draperies was sometimes used for bed coverings, furniture upholstery, and walls. Venetian blinds came into use during the 1760's.

Furniture played an important rôle in interior decorating. Like architecture, furniture design came from abroad—mostly England—and was expertly copied in America. Some of the most important furniture styles during the colonial period were Queen Anne, Adam, Windsor, and Chippendale from England, and Louis XV from France.

American furniture was generally stained in walnut or mahogany; occasionally it was ornamented.

Japanning, a paint and varnish method of imitating Oriental lacquer for decorative work, was influenced by the colonists' interest in Oriental adornment. Japanning was usually applied to cabinets, grandfather clocks, mirror frames, and serving trays. Oriental folding screens and prints were also popular.

The Pennsylvania Dutch settlers brought with them their "peasant" art, depicting delightful, cheerful designs of flowers, birds, and hearts, which they painted on their furniture for the sheer love of color and decoration. However, this furniture art was not accepted by the bourgeois of the 18th century.

Accessories were proudly, and conspicuously, displayed on the numerous mantels and in corner cabinets. Fine imported porcelain chinaware and figurines came from England, France, Germany, and Italy. Waterford crystal glasswares and chandeliers came from Ireland. American production of glazed stoneware and woodenwares began late in the century. In Pennsylvania, Henry Stiegel was one of the first glassmakers to produce crystal-like Stiegel glass (1765–1774).

Silverwares were manufactured at home and used abundantly both decoratively and pragmatically. Pewter, brass, copper, and wrought iron were used to make accessories, lamps and chandeliers, and eating and cooking utensils.

No home was complete without a grandfather clock, a Bible box, and a footwarmer. Beautiful clocks of several styles and types were used abundantly throughout the house, especially on fireplace mantels. And the spinning wheel, weaving loom, butter churn, and washtub and scrub board were all absolute necessities.

Home crafts, such as quilting, embroidery, rug-braiding, needlepoint, and wood carving, were practical as well as decorative in 18th century households. Today, there has been a tremendous resurgence of these crafts in our homes.

The People and What They Wore

People emigrated to the new country from all over Europe. Families were large and close-knit. Food preparation, spinning, weaving, and related domestic activities were centralized in the kitchen and service quarters. Lack of speed and conveniences in the 18th century kitchen was compensated for by a domestic staff, which was readily accessible to the lady of the house so that she could indeed be a lady of leisure. With such an abundance of spare time, families of means could enjoy much leisure, comfort, and elegance in their homes. They also could pursue all the latest fashions from abroad.

Costume design in the 18th century reached unprecedented elegance. It was also a time of such extravagant extremes in design that doors, stairways, and carriages had to be modified in order to accommodate the voluminous clothing. The clothes were beautiful, but they were seldom comfortable to wear.

High fashion styles for both women and men came from England and France. But the American women were far more fashion-conscious, often to the point of obsession, than the Europeans.

Prior to the French Revolution in 1789, women's gowns were ankle length to reveal the slippers slightly; sleeves were three-quarter length, usually terminating in wide flowing ruffles; bodices were long-waisted, ending in a V-shape; and necklines were daringly low.

Men's clothing basically included a coat, waistcoat, breeches, silk stockings, buckled shoes, and tricorne hat. Men's clothing was much more elaborately cut, embroidered, and costly than the women's. But it never became as extreme and ridiculous.

Early in the century, women wore the sack-back, or Watteau, gown, which had a train flowing from the shoulders to the hem. Round hoops, made like a cage, were worn to make the myriad of skirts stand out, sometimes to six feet in diameter. The overdress opened at the waist to show the petticoat, which was usually of contrasting color and fabric. Corsets, made of whalebone, were laced in back to mould the desired shape of the body. For outdoors, women wore a red-hooded cloak.

Men wore a collarless, double-breasted greatcoat with huge embroidered cuffs and large pockets. The waistcoat was often elaborately hand-embroidered in either a matching or contrasting color and fabric. Large lace cravats, lace-frilled shirt cuffs, and cocked hats were all important in this era. Breeches were worn throughout the century.

Women's hair was simply swept off the face with either short curls worn close to the head or long curls draped down in back. Headwear was generally small lace caps.

Very early in the century, men wore the full bottom wig, a mass of curls falling at the shoulders and in back, but later they adopted the smaller, pigtail wig for neatness and convenience.

Women carried folding fans; men carried swords. Both wore silk stockings and buckled, high heel shoes, although the men's were slightly lower than the women's heel. The men also wore top boots.

Make-up applied sparingly, perfume, and face patches (imitation beauty spots) were worn by both women and men. The gentlemen padded out their thin calves much like 20th century women pad out their flat chests. Wigs of varied styles were worn by both sexes until the very late 18th century.

In the mid-18th century, feminine fashions called for extravagantly wide, oval hoops which were worn to make the skirts stand out to ridiculous proportions. Overskirts were panniered (drawn up into hoops at the sides) to reveal more of the petticoat which was often decoratively quilted. Mob caps, lace aprons, and fichus (a three-cornered cape) distinguished the "milkmaid" fashion that was popular with all classes. Stomachers, ornamented with laces or lacings, were worn as coverings for the chest. Small capes (mantelets) and muffs for cold weather, as well as umbrellas and handkerchiefs, all appeared during this period. Fichus were worn both for warmth and for decency because the necklines were so low.

The men's greatcoat in the Cossack style became single-breasted, with the fullness of the coat comparable to that of the women's skirts. Cuffs were still large, but narrow Cravats became smaller. Both the coat and the waistcoat were more lavishly embroidered than ever before.

Women's coiffures heightened as the skirts widened. The hair was swept off the face and piled high from the forehead over a padded wire frame, with long curls hanging down at back and over the shoulders, and powdered white for a formal look. Wigs and wool were necessary to supplement the hair for the desired style. The hair-do was topped with feathers, beads, ribbons, or a small lace cap. Mob caps, made famous by Martha Washington, were worn at night to protect the elaborate hair-do that was a work of art indeed!

The height of men's hair-dos (called cadogans) matched the elevation of women's pompadours. Tricorne hats became smaller and were often carried rather than worn.

From the mid- to late-18th century, American women began to turn more to French designers, whereas previously England was leader of the fashion world. Panniers were not drawn up to bulge out so much, but ruffles and lace were used lavishly. The sleeves, as well as the overskirt along the front diagonal edges, and the underskirt above the hem, were all trimmed in matching ruffles or laces. The two skirts were made of either matching or contrasting color and fabric. By 1780, the hoop disappeared, but the polonaise style dress remained basically the same, except that the bustle, a padding to fill out the upper back of the skirt, replaced the panniers. The pelisse, a cloak edged with fur, was used for outdoor wear.

Men wore single-breasted, silk-lined, "cutaway" coats with tails in back, narrow sleeves with no cuffs, and no embroidery. The waistcoat became longer and was less frequently embroidered. The cravat was replaced by the black ribbon solitaire.

Both the pompadour and the cadogan continued to rise, reaching their highest in the 1770's. The big bouffant bonnet, Gainsborough hat, and mob cap were in vogue for the women. The "Napoleonic" style cocked hat introduced at this time had the front and back brim turned up, and remained popular into the 19th century.

Beautifully carved walking sticks were carried by both the women and the men.

Throughout the 18th century, there was little change in styles of clothing, as we know change today, until very late in the century when the French Revolution (1789) brought a halt to elegant extravagance in clothes, and country living, popular in England, led to informal, rural living. It was inevitable then that the simplicity, and comfort, adopted by the English would have an impact on fashions in America.

Women's skirts were straight; the waistline was short; the sleeves were either short-puffed, or three-quarter length and unadorned. The total look was classic and "Grecian." Large, fur muffs, shawls, and Spencer coats (waist-length jackets) appeared late in the century. Hats assumed various styles. The handbag was introduced, and has been women's most indispensable accessory ever since.

The new look for men included a double-breasted coat which was cut horizontally at the waist and diagonally from the hips to the long, double tails in back. The collar was a small, stand-up type around which scarves could be wrapped. The double-breasted waistcoat was shortened to the waist. No embroidery was used. The new hat was a small brim with high crown. Watches were worn dangling out of the pocket.

Women's hair fashions became reminiscent of the Charles I style—that is, a mass of short, loose curls fell around the forehead and temples, with longer curls cascading to the shoulders and back. Powder was no longer used on the hair.

Men wore their natural hair in a pigtail in back with horizontal ringlets at the sides to look like a wig.

The high heel drastically lowered in both the women's and men's shoes, now without the buckle, and helped to make walking a fashionable pastime.

Throughout the century, children were clothed much like their parents. Little boys wore clothing like the little girls up to the age of six, after which they were dressed like their fathers. Very late in the century, little boys wore "sailor trousers" (much like today's pants) with sash and lingerie blouse.

You will get a true picture of the homes and clothes of 18th century America, as they have been presented here, as you read through the rest of this book.

The Basic Tools, Equipment, and Materials

A work area with a carpenter's bench, such as a garage, or a part of a basement, is necessary for at least the sawing, sanding, and drilling.

You should set aside another work area, preferably in the house, for assembling and glueing the furniture pieces and accessories, and for staining, painting, upholstering, decorating, and sewing. You will probably work on your dollhouse project more consistently if you do not have to clear off and clean up the work area at the end of each work session. Most of the work, however, can be done on a small table, portable tray, or even a shallow box while you are watching television. Portable trays or shallow boxes are especially good to use because you can store them out of sight after you have finished working on the project for the day.

You should also set aside some storage space, such as boxes, drawers or cabinets, for storing, collecting, and identifying the furniture pieces, and the accessory, upholstery, sewing, and decorating materials and equipment. This way, everything can be readily available and well organized.

Following is a listing of the tools, equipment and materials used to make the Woodruff Dollhouse.

Carpentry, Decorating and Sewing Tools and Equipment

High-speed power jig saw: for cutting all the dollhouse parts and furniture pieces;

Blades: in sizes 14 teeth to the inch (for $\frac{1}{2}$-inch plywood), 24 (for $\frac{3}{16}$-inch plywood), and 32 (for $\frac{1}{4}$- and $\frac{1}{8}$-inch plywood);

Drills: with various-sized bits;

Pliers: to cut 20-gauge and coat hanger wire; to screw on eye hooks;

Paint and stain equipment: turpentine for removing paints and stains; shellac thinner for removing shellac; water for removing acrylics; several inexpensive brushes in various sizes; lots of rags for staining and wiping;

Sewing machine (optional): for sewing the dolls' costumes; although most, if not all, of the sewing can be done by hand (all bed coverings and drapes were sewn by hand);

Sewing notions: such as threads and needles, a measuring tape, two pairs of scissors (one pair that you can afford to ruin for cutting sandpaper);

Other tools and equipment: carbon paper, pencils, and a straight-edge ruler and tracing paper for tracing the patterns to plywood for sawing; utility knife (or razor blade) for scoring the floors; tiny nails about $\frac{5}{8}$-inch long for hanging pictures; a small hammer (optional) for the tiny nails; a screwdriver for putting on hinges; a lot of white glue.

Wood

Plywoods: $\frac{1}{2}$-inch thick of the best quality plywood for all the walls, floors, ceilings, and roof; $\frac{3}{16}$-inch plywood for most of the furniture (one standard wood panel, 4 feet × 8 feet × $\frac{3}{16}$-inch, available fairly inexpensively at a lumberyard, is enough to make furniture for two dollhouses); a few scrap pieces of the $\frac{1}{4}$- and $\frac{1}{8}$-inch plywoods (all the shutters are of $\frac{1}{8}$-inch thick plywood);

Dowels: about 6 feet of $\frac{1}{4}$-inch dowelling for fitting the walls, floors, ceilings, and roof (can also be used for furniture legs and coat-and-hat rack); about 2 to 3 feet of $\frac{1}{8}$-inch dowelling for drapery rods, wardrobe closet bars (cotton swab sticks can be used in some instances); about 50 ($\frac{1}{4}$-inch diameter, $2\frac{1}{2}$-inch high) turned dowels for staircase balusters;

Artist's plaques (optional): for panelling the walls and for table tops (although you can cut these out of $\frac{1}{8}$-inch plywood or heavy cardboard);

Veneer stripping: about 10 to 12 feet (comes in $\frac{1}{2}$- to 1-inch widths) for window glazers, around fireplace openings, and wherever you want inlay work;

Other tools and equipment: wood filler to fill irregularities in wood; sandpaper in various grades for sanding all wood pieces and for brickwork in the kitchen; white glue (in bulk quantities); acetate for the see-through windows; light-weight cardboard for the gold-leafed French chairs, valances, dressing table, and chair seats to be padded and upholstered;

Decorator plaques: four on the folding façade doors for architectural interest (approximate size for the ones shown on page 19 is 8 × 24 inches).

Hardware

Hinges: eight for the folding façade doors; four miniature-sized ones for the two wardrobes;

Small eye hooks: nine to hang the chandeliers in each room; 12 to hang the drapery rods; two to hang the fireplace crane; two for the swinging wardrobe bar (in the dressing room);

Wire: 20-gauge for the clothes hangers in the wardrobes; coat hanger wire for fireplace accessories;

Combination lock (optional): for the folding façade doors.

Paints and Stains

Stains: a variety of about four to five different kinds for the collected look; suggested stains are mahogany, fruitwood, walnut, maple, and teakwood;

Acrylic paint: you need about a half gallon for painting the outside of the dollhouse, the walls, and some of the furniture pieces (acrylic paint results in a flat finish and is extremely fast-drying in comparison to enamels; you can use it instead of hobby paints or enamels);

Hobby paints (enamels): get very small-sized jars of gold, brass, silver, copper, flat black, and pewter to simulate the various metals popular during the 18th century; optional: small jars of off-white, light blue or teal, navy, and red for a few furniture pieces for variety;

Shellac: one quart for protecting all the stained furniture and floors; you can also use shellac for decoupage work.

Decorating Materials

Con-Tact paper and/or gift-wrap paper: for wallpapering walls, covering a hat box or toy box, and lining drawers or closets;

Scenic magazine cut outs: for murals or wallpaper;

Stones (small, flat ones): for studding a fireplace or a wall;

Laces and trims: for ceiling trims and borders; for creating a carved-wood look;

Plastic doilies: for rosette ceiling mouldings; for creating a carved-wood look;

Crocheted doilies: for rugs, tablecloths, and bed coverings;

Fabrics: for covering walls;

Plastic foam: for chandeliers and books; also excellent for chair seats;

Other decorating supplies: placemats, potholders, and handkerchiefs for rugs and bed coverings; decorative picture hooks for furniture decorations; hardware discs for sconces.

Clothing and Upholstery Materials

Fabrics (remnants or old clothing): for upholstery, rugs, tablecloths, dolls' costumes, bed linens and coverings, and drapes;

Laces and trims: for costume and upholstery decoration;

Yarns and embroidery threads: for upholstery and upholstery trims, drapery trims and dolls' wigs; for hanging pictures, and for all needlework;

Foam rubber: for padding upholstery pieces;

Tiny beads: for buttons and trims.

Materials for Accessories

Bottle caps: all sizes and types to make a vase, bowl, compote, cake cover, wastepaper basket, candy dish, coal bucket, hat box, toy drum, lamp base, lamp shade, horn of plenty, chamber pot, footstool, basket, candleholder, drinking beaker, water tumbler, wash basin, hat base, newspaper rack, frying pan, or much more (see also the chapter "Accessories" on page 132);

Buttons: for dishes and bowls;

Plastic moulds (that manufacturers use to protect their products): for dishes, and pots and pans;

Tin-can lids: for trays, table tops, picture frames, and chandeliers;

Dishwasher soap dispensers: for spindled newspaper rack, wastepaper basket, and bird cage;

Cosmetic brushes: for fireplace brushes and brooms;

Plastic tubing: $\frac{1}{8}$-inch diameter for napkin holders; $\frac{1}{4}$- to $\frac{1}{2}$-inch for hurricane lamps;

Sample lipstick tubes: for tumblers, beer steins, and drinking beakers;

Shoe buckles: for firescreens;

Tin-can lift rings: for towel rings;

Pillboxes: for bedwarmers and Bible boxes;

Mirror discs: $\frac{1}{2}$-inch diameter for mirrors, folding screens, and sconces;

Thread spools: for umbrella stand, table base, and lamps;

Old costume jewelry (beads, filigrees, chains, glitter, push pins): for lamps, chandeliers, perfume bottles, candleholders, pictures, fruit, mirror sconces, buttons on costumes, doorknobs, drawer pulls, Christmas tree baubles, and many other items;

Ornate, plastic, fruit baskets: for fireplace grates and andirons;

Other materials for accessories: cake decorations, party gifts, food and candy prizes, charms, magnetic memo holders, cocktail stirrers, and costume jewelry often come in almost any shape from frying pans to various fruits in miniature size suitable for the dollhouse; this is a very good, economic way to collect a great many fine accessories for your dollhouse.

The Basic Cabinet Dollhouse

The advantages of a basic cabinet-type dollhouse are primarily two-fold: it is economical and easy to construct due to the simplicity of its design; and it is compact so you can display it against a wall without having to set it in the middle of the room since it does not need to be viewed all around as a two-sided dollhouse does.

A one-inch to one-foot scale was used for practical reasons. One-inch scale dollhouses and miniatures are more popular, sought after, and valuable than any other scale miniatures. Thus, if you are planning to make only some of the miniatures, and buy the rest, you will be able to buy things in the proper proportionate sizes.

Another reason for choosing the one-inch scale is for economy of space. The Woodruff Dollhouse is 46 inches wide, 49½ inches high, and 15½ inches deep. Thus, it does not require much space to store.

One-half inch, fine quality plywood was used for the construction of the entire house. Flat, white acrylic paint was used to give the house a stately New England look. No nails or glue were used in building the actual dollhouse itself. The house is completely dowelled so that it can be disassembled to facilitate decorating the walls, floors, ceilings, and windows. If you have ever decorated a dollhouse that could not be dismantled, you well know what a difficult job decorating the dollhouse can be. Another advantage to the dowelling is that you can easily take the dollhouse apart for packing and travelling, if necessary.

The house has nine rooms and three stories. For storage purposes, there is also an attic, accessible by lifting the dowelled roof. The first and third floor ceilings are 10 inches high; the second storey ceiling is 12 inches high. The elaborate, circular "flying" staircase is described in the chapters covering the Entrance Hall, the Sitting Room, and the Master Bedroom.

All the outside rooms have see-through windows made of heavy acetate plastic for the glass, and $\frac{1}{16}$-inch strips of veneer for the window glazers. For the window moulding, ¼-inch strips of veneer were used around the interior and exterior windows. All the draperies hang from ⅛-inch thick rods that run through the top hem of the draperies and a pair of eye hooks on either side of the window. Brown wood shutters complement all the outside windows of this New England colonial mansion.

The shingles are 1¾ inches by 1¼ inches cut from coarse sandpaper and glued on in the same pattern that real shingles would be installed. Approximately 475 shingles were used for the roof. The apex is finished off by folding sandpaper over the apex to conform to the depth of the shingles.

In keeping with true authenticity, the dollhouse is not wired for electricity. For light, the dollhouse has nine, real candle-burning chandeliers, one for each room of the house.

The façade is a pair of simple, hinged folding doors on which are mounted decorator plaques for a Queen Anne architectural effect. On one of the plaques, you can put the initials of the owner of the dollhouse. A miniature combination lock is optional. This type of simple folding door façade on a cabinet-type dollhouse has been a very popular adaptation used on many famous museum dollhouses throughout the history of dollhouses.

The Woodruff (Woodroffe) family coat-of-arms adorns the pediment. If your family does not have a coat-of-arms, you can use any other decoration here—or none—that you want. Remember that whatever you choose should agree with the period style of your dollhouse.

A basic cabinet-type dollhouse closes up compactly when it is not being used. You can decorate the front with the owner's initials, and with the family coat-of-arms as well.

Patterns and Instructions for the Basic Cabinet

Pattern for the First Floor or Base

Cut one piece from 1/2" thick plywood.

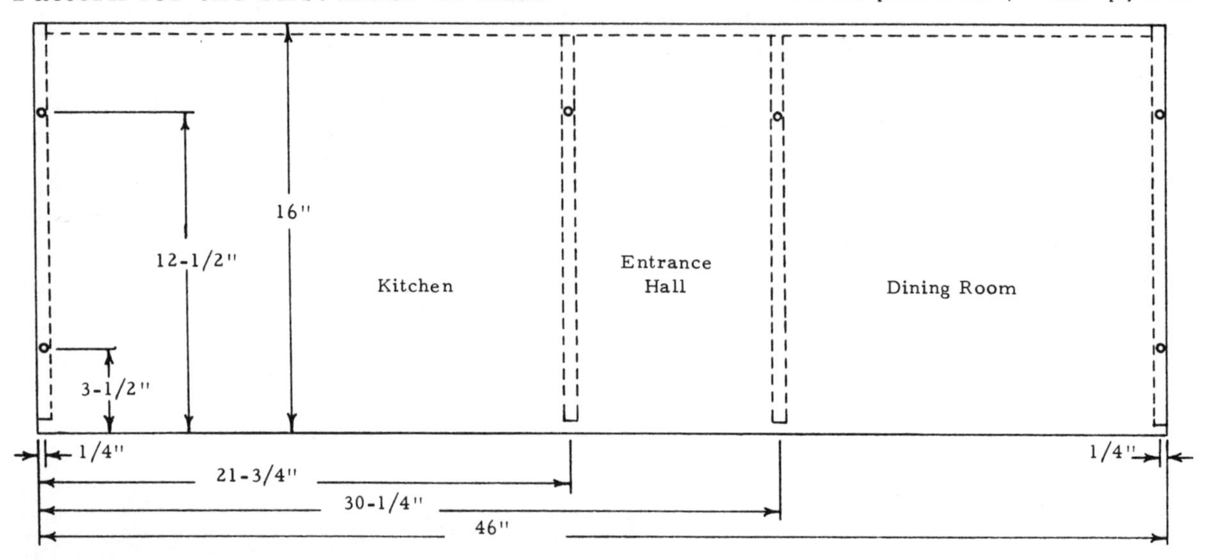

The sides fit into the holes at both sides. The back fits into the holes in the sides. Add rubber feet or felt pads to the underside of the base to prevent scratching furniture or floors.

Pattern for the First-Floor Ceiling and Second Floor.

Cut one piece from 1/2" thick plywood.

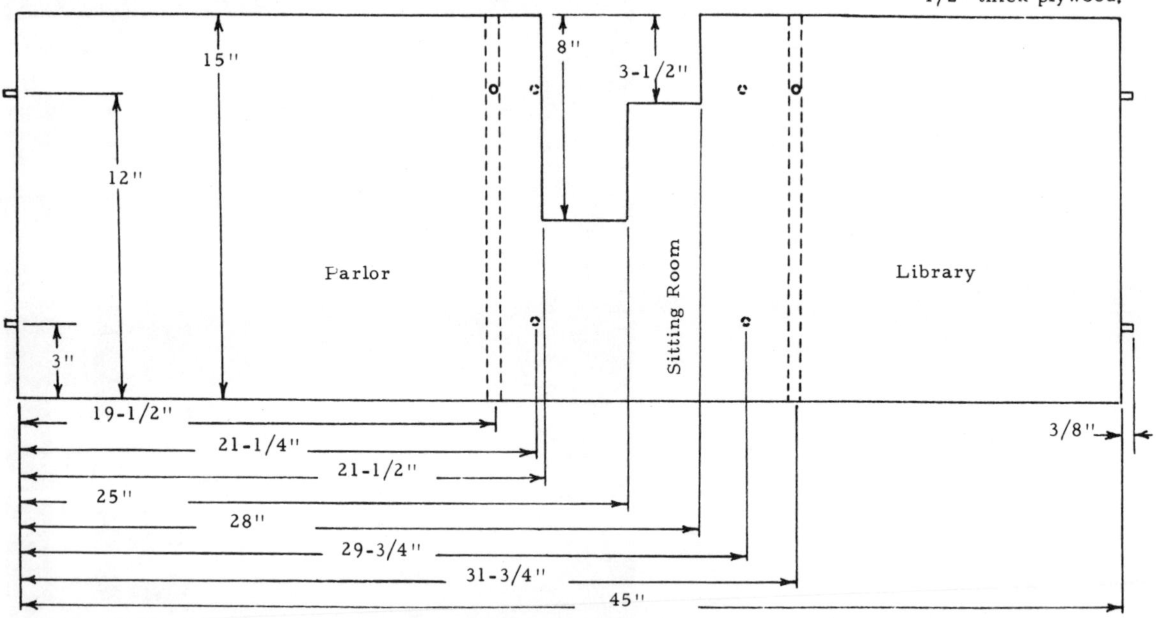

Holes at the 19-1/2" and 31-3/4" dimensions are 9/32" in diameter by 13/32" deep. Holes at the 21-1/4" and 29-3/4" dimensions are in the underside or ceiling side. The pegs are 1/4" in diameter and are recessed 1/2" and glued.

Pattern for the Second-Floor Ceiling and Third Floor

Cut one piece from 1/2" thick plywood,

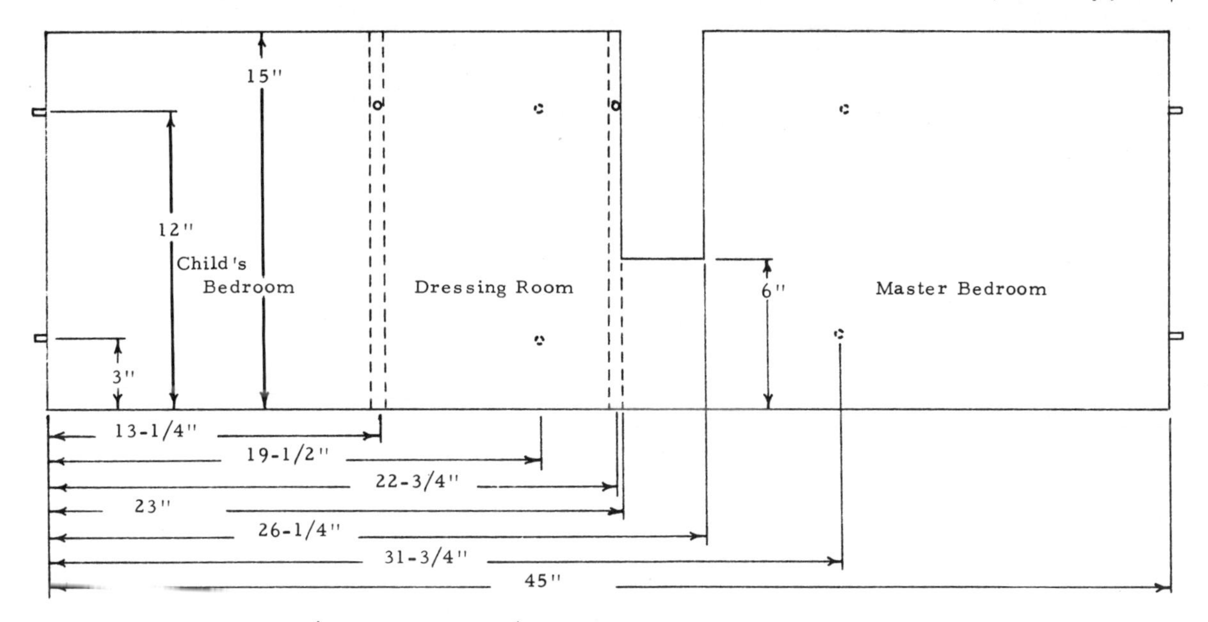

Holes at the 19-1/2" and 31-3/4" dimensions are in the underside or ceiling side.

Pattern for the Third-Floor Ceiling

Cut one piece from 1/2" thick plywood.

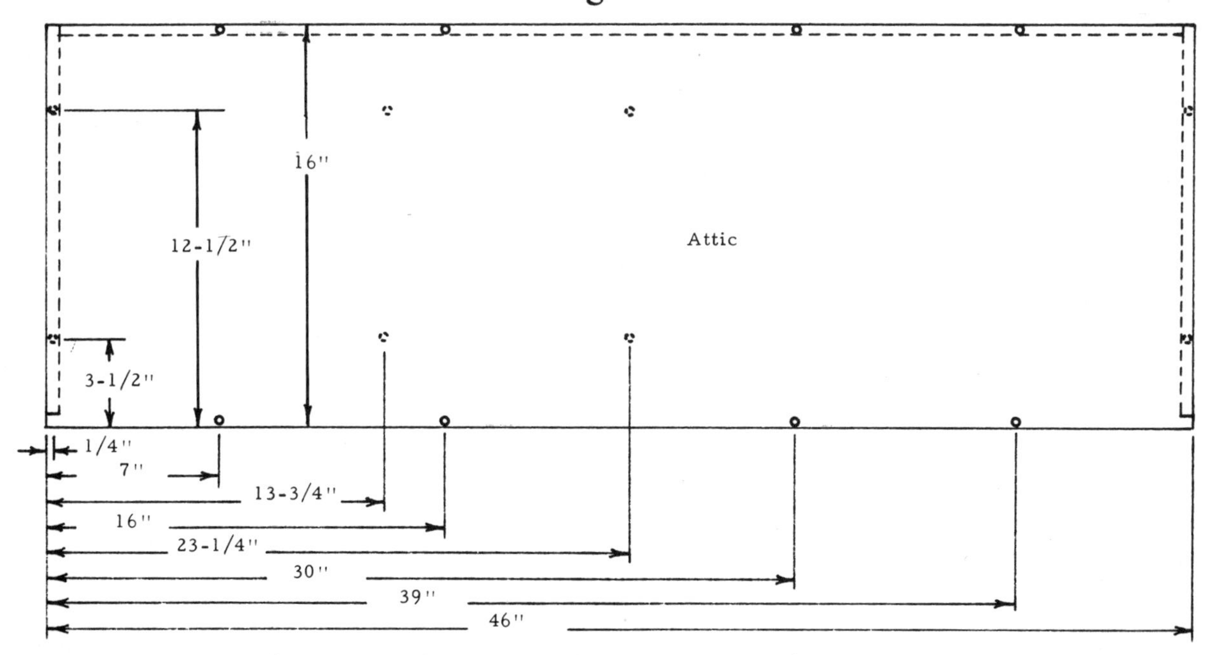

Holes at the 1/4", 13-3/4", 23-1/4", and 45-3/4" dimensions are in the underside or ceiling side. All other holes are on the top and are for the pediments.

Pattern for the Right Side and the Left Side

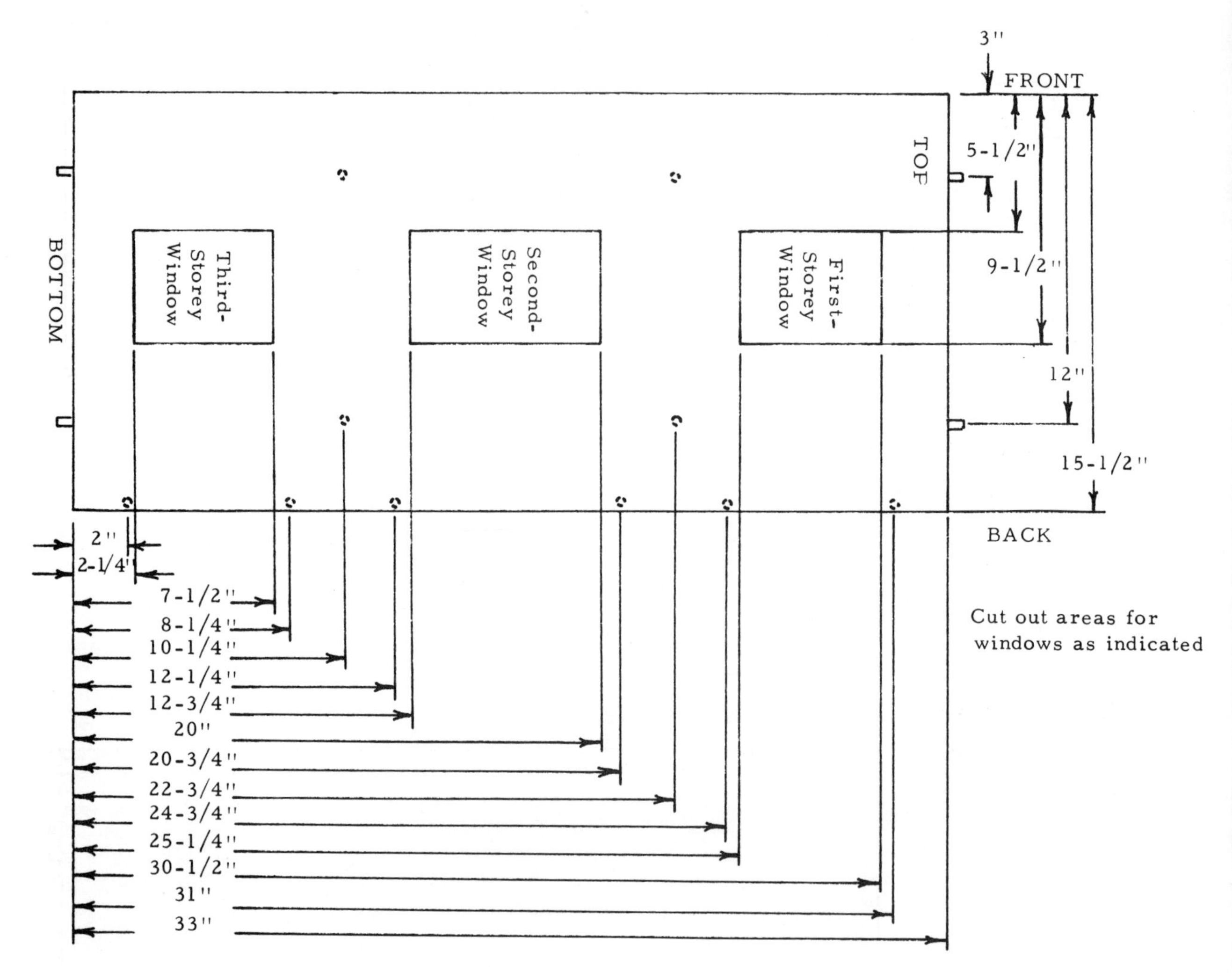

For the right side, cut one piece from 1/2" thick plywood. For the left side, cut one piece the mirror image of the right side.

Pattern for the Back Wall for the Bottom Level and for the Top Level

Cut two pieces from 1/2" thick plywood.

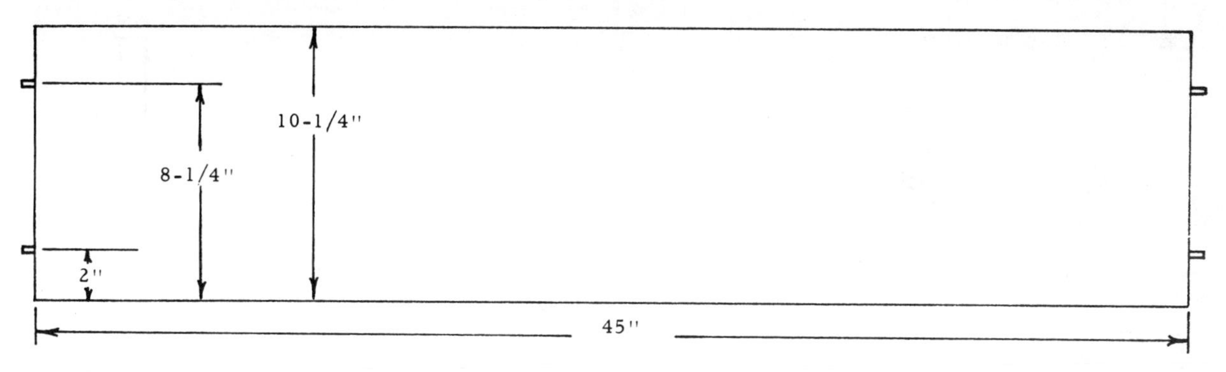

Pattern for the Back Wall for the Middle Level

Cut one piece from 1/2" thick plywood.

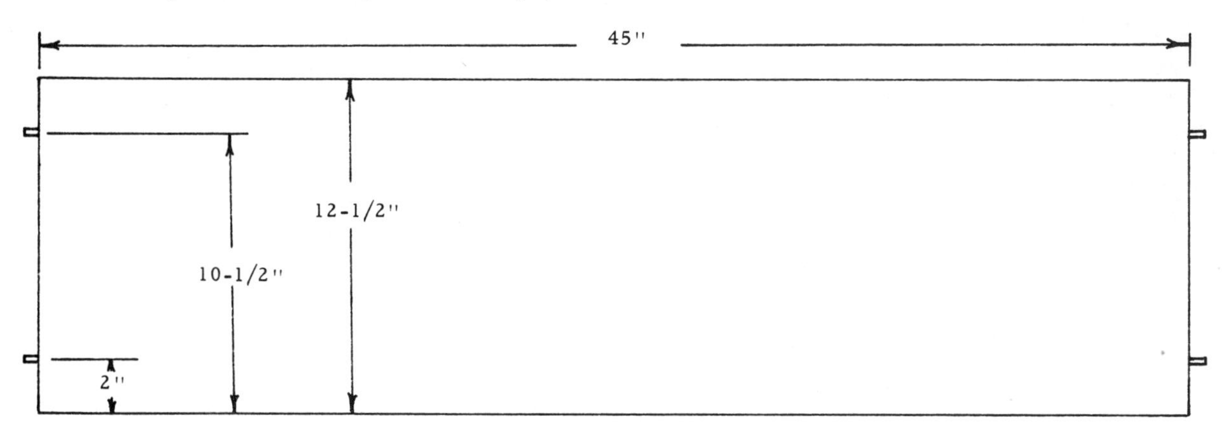

Pattern for the Front and Back Pediment

Cut two pieces from 1/2" thick plywood.

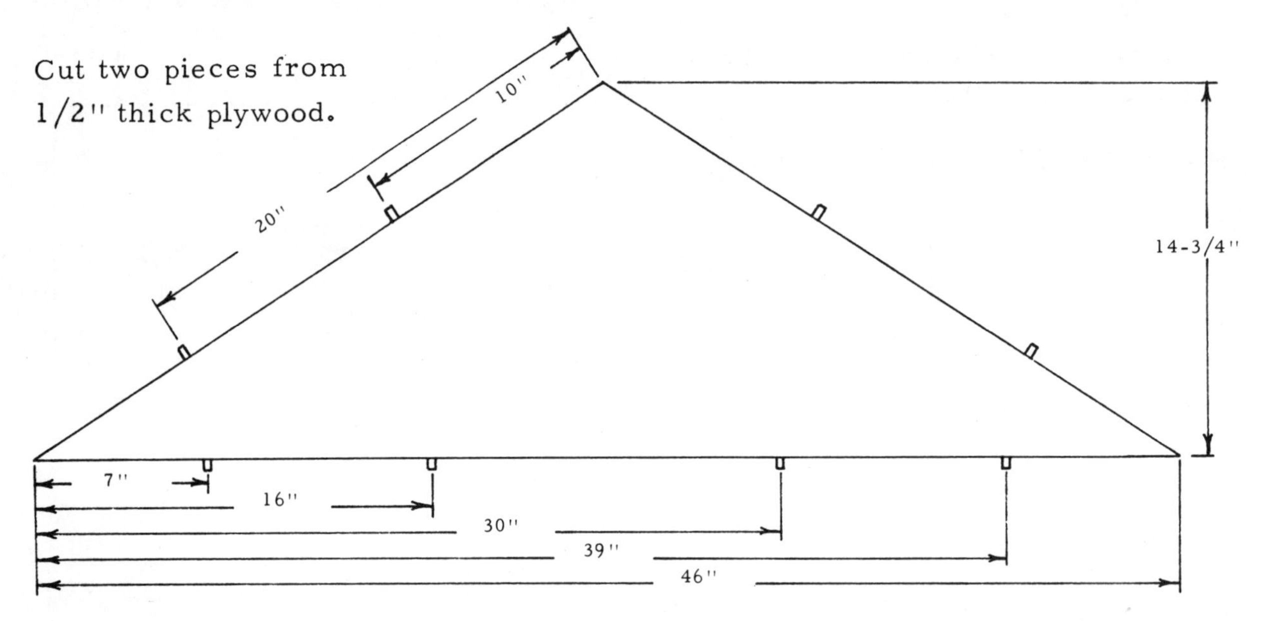

Decorate the front pediment with your family crest, or with moulding appropriate to the 18th century. A Betsy Ross American flag, to show that the doll family is in residence, would also be nice.

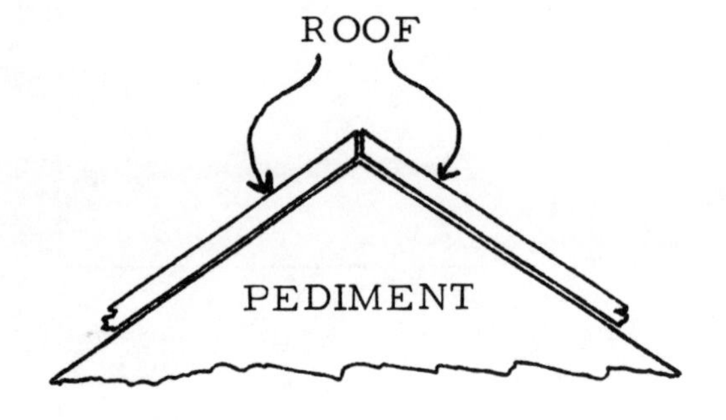

Instructions for the Basic Cabinet

The shingles are $1\frac{3}{4}$-inch × $1\frac{1}{4}$-inch pieces of coarse sandpaper. Glue them on the roof in the same pattern you would use to install real shingles. You need approximately 475 shingles. Finish off the apex by folding sandpaper the width of the roof over the apex to conform to the depth of the shingles. Do not glue this piece.

You can make an attic by lifting the dowelled roof and using the third-storey ceiling as the floor of the attic for storage purposes.

Decorate the pediment with your family crest, or with moulding appropriate to the 18th century.

Pattern for the Underside of the Roof (Right and Left)

Cut two pieces from 1/2" thick plywood.

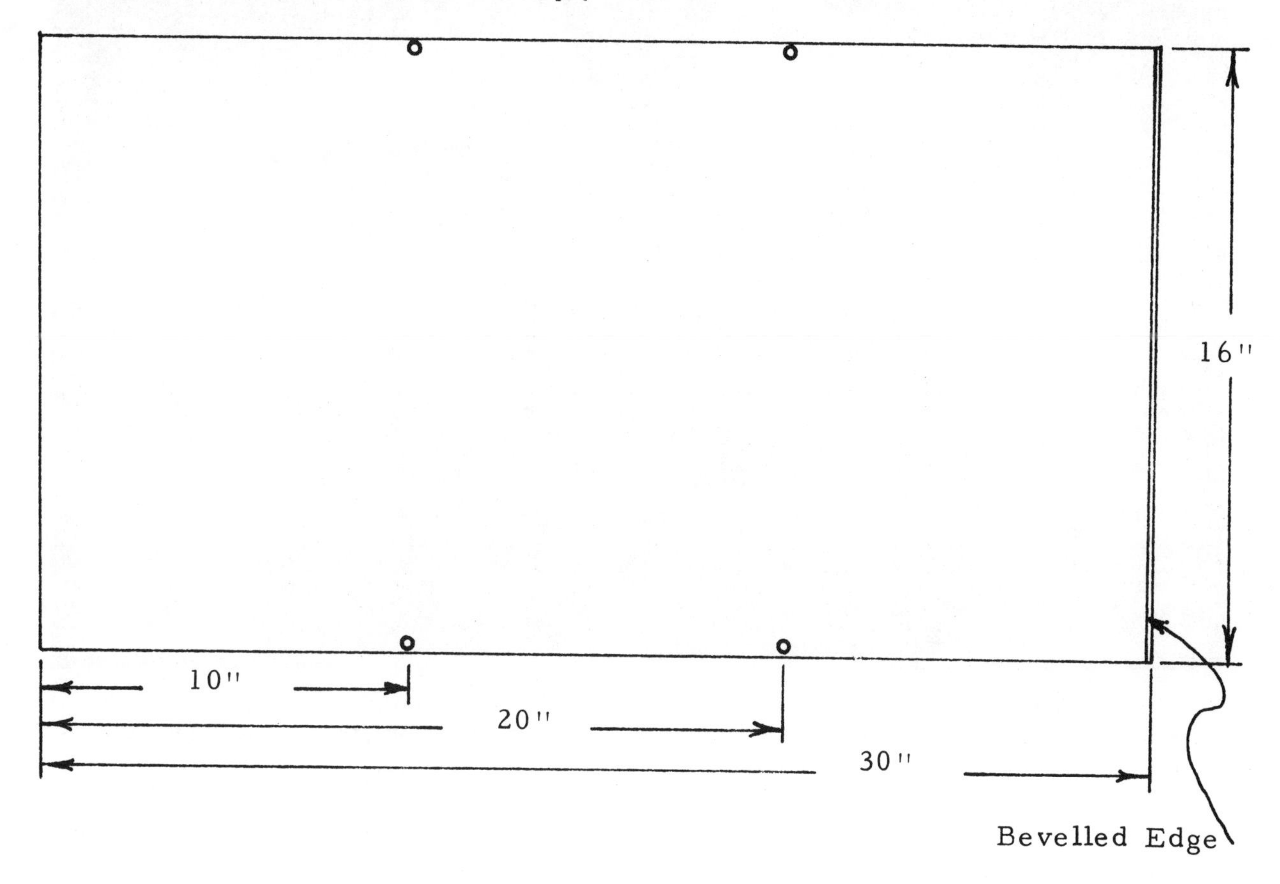

This is a full view of the interior of the Woodruff Dollhouse. From left to right, the rooms are: first floor: kitchen, entrance hall, dining room; second floor: parlor, sitting room, library; third floor: child's bedroom, dressing room, master bedroom.

Pattern for the Front Door (Façade)

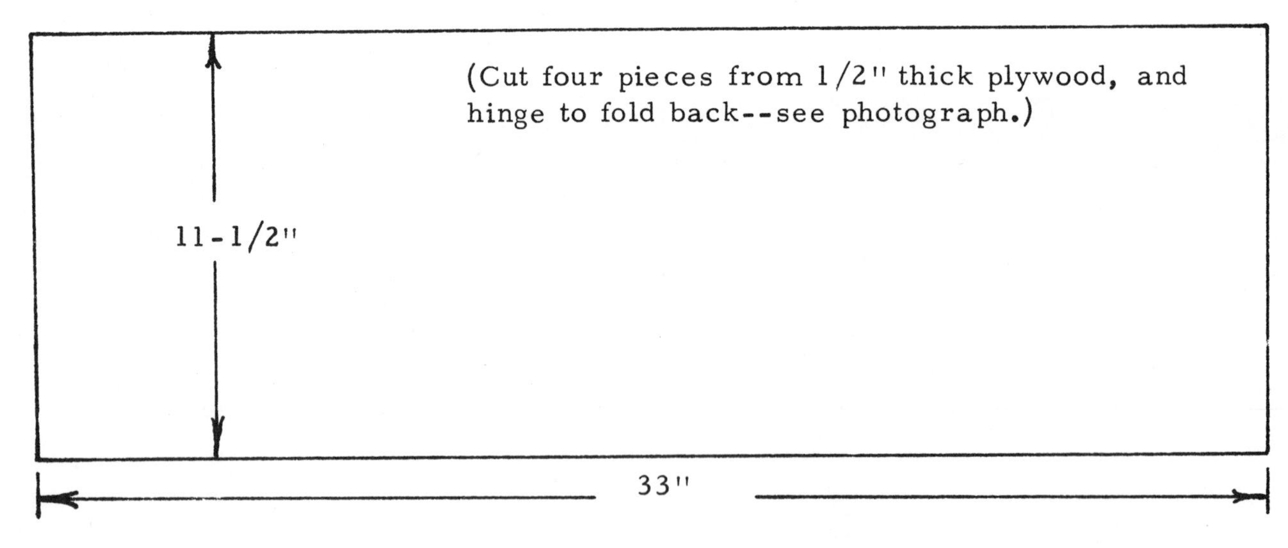

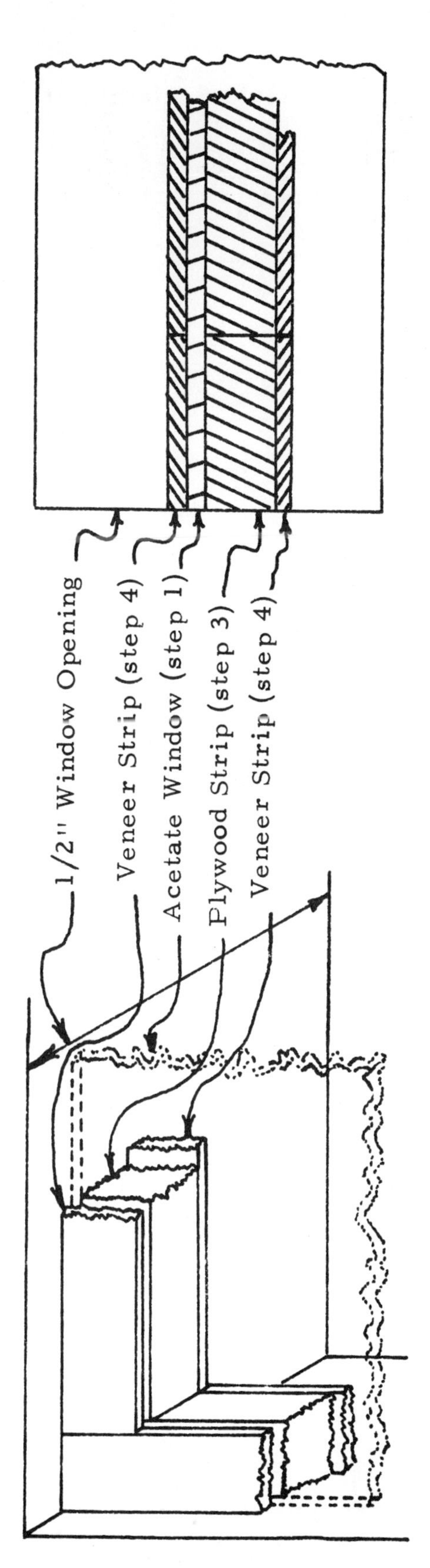

Blown-up isometric view inside the 1/2" thick cut-out window area.

Instructions for Installing the Windows

1. Cut from clear acetate four small windows ($4 \times 5\frac{1}{4}$ inches) and two large windows ($4 \times 7\frac{1}{4}$ inches).

2. Glue $\frac{1}{16}$-inch wide, paper-thin glazers (cut from *self-adhesive* veneer strips) on both sides of the acetate window panes (two glazers vertically on all windows, and three glazers horizontally on the small windows and five glazers horizontally on the large windows).

3. Glue $\frac{3}{16}$-inch thick, $\frac{1}{4}$-inch wide plywood strips *inside* the $\frac{1}{2}$-inch thick cut-out window area (see the illustration).

For the four small windows, cut eight 4-inch strips and eight $4\frac{3}{4}$-inch strips; for the two large windows, cut four 4-inch strips and four $6\frac{3}{4}$-inch strips. These are to hold (with glue) the acetate, see-through windowpanes (see the illustration).

4. Trim the windows with $\frac{1}{4}$-inch-wide moulding (cut from *self-adhesive*, paper-thin veneer strips) all around the window inside and outside the window frame. These mouldings will cover the exposed mouldings (in step 3) and the glue; therefore, their length-wise and width-wise dimensions are the same, except, of course, that they are cut from paper-thin veneer strips.

5. Add $\frac{1}{8}$-inch thick wood shutters to the outside windows.

Patterns for the Large and Small Windows

Actual Scale Shown

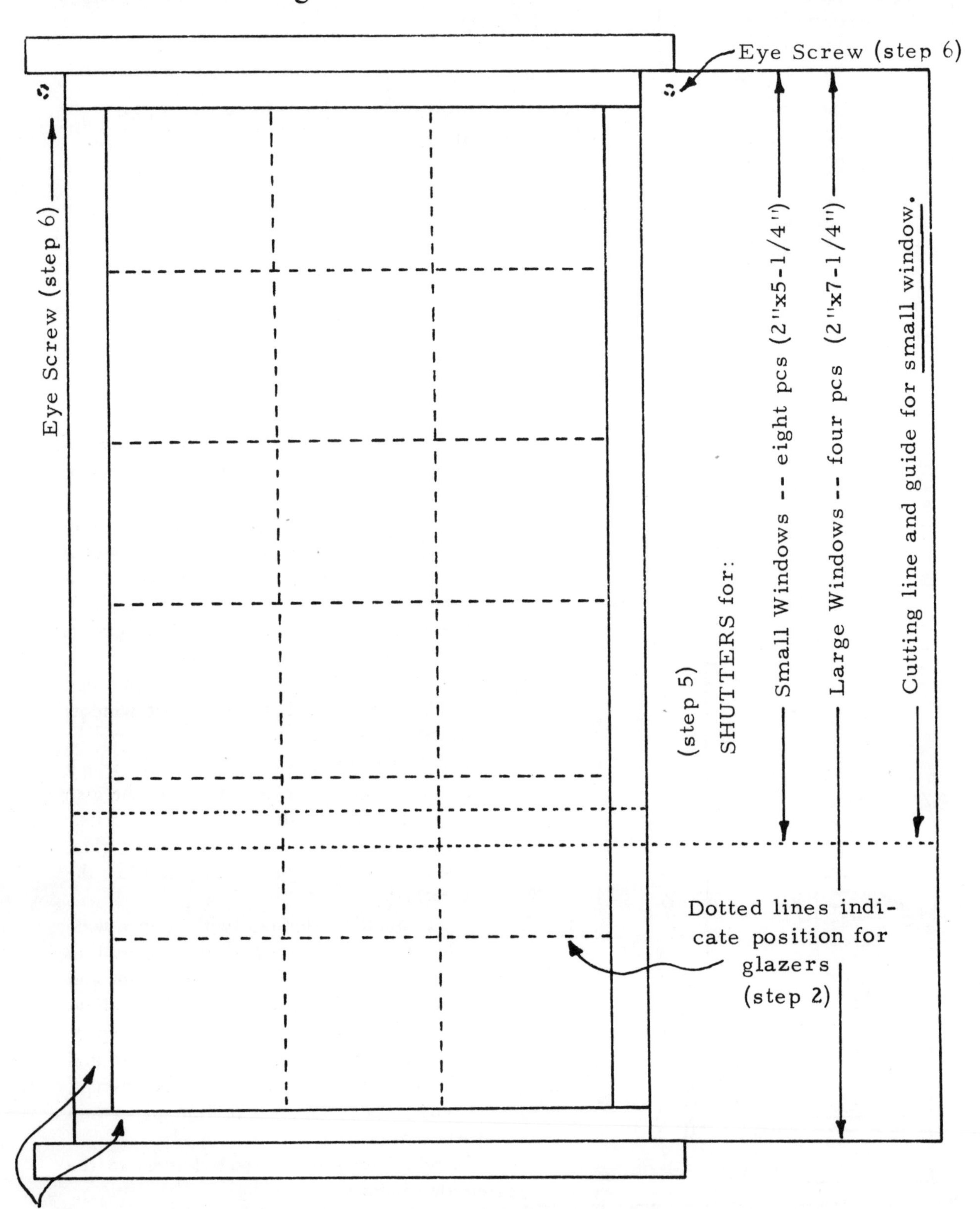

For the small windows, cut eight pieces 2 × 5¼ inches; for the large windows, cut four pieces 2 × 7¼ inches.

Stain the shutters as you want, and cover them with two coats of shellac, sanding lightly between each coat. You may glue the shutters onto the dollhouse.

6. Screw in eye screws for the inside windows (as shown in the illustration) for the drapery rod. Pass through a ⅛-inch diameter dowel, approximately 4½ to 5 inches long, for hanging the draperies.

7. Hang draperies in all the windows. See the chapter "Patterns and Instructions for the Draperies" on page 140 for how to make fine draperies.

Close-up of a kitchen window from the outside of the dollhouse.

The largest room in the dollhouse, this kitchen is usually a hub of activity. Contrasting enamelled and wooden stained furnishings make the room especially charming. A red and white checked tablecloth and curtains to match add a splash of color and additional warmth to the room.

The Kitchen

Whereas most of the Woodruff dollhouse is decorated and furnished in a graceful and grand 18th century manner, the kitchen is homey, comfortable, and warm. It has a rustic grandeur, but without any of the refined elegance that dominates the rest of the dollhouse. Family closeness and warmth is achieved by the use of warm reds and stark whites, which harmonize with and contrast to the rich, mellow browns of the furniture and floors, and the rough "brickwork" of the fireplace wall. The kitchen is the largest room in the dollhouse.

The two side walls and the ceiling are painted with flat, white acrylic to give them a white-washed, plaster-wall appearance. To maintain a rustic authenticity in the kitchen, the fireplace wall is covered with tiny $\frac{3}{8}$ inch × $\frac{5}{16}$ inch "bricks" cut from very fine sand-paper. Two different shades of sandpaper were used to achieve the used-brick effect. The huge floor-to-ceiling kitchen fireplace with its segmented arched Dutch oven is portable, and is covered with the same "bricks" as the fireplace wall. It was inspired by the fireplace-oven in the kitchen of the Tryon Palace in New Bern, North Carolina, built in 1767 to 1770. Over 3,000 "bricks" were used for the back wall and the fireplace-oven.

For the functional fireplace set, the wood carrier, which is a ceramic basket, the shovel set, and the broom are from Mexico. The mop is made from yarn and a cotton swab stick. The coal bucket is an eyewash cup that holds real coal from a fish aquarium filter.

The fireplace grates were cut from an ornate, plastic, fruit basket and painted black. Real wood cut from tree twigs "burns" in the fireplace. Red cellophane paper simulates the flames; real ashes tell a convincing story!

All the black "wrought-iron" cooking utensils and fireplace accessories, including the moveable hanging crane, were hand-wrought from 20-gauge wire or from coat hanger wire. Black cooking pots and frying pans are available from the Grey Iron Casting Company in Wrightsville, Pennsylvania (see page 174 for the address); you can also make them from bottle caps and wire sprayed black. The "copper" pots hanging on the fireplace-oven are magnetic memo holders.

On the mantel is a candleholder fashioned out of a cardboard disc, plastic tubing, and sewing thread (for the handle), all painted with brass-colored paint.

The see-through, 12-panel window, draped with red and white gingham kitchen curtains, is on the east to welcome the morning sun.

The kitchen floor was scored with a utility knife to give it the appearance of wood

About 3,000 sandpaper "bricks" cover the back wall and this authentic fireplace-oven. "Wrought-iron" cooking utensils (20-gauge or coat-hanger wire) decorate the fireplace, while two copper pots (magnetic memo holders) hang above it. "Fresh" bread is baking in the oven.

planks. It was then stained walnut-color to contrast dramatically with the white-washed walls and to harmonize with the "used-brick" wall and fireplace-oven. The red and white hearth rug was hand-woven on a mini-loom.

Furnishings in the kitchen are generally 17th century antiques and early to mid-18th century pieces. The furniture is finished in stains of walnut, mahogany, fruitwood, oak, and maple for the collected look. A few pieces are enamelled for varied interest.

Four mahogany-colored William and Mary slatback chairs are arranged around a natural wood sawbuck table which the dolls use for their informal meals, usually breakfast and luncheon. A red and white checkered tablecloth of the same fabric as the curtains covers the table. The slatback chairs are padded with "rush" seats, imitating woven fibre seats, but worked in beige Persian wool for comfort.

The table is set for luncheon of hot soup and fresh, home-baked bread. Earthenware soup mugs found in Mexico, and a "pewter" soup bowl and ladle, available from Shackman in New York (see page 175 for the address), are the eating implements. The bread is made from baker's clay. (To make baker's clay, mix 4 parts flour, 1 part salt, and $1\frac{3}{4}$ parts water. Knead for 20 minutes. Shape into loaves to fit the miniature pan and let air-dry for about 24 hours. Paint the "baked" bread a golden brown bread

Mahogany-stained William and Mary slatback chairs are arranged around this natural wood sawbuck kitchen table. Crockery, pewter, and other functional and decorative kitchen items fill the open-shelf cupboard and knick-knack shelf.

color. For unbaked bread, leave it unpainted.) The bread pans are tiny, clear plastic moulds (used by manufacturers to package and to protect their merchandise) cut to the shape of miniature bread pans and painted tin color for authenticity. More bread is baking in the oven. Fresh butter for the new bread was made in a churn which consists of a yeast bottle and a cotton swab stick.

The horn of plenty is a bottle cap; the fruit is a cluster of beads glued together.

The open-shelf cupboard is actually typical of both the 17th and 18th centuries, and holds everyday kitchenware and foods. Crockery and glazed earthenware cups and dishes were found in Mexico. The "pewter" bowls are the bases for the type of buttons you cover with fabric. The "copper" containers, tea sets, and kitchenware in the cupboard are magnetic memo holders. Many of the bowls and plates were originally bottle caps and buttons that were painted to look like copper, silver, pewter, brass, black wrought iron, or glazed enamelware, all of which were popular in 18th century New England. On top of the cupboard, the large brown bottles with rubber stoppers are authentic. They are for "storing" the doll family's food in bulk. The various woven baskets are from The Last Straw in Solvang, California (see page 175 for the address).

The oak knick-knack hanging wall shelf on the left wall is a late 17th to early 18th century piece, and holds decorative, but functional miniature bric-a-brac.

The Jacobean stretcher table used for cooking and baking is a late 17th century antique. The wooden kitchen implements are from Shackman in New York (see page 175 for the address). The enamelled clay bowl is from Mexico.

Against the fireplace wall is a hutch table-chair that is authentic right down to the pivoting table top so that the piece can be used as either a table or a chair. It has a natural finish and is padded with a beige wool "rush" seat.

The high-back settle also has a natural finish. Although not particularly comfortable by 20th century standards, the settle is the most popular piece of furniture in this colonial New England kitchen. Frequently the dolls place their headwear on the top of the settle, while they use the under area for footwear. A cross-base hat-and-coat rack in the right-hand corner is used by the dolls to hang up their clothes.

In contrast to the rustic settle are the pair of pretty Pennsylvania-German peasant chairs enamelled white and decorated with cut-out hearts painted red inside.

A William and Mary white enamelled rocking chair completes the seating arrangement around the fireplace. Both the rocker seat and back are padded with "rush" seat upholstery worked in red Persian wool.

The spinning wheel from Shackman in New York (see page 175 for the address), which really turns, also aids in creating the domestic mood in this authentic 18th century kitchen.

Above the settle hangs a japanned tray made from a cocoa can lid which was oil-painted in "red Japan" colors. It is used by the dolls both as a decorative item and as a functional serving utensil.

Like the japanned tray, the rifle over the hutch table is also both decorative and functional. It is made from plywood, a cotton swab stick, and a piece of leather.

On the left "white-washed" wall hangs a linen sampler embroidered in red that says,

"God Bless This Home." (Do not forget to include your initials and the date on any samplers you make.)

The black "wrought-iron" candle chandelier, made from a tea-can top, costume jewelry chain, and birthday candles, is the source of light in the kitchen. It hangs from a tiny eye hook so that the chandelier may be easily taken down if necessary. The design for this simple chandelier was inspired by the chandelier in the Great Hall of The Miller's House, Millbach, Pennsylvania, built in 1752.

Patterns and Instructions for the Kitchen

Instructions for the Fireplace-Oven

1. Cut out the following pattern pieces from $\frac{3}{16}$-inch plywood:
a. one fireplace-oven front ($6 \times 9\frac{1}{2}$ inches);
b. one fireplace-oven back ($6 \times 9\frac{1}{2}$ inches);
c. two fireplace sides for the outside walls ($1\frac{1}{4} \times 9\frac{1}{2}$ inches);
d. one fireplace top ($1\frac{5}{8} \times 5\frac{5}{8}$ inches); this piece is optional—the fireplace-oven goes up to the top of the kitchen ceiling; therefore, this piece would not show if it were omitted;
e. one fireplace hearth ($3\frac{1}{2} \times 6$ inches);
f. one mantel and one pair of brackets;
g. two fireplace sides for the *inside* walls ($1\frac{1}{4} \times 6\frac{1}{2}$ inches);
h. two pieces for the oven top and bottom ($1\frac{1}{4} \times 4$ inches) for the *inside* of the fireplace-oven;
i. one oven side ($1\frac{1}{4} \times 1\frac{3}{4}$ inches) for the *inside* of the fireplace-oven.

2. Sand all the pieces.

3. Position and glue on the wrong side of the fireplace-oven the following *inside* walls as shown along the dotted lines: the one oven side (i); the two pieces for the oven top and bottom (h); the two fireplace sides (g).

4. Position and glue the two fireplace-oven sides for the *outside* walls (c); the fireplace back; the hearth; and the mantel and brackets.

5. Sand any overlapping edges with coarse sandpaper and finish with fine.

6. Paint the fireplace-oven with flat, white acrylic paint or enamel inside and out. Let it dry.

7. Sand lightly with very fine sandpaper.

8. Cover the fireplace-oven with two different shades of $\frac{3}{8}$- $\times$ $\frac{5}{16}$- inch sandpaper "bricks" for a used-brick effect. (For a really striking effect, cover the entire fireplace wall of the kitchen with the same sandpaper "bricks.")

9. Screw in two miniature eye hooks (painted black) into the left inside fireplace wall for the moving crane; decorate the fireplace with hanging pots and pans or a rifle; fill the mantel with breads and period bric-a-brac; make fireplace accessories (see the chapter "Accessories" on page 132).

You can leave the fireplace-oven flat white, if you are short on time. For a rough, whitewashed plaster look, add very fine white sand to the acrylic or enamel before you paint the fireplace-oven. However, it only takes about 14 leisure hours (for instance, while watching television) and approximately 3,000 sandpaper "bricks" to cover both the fireplace-oven and the entire back kitchen wall. The effect is well worth it.

Patterns for the Fireplace-Oven [c. mid-18th century]

(For full size, enlarge to 6 × 9½ inches.)

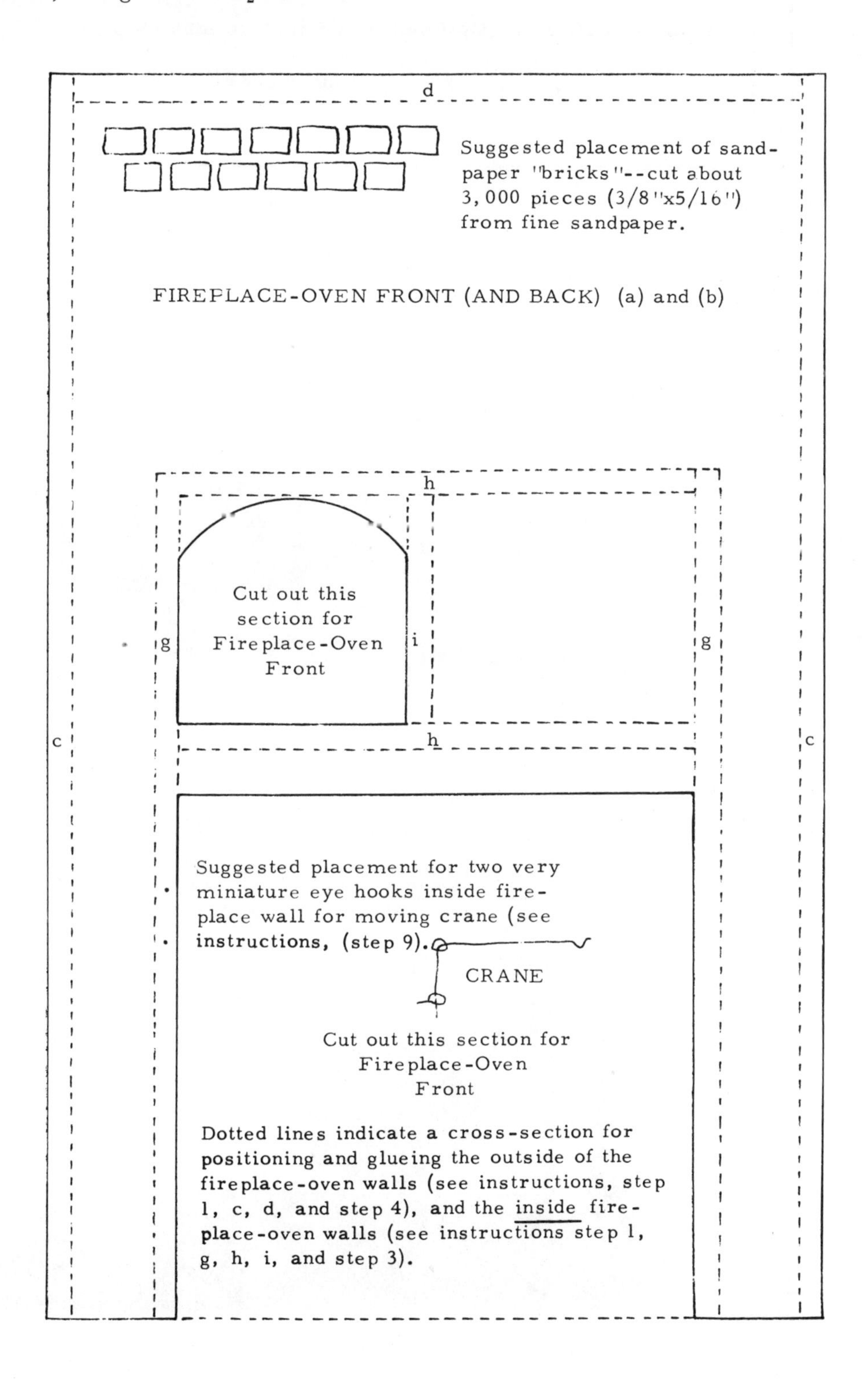

FIREPLACE TOP (Optional - see instructions step ld.

(one piece)

(f)

MANTEL - pattern is overlapped

(one piece)

FIREPLACE SIDE

(two pieces)

(c)

For full size patterns, see Instructions for the Fireplace-Oven, page 34.

Close-up of the fireplace-oven.

You could also make an authentic, stone-studded fireplace-oven by using very tiny real stones. Fabric or paper with stone, brick, or plaster patterns can also be used. Whatever decorative method you choose, it is nice to have the fireplace-oven and the fireplace-oven kitchen wall covered with the same materials for a uniform and pleasing effect.

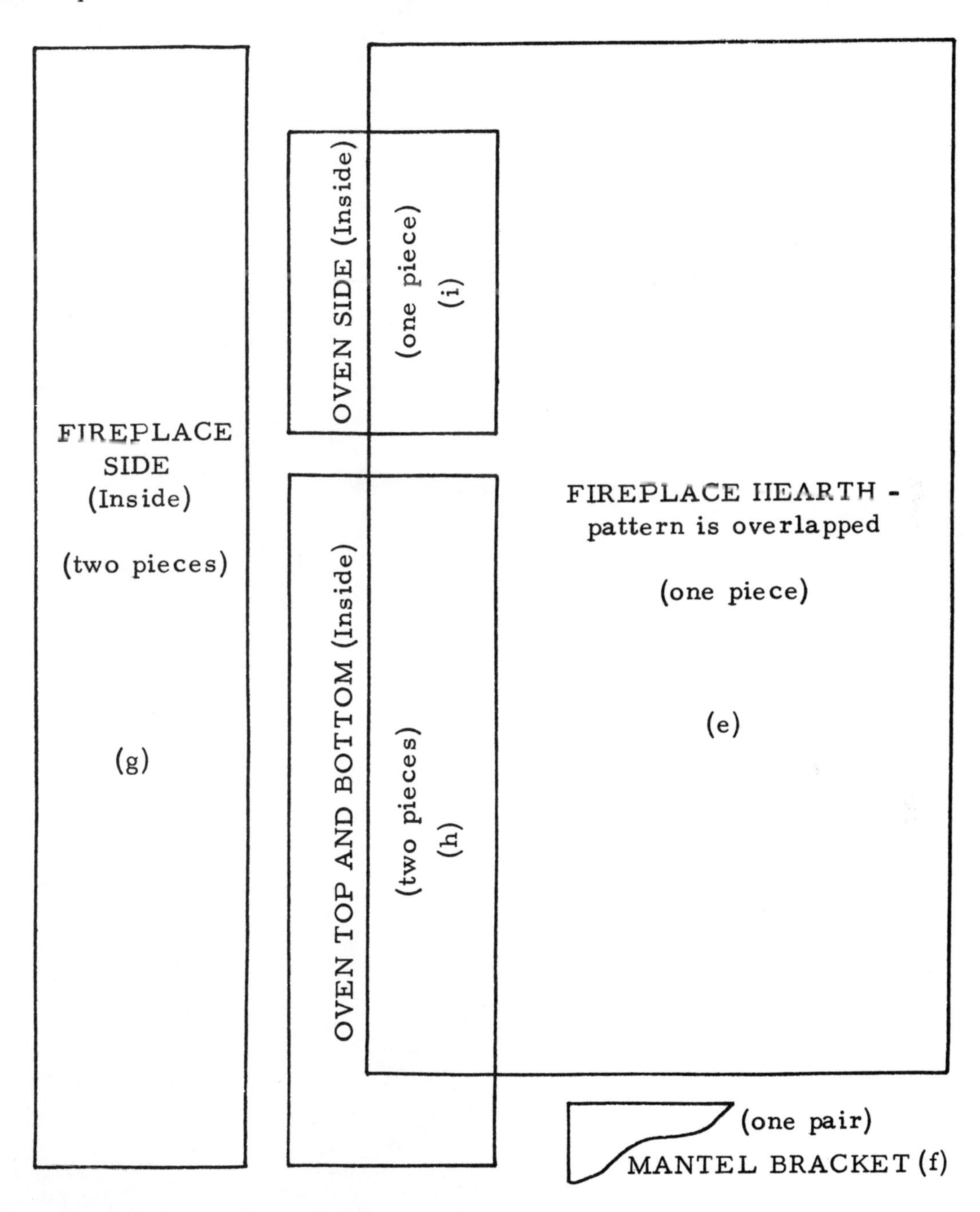

Patterns for the Sawbuck Kitchen Table [c. 1720]

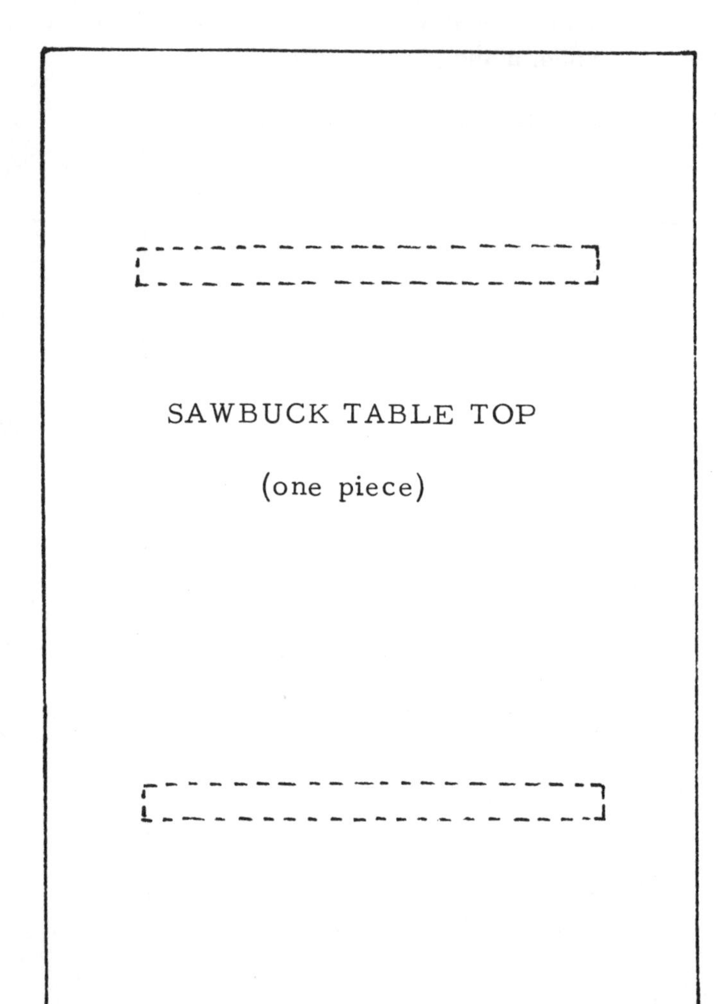

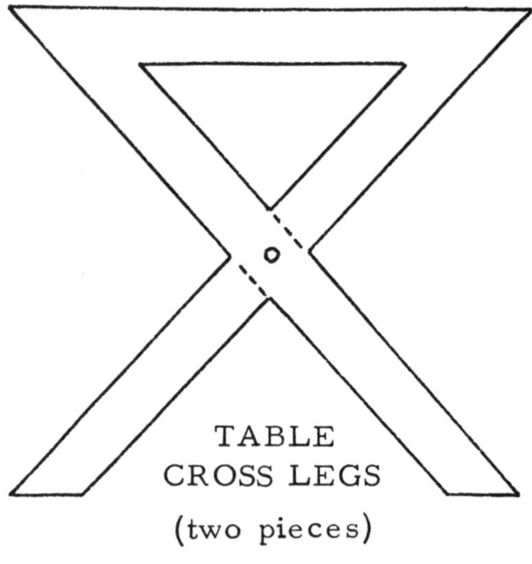

(Below) Close-up of the sawbuck kitchen table.

Instructions for the Sawbuck Table

1. Cut, from $\frac{3}{16}$-inch plywood, one table top ($3\frac{1}{2} \times 5$ inches) and two table cross legs.
2. Sand all the pieces and score them with a knife along the dotted lines on the legs.
3. Position and glue the cross legs along the dotted lines on the underside of the table.
4. Stain and cover with two coats of shellac. Sand lightly between each coat.

Patterns for the Jacobean Stretcher Table [c. 1690-1725]

STRETCHER TABLE TOP
(one piece)

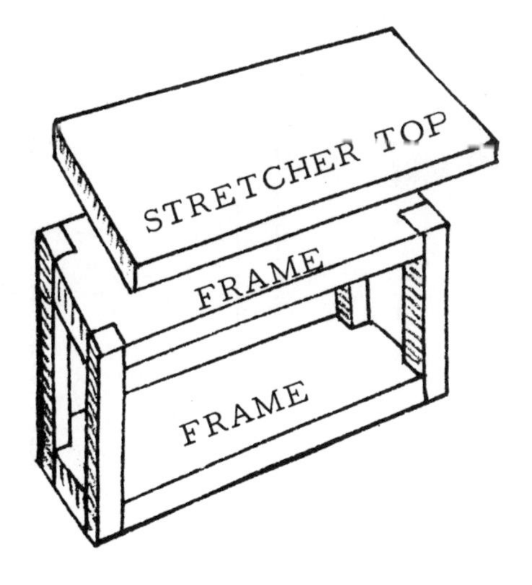

STRETCHER FRAME
(two pieces)

STRETCHER TABLE
LEG (four pieces)

Instructions for the Jacobean Table

1. Cut the following from $\frac{3}{16}$-inch plywood:
a. two notched frames ($1 \times 2\frac{1}{2}$ inches);
b. one table top ($1\frac{1}{2} \times 3$ inches);
c. four legs (2 inches long).
2. Sand all the pieces.
3. Position and glue the legs into the frame notches at the top and bottom.
4. Glue the table top to overlap the top frame.
5. Sand, stain, and cover with two coats of shellac. Sand lightly between each coat.

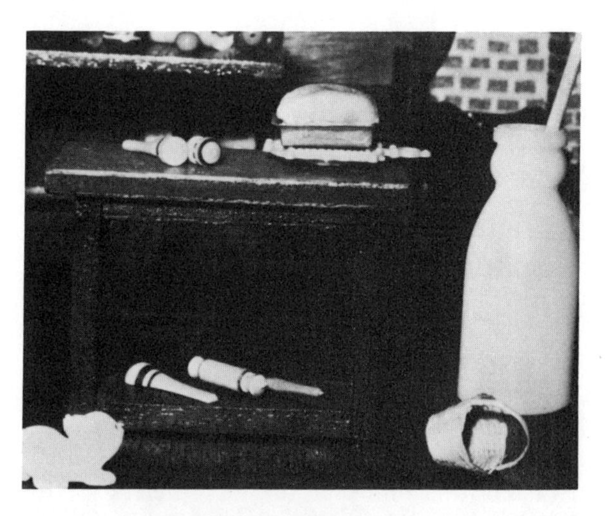

Close-up of the Jacobean stretcher table.

Patterns for the Open Shelf Kitchen Cupboard [c. mid-18th century]

CUPBOARD BACK

(one piece)

This pattern may also be used for a bookcase in the library, or in the bedroom, or for an open shelf cupboard in the dining room to display fine china and accessories.

CUPBOARD SIDE

(two pieces)

CUP-
BOARD
SHELF

(six pieces)

Instructions for the Open Shelf Kitchen Cupboard

1. Cut the following from $\frac{3}{16}$-inch plywood:
a. one cupboard back (4 × 6 inches);
b. two cupboard sides ($1\frac{3}{16}$ × 6 inches);
c. six shelves (1 × 4 inches).

2. Sand all the pieces.

3. Position and glue the four shelves to the cupboard back along the dotted lines. Add one shelf for the top, and one for the bottom of the cupboard. Glue the sides on last.

4. Sand lightly. Stain and cover with two coats of shellac. Sand lightly between all coats.

5. Fill with functional 18th century kitchenwares. See the chapter "Accessories" on page 132 for ideas.

Patterns for the Settle
[c. 1720-1780]

SETTLE BACK(5-1/2"x5-1/2")
(one piece)

Guide for positioning settle seat to back

SETTLE TOP

(one piece)

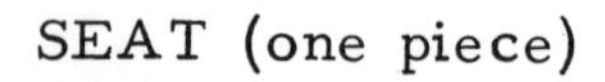

SEAT FRONT (one piece)

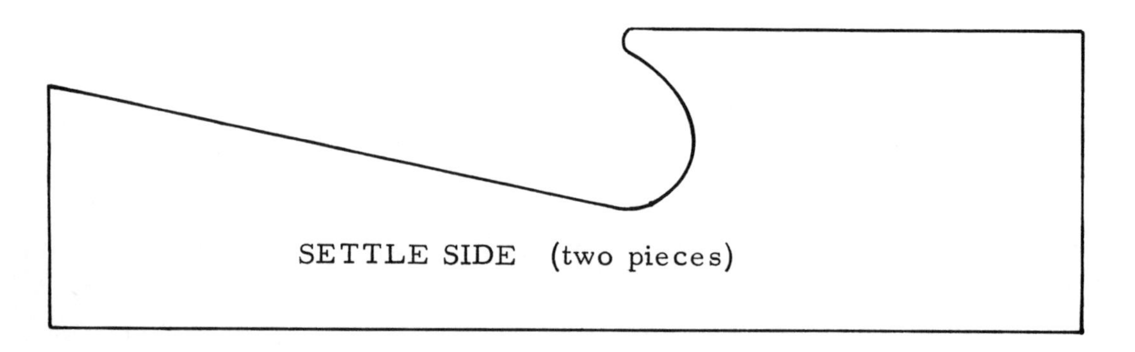

Instructions for the Settle

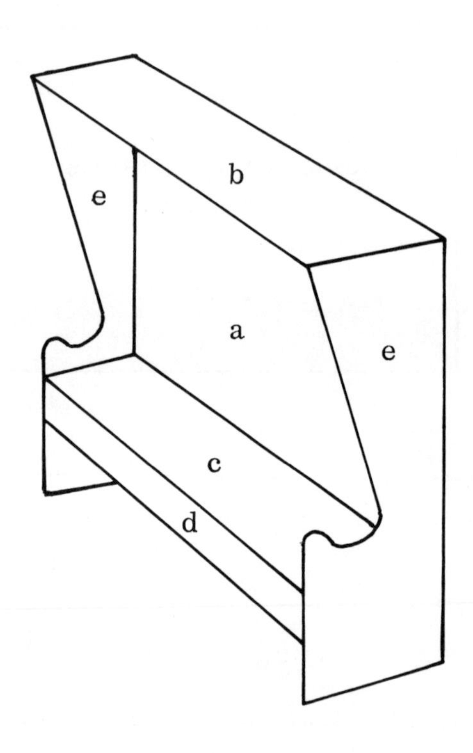

1. Cut the following pattern pieces from $\frac{3}{16}$-inch plywood:
a. one settle back ($5\frac{1}{2} \times 5\frac{1}{2}$ inches);
b. one settle top ($1\frac{1}{4} \times 5\frac{7}{8}$ inches);
c. one seat ($1\frac{5}{16} \times 5\frac{1}{2}$ inches);
d. one seat front ($1 \times 5\frac{1}{2}$ inches);
e. two settle sides ($1\frac{1}{4}$ to $1\frac{1}{2} \times 5\frac{1}{2}$ inches).
2. Sand all the pieces.
3. Position and glue the settle seat to the settle back along the dotted guide lines.
4. Add the seat front, the settle sides, and the top.
5. Sand, stain maple-color, and cover with two coats of shellac. Sand lightly between all coats.

Patterns for the William and Mary Slatback Rocker/Armchair [c. 1730-1760]

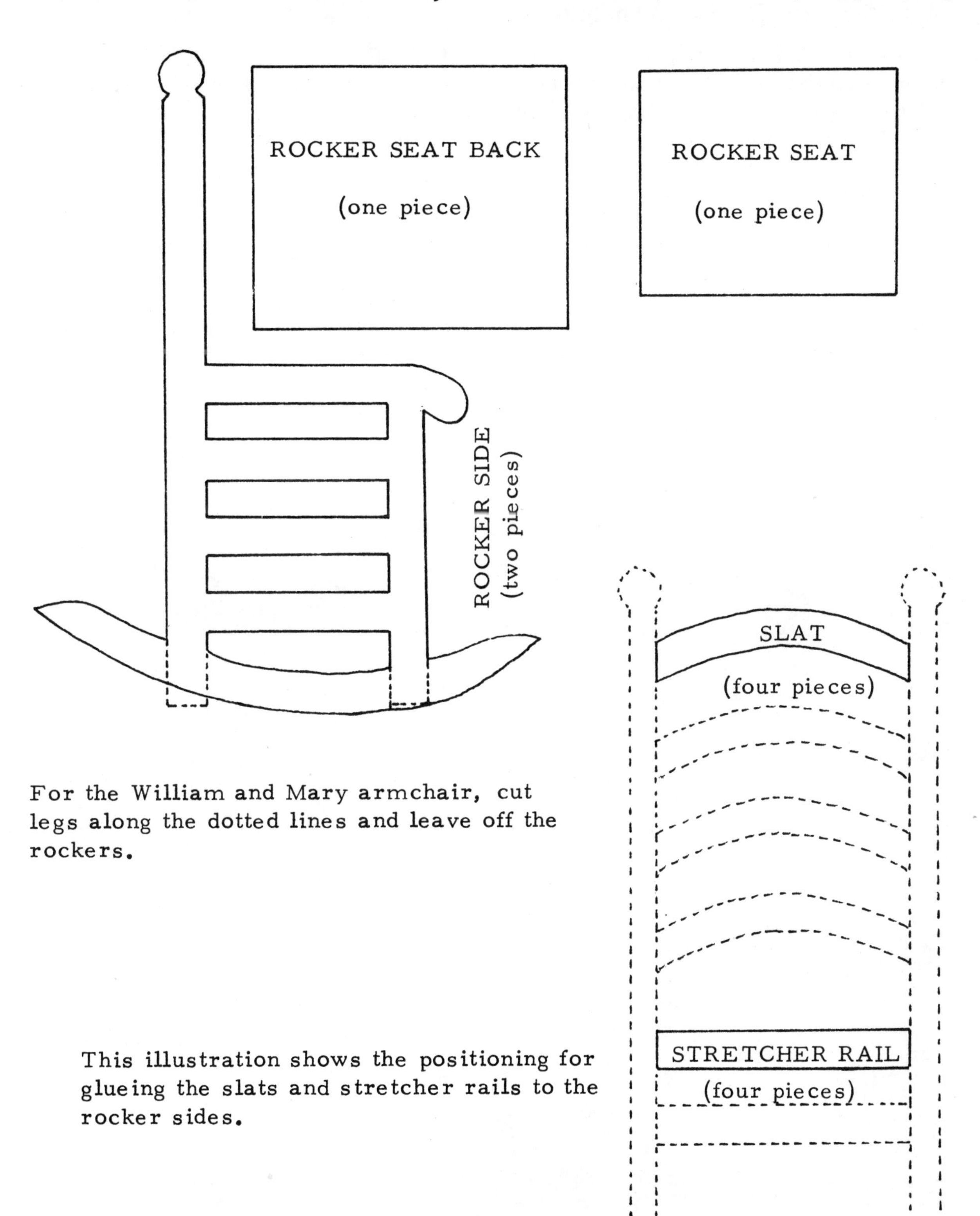

For the William and Mary armchair, cut legs along the dotted lines and leave off the rockers.

This illustration shows the positioning for glueing the slats and stretcher rails to the rocker sides.

Instructions for the William and Mary Slatback Rocker/Armchair

1. Cut the following from $\frac{3}{16}$-inch plywood:
a. two rocker sides (you can cut the ball finials at the tops of the sides from plywood as part of the rocker sides, or you can cut the tops off and then glue on wood ball or bead finials when the rocker pieces are assembled);
b. four rocker slats;
c. four stretcher rails ($\frac{1}{4} \times 1\frac{3}{4}$ inches).

2. Sand all the pieces.

3. Cut the following from cardboard:
a. one seat ($1\frac{1}{2} \times 1\frac{3}{4}$ inches);
b. one seat back ($1\frac{3}{4} \times 2\frac{1}{8}$ inches).

Upholster both pieces with fabric or make wool "rush" seats (see page 152 in the chapter "Needlecrafts").

4. Position and glue the slats to the rocker sides (as shown in the illustration), and assemble and glue all the stretcher rails to line up with the side rails (which are part of the rocker sides).

5. Sand lightly; stain or enamel. If you use stain, then cover with two coats of shellac. Sand lightly between all coats.

6. Glue or tie on the upholstered seat; then tie on the upholstered seat back.

(Above). Close-up of the William and Mary slatback chair.

(Left). Close-up of the William and Mary slatback rocker/armchair.

Patterns for the William and Mary Chair/Stool [c. 1730-1760]

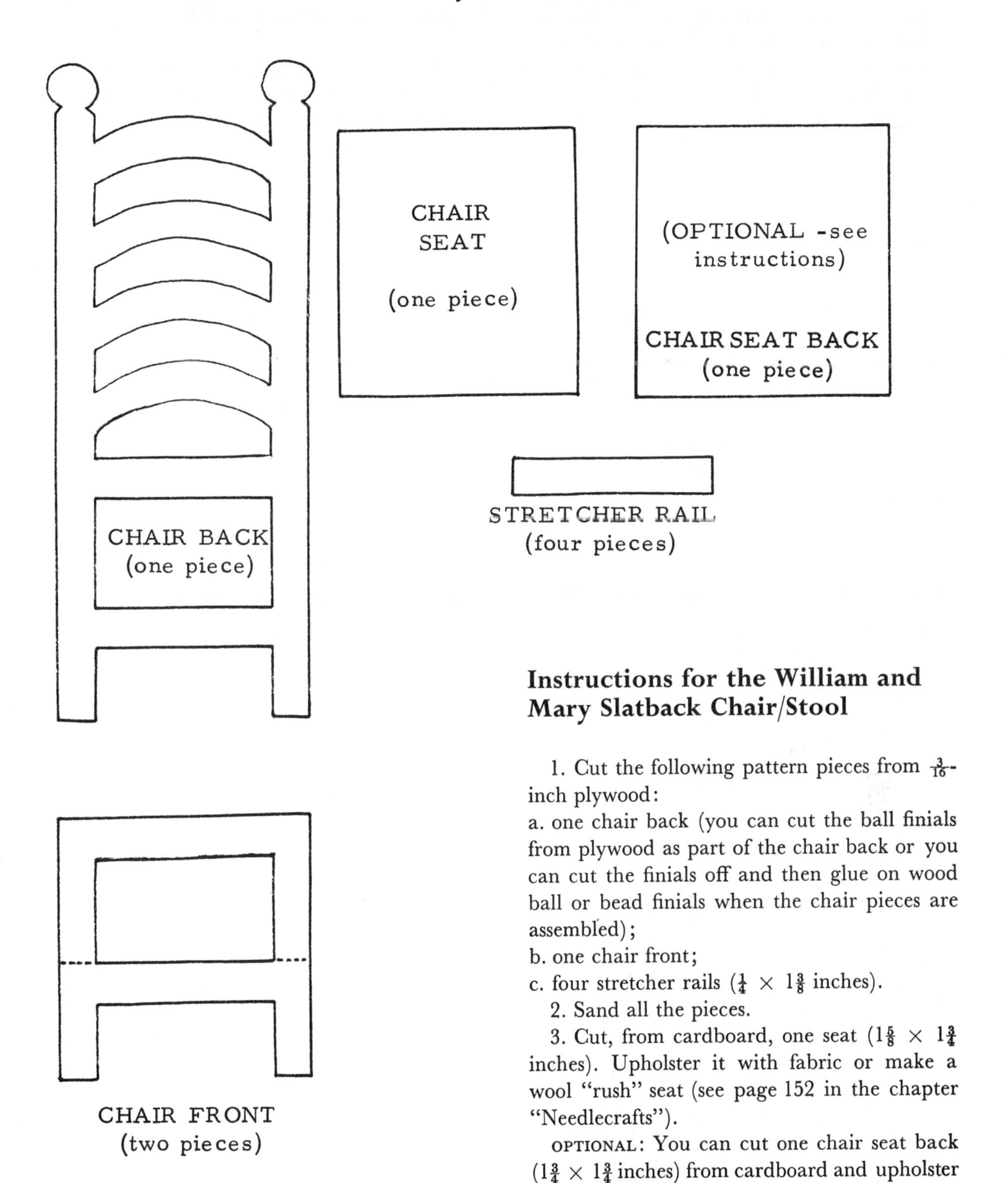

Instructions for the William and Mary Slatback Chair/Stool

1. Cut the following pattern pieces from $\frac{3}{16}$-inch plywood:
a. one chair back (you can cut the ball finials from plywood as part of the chair back or you can cut the finials off and then glue on wood ball or bead finials when the chair pieces are assembled);
b. one chair front;
c. four stretcher rails ($\frac{1}{4} \times 1\frac{3}{8}$ inches).

2. Sand all the pieces.

3. Cut, from cardboard, one seat ($1\frac{5}{8} \times 1\frac{3}{4}$ inches). Upholster it with fabric or make a wool "rush" seat (see page 152 in the chapter "Needlecrafts").

OPTIONAL: You can cut one chair seat back ($1\frac{3}{4} \times 1\frac{3}{4}$ inches) from cardboard and upholster it to match the chair seat.

4. Assemble and glue the side stretcher rails to line up with the front and back stretcher rails (which are part of the front and back pieces).

5. Sand, stain, and cover with two coats of shellac. Sand lightly between all coats.

6. Glue on the upholstered seat; tie the chair seat back (optional).

INSTRUCTIONS FOR THE STOOL

1. For the stool, cut two pieces along the dotted lines of the bottom portion of the chair front and two stretcher rails.

2. Follow the assembly, finishing, and upholstery instructions as for the slatback chair above.

You can use this stool pattern with virtually any other chair in the dollhouse. Match the stain and upholstery to the chair.

Instructions for the Pennsylvania-German Chair

1. Cut the following from $\frac{3}{16}$-inch plywood:
a. one chair back (you can cut out the heart or glue on one cut from a magazine);
b. one chair seat;
c. one pair of front legs.

2. Sand all the pieces.

3. Position and glue the chair seat to the back along the dotted lines. Add the legs in front.

4. Paint with white enamel. Then paint the inside of the heart cut-out red.

You can paint folk art, or "peasant" art, made popular by the German settlers in colonial America, on the chair, or you can cut out decorations from magazines and decoupage them onto the chair.

This chair can also be used in the child's bedroom.

Patterns for the Pennsylvania-German Chair [c. mid-18th century]

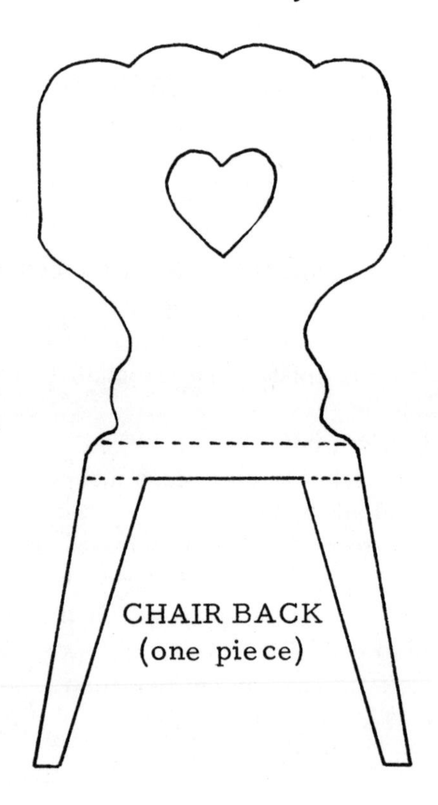

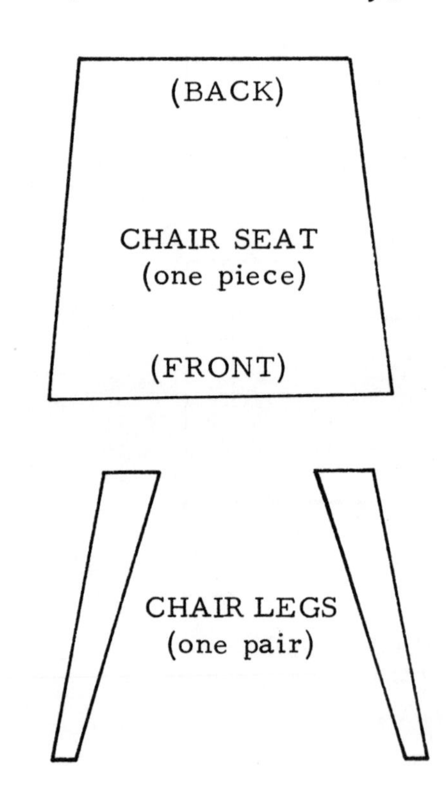

Patterns for the Knick-Knack Shelf [c. early 18th century]

SHELF
(three pieces)

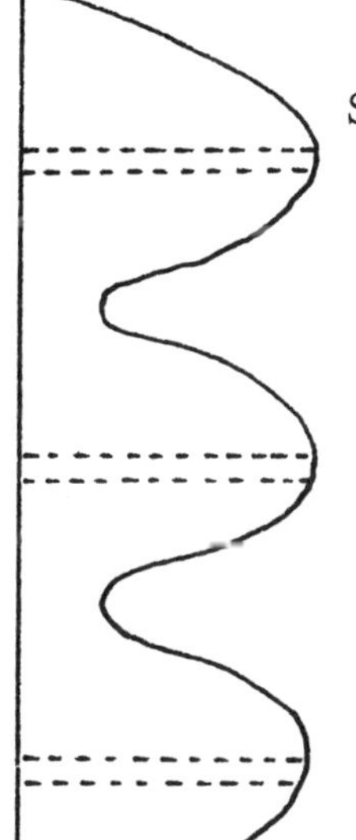

SHELF SIDE (two pieces)

Instructions for the Knick-Knack Shelf

1. Cut two shelf sides from $\frac{3}{16}$-inch plywood.
2. Cut three shelves (1 × 3 inches) from $\frac{1}{8}$-inch plywood.
3. Sand all the pieces.
4. Position and glue the shelves along the dotted lines inside the two shelf sides.
5. Sand, stain, and cover with two coats of shellac. Sand lightly between all coats.
6. Fill with 18th century bric-a-brac. See the chapter "Accessories" on page 132 for ideas.

Close-up of the Pennsylvania-German chair.

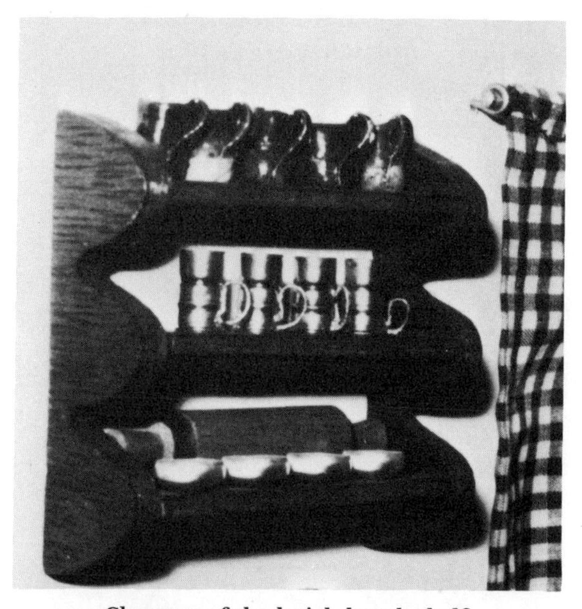

Close-up of the knick-knack shelf.

Patterns for the Hutch Table/Chair [c. early 18th century]

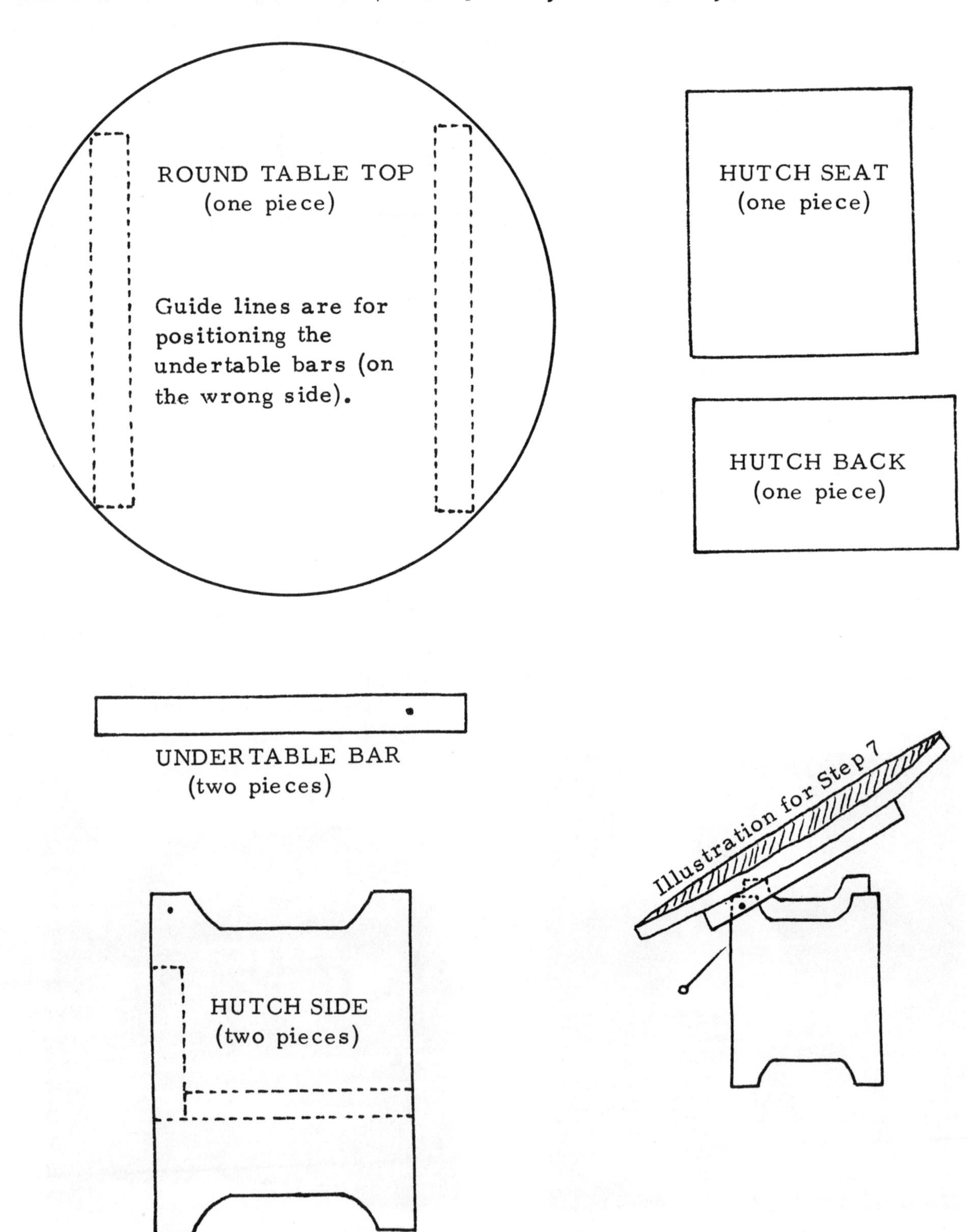

Instructions for the Hutch Table/Chair

1. Cut the following from $\frac{3}{16}$-inch plywood:
a. one circle approximately $3\frac{1}{2}$ inches in diameter;
b. two table sides;
c. one back ($1 \times 1\frac{3}{4}$ inches);
d. one seat ($1\frac{1}{2} \times 1\frac{3}{4}$ inches);
e. two undertable bars ($2\frac{1}{4} \times \frac{1}{4}$ inches).

2. Sand all the pieces.

3. Drill pin-sized holes (big enough to hold a dressmaker's stickpin) in the undertable bars and the hutch table sides as indicated by the dots.

4. Position and glue the back and seat pieces to the two hutch table sides (see the cross-section of the table side).

5. Glue the two bars underneath the table top (on the wrong side) along the dotted lines.

6. Sand lightly, stain, and cover with two coats of shellac. Sand lightly between all coats.

7. Line up the drilled holes of the undertable bars with the drilled holes of the table sides. Pass a stickpin through the hole of the undertable bar and the table side on both sides so that the hutch table/chair can swing into position as a hutch chair or a hutch table. Leave the head of the pin on the outside so that the pin will be secure in place. (See the illustration.)

OPTIONAL: You may upholster the hutch chair seat as follows:

1. Cut one seat from cardboard ($1\frac{1}{2} \times 1\frac{3}{4}$ inches).

2. Cover the cardboard seat with fabric or a wool "rush" seat (see page 152 in the chapter "Needlecrafts"). Position the seat in place on the wood seat of the hutch table.

Close-up of the hutch table.

Close-up of the hutch chair.

A gold-leafed Louis XV chair, a pearl and crystal chandelier, and a working grandfather clock set the elegant tone in this grand entrance hall.

The Entrance Hall

As in most homes, the entrance hall here sets the mood of the rest of the house: a grand, and elaborate 18th century American manor steeped in family tradition. Authentically, the entrance hall extends to the back of the house, with the staircase ascending through the middle of the house, flanked with living quarters on both sides on all floors. But it is not just an entrance hall; it is also the first floor of a three-storey, "flying," portrait gallery.

The floor is stained walnut and shellacked for a highly polished look.

All the walls and ceiling are simply "white-washed" with flat, white acrylic to accommodate, but not compete with, family portrait pictures.

The grand, circular staircase serves all three stories and is the focal point of the doll-house. It is stained mahogany and is carpeted with white, old velvet fabric. White balusters are connected with gold thread to represent brass. This staircase is highlighted by an elegant pearl and crystal chandelier which is made from half a plastic foam ball, a string of pearls, costume jewelry crystal beads, pins, and birthday candles.

In the entrance hall, as in the second floor sitting room and the master bedroom around the stairwell, are hung portraits of the dollhouse owner's ancestors. The idea was to create a "flying" staircase picture gallery that would extend to and be a part of all three floors of the dollhouse. The gold, rose-studded picture frames are from Lillian Vernon, Mt. Vernon, New York (see page 175 for the address). Each frame has a name plate engraved with the name of the family member whose portrait is featured. All the dolls, discussed later in this book (see page 157), also represent various family ancestors, although not necessarily of the 18th century.

The tall-case grandfather clock is Queen Anne style and has a genuine, working, man's wristwatch for the face.

The French Louis XV chair is made from cardboard, papier-mâchéd, gold-leafed, shellacked, and upholstered in pink silk.

The umbrellas are party prizes set in an umbrella stand which is a large thread spool enamelled and decorated with gold braid.

Patterns and Instructions for the Grand Staircase and Entrance Hall

SCALE: 1/2" = 1"

Patterns for the First-Floor Staircase

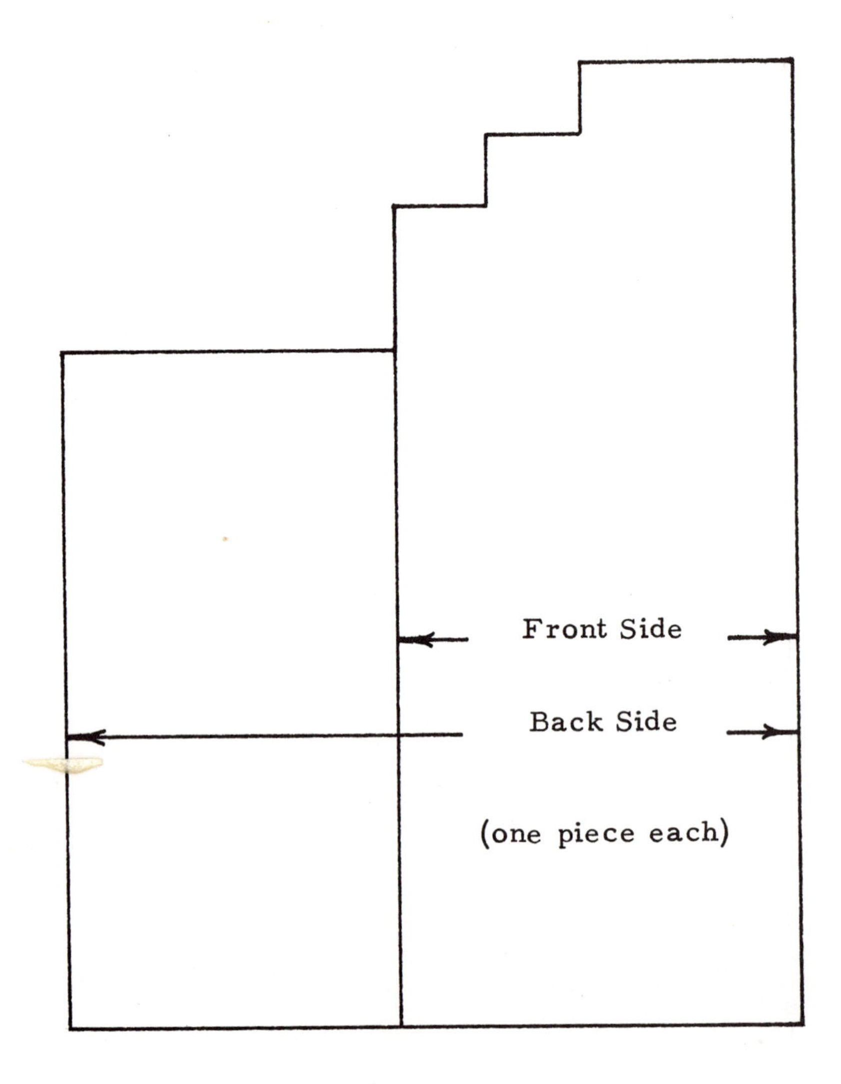

Instructions for the First-Floor Staircase

1. Cut, from $\frac{1}{8}$-inch thick plywood, one piece of each staircase part *except* all the steps.
2. Cut, from $\frac{3}{4}$-inch thick plywood, the three types of steps shown in the patterns.
3. Assemble the staircase according to the isometric view of the first-floor staircase.
4. Finish as desired and carpet, following the instructions on page 60.

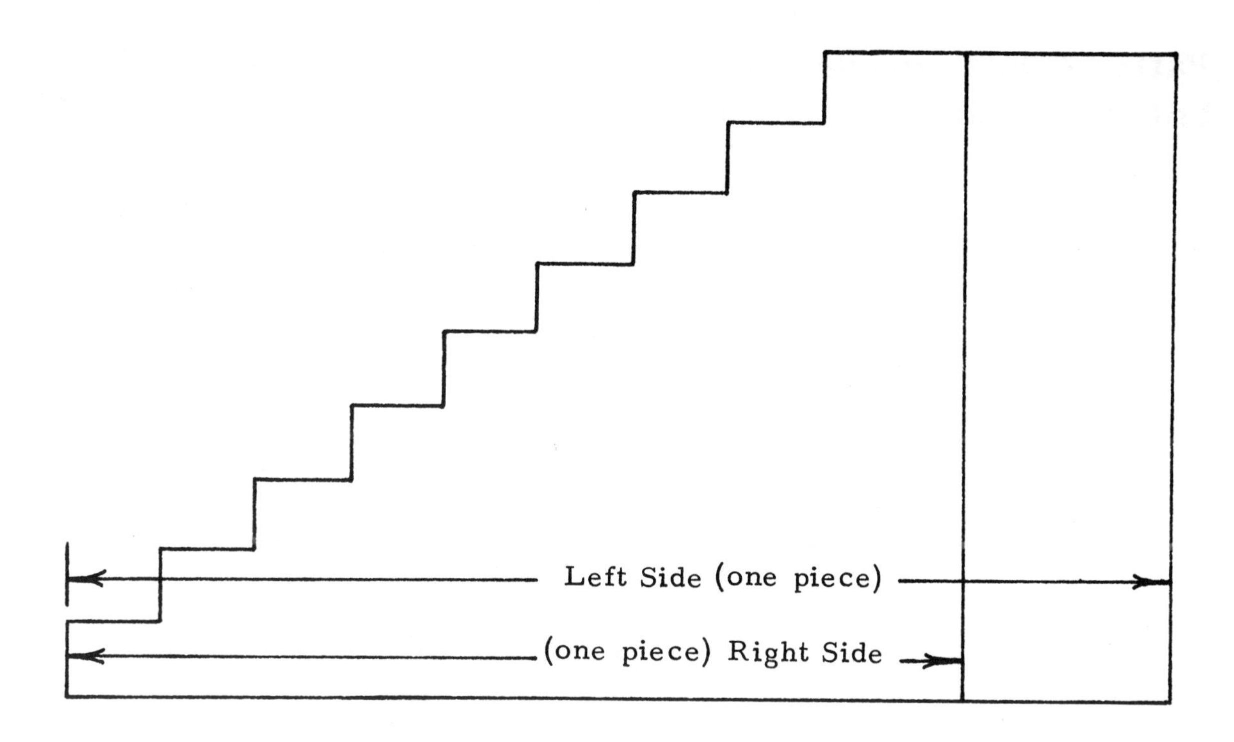

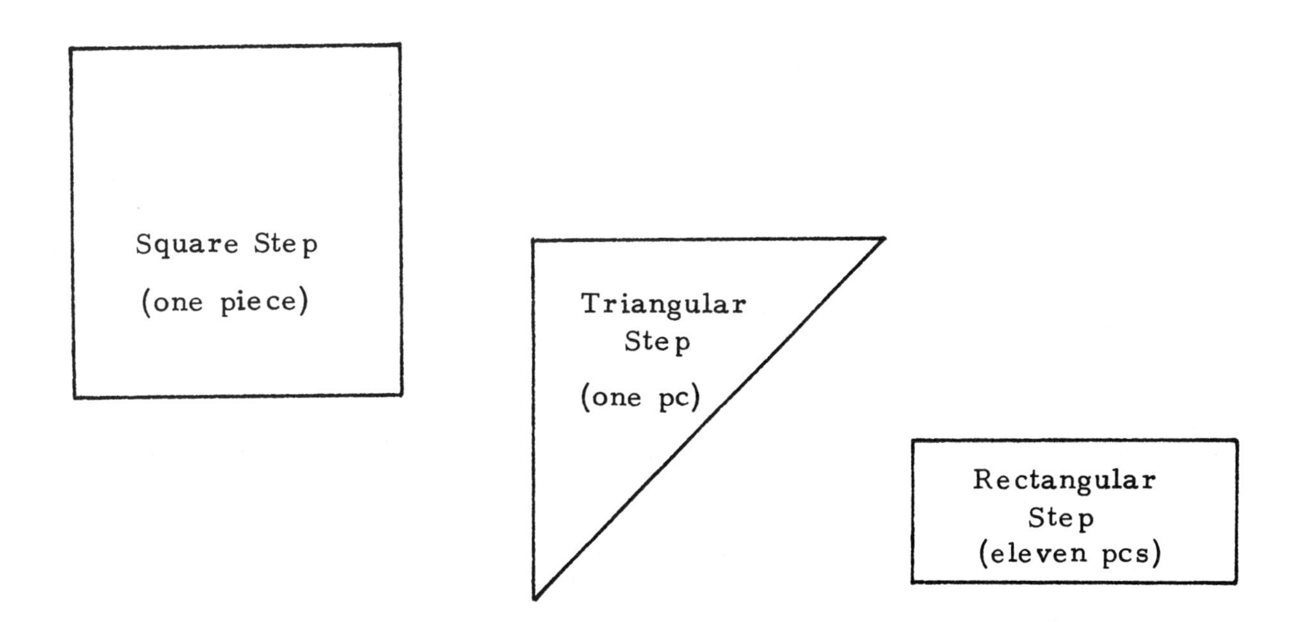

The steps to be cut from 3/4" plywood are the square, triangular, and rectangular.

FIRST-FLOOR STAIRCASE
Isometric View

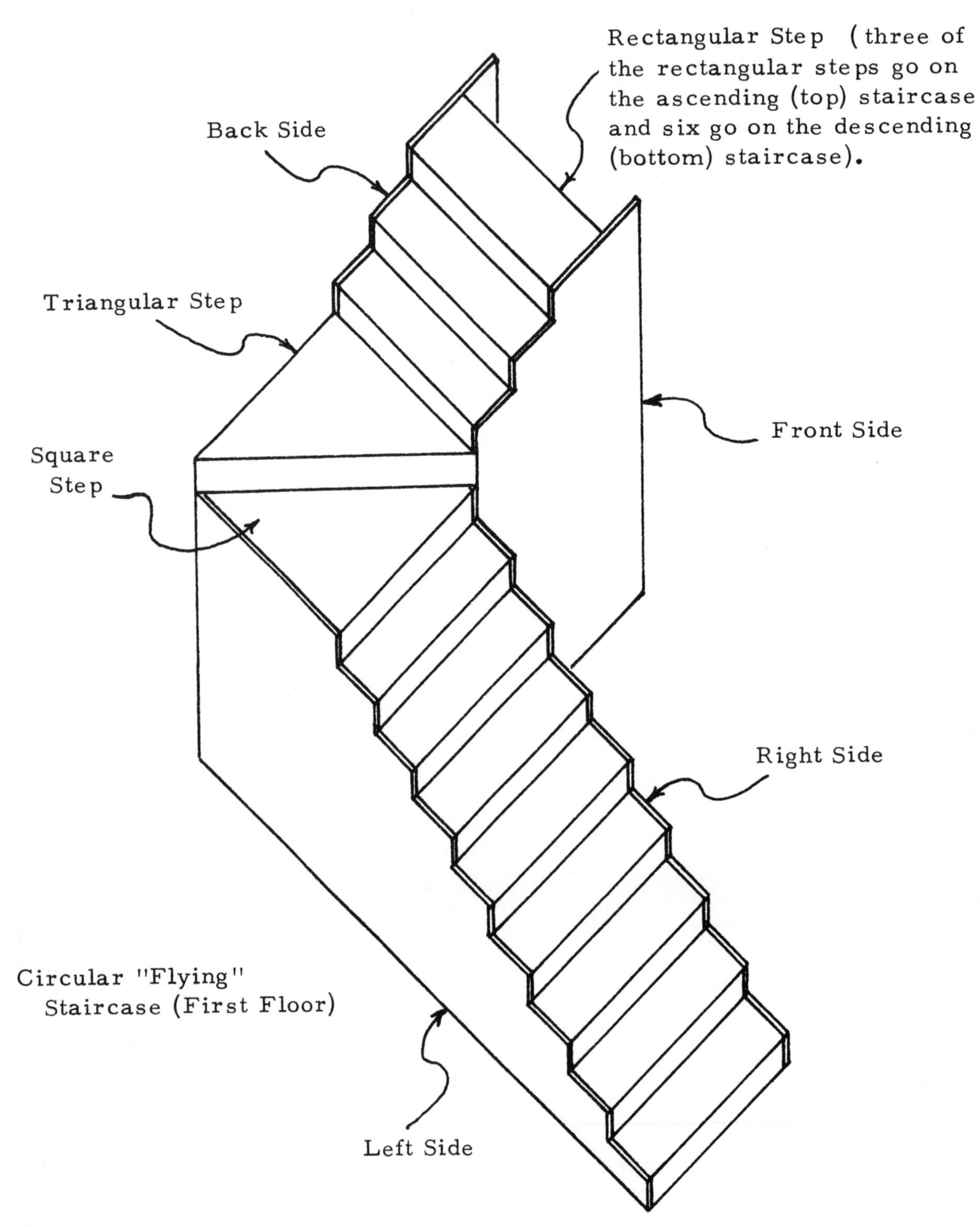

Patterns for the Second-Floor Staircase

SCALE: 1/2" = 1"

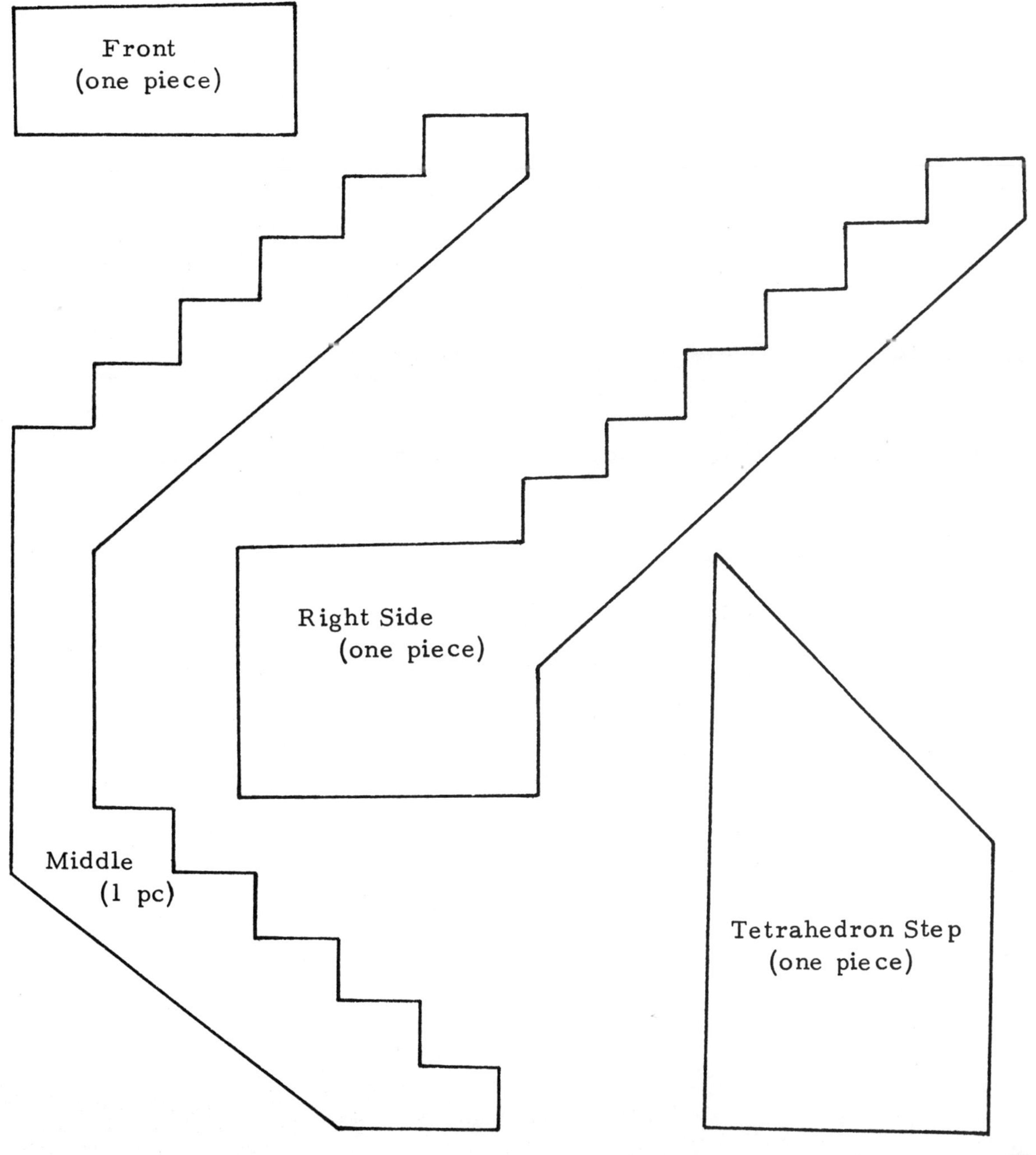

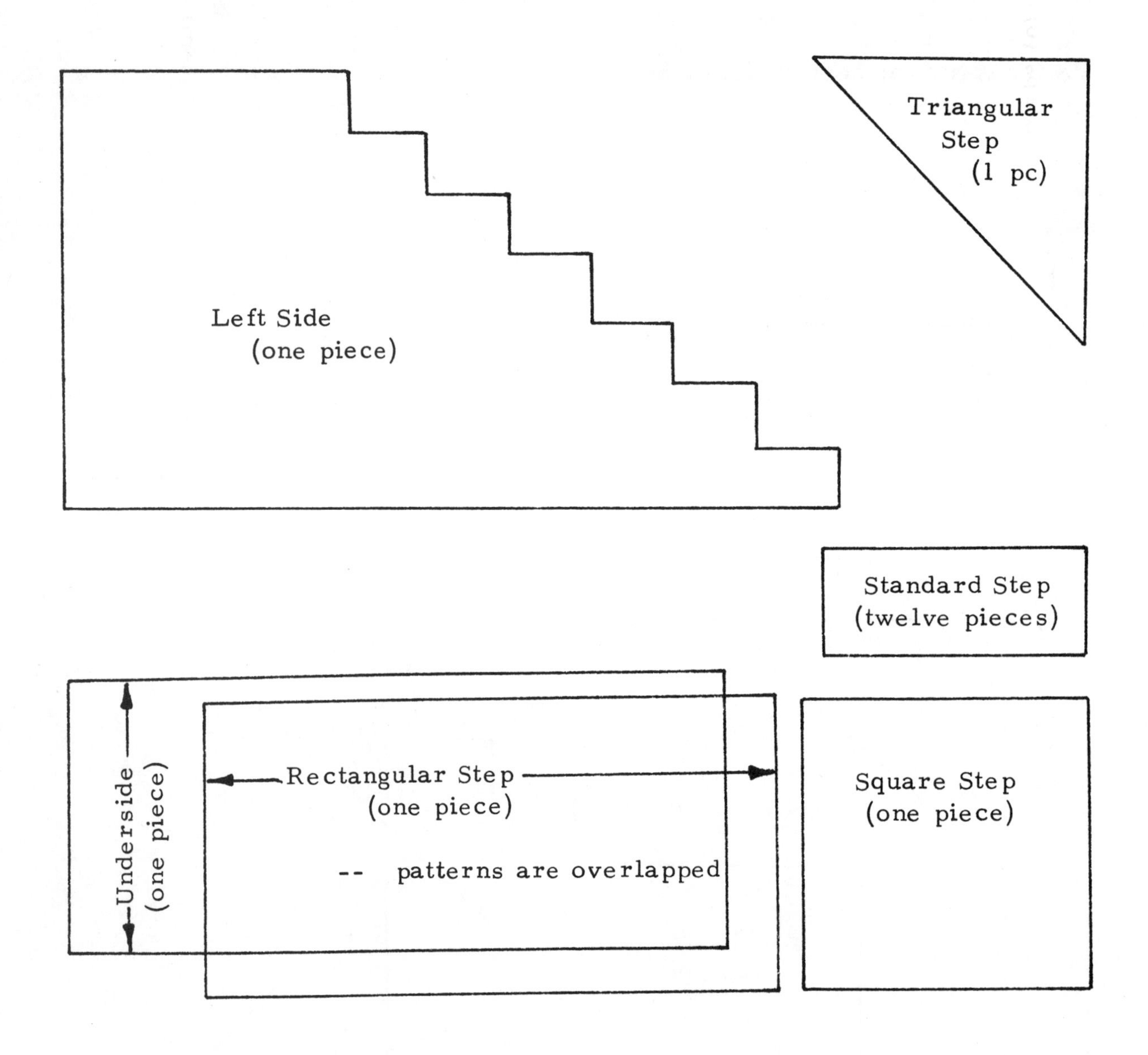

Cut all pieces from 1/8" plywood EXCEPT all the steps (rectangular, square, standard, and tetrahedron), which you cut from 3/4" thick plywood. Assemble according to the isometric view of the second-floor staircase. Finish as desired. Follow upholstery instructions for carpeting.

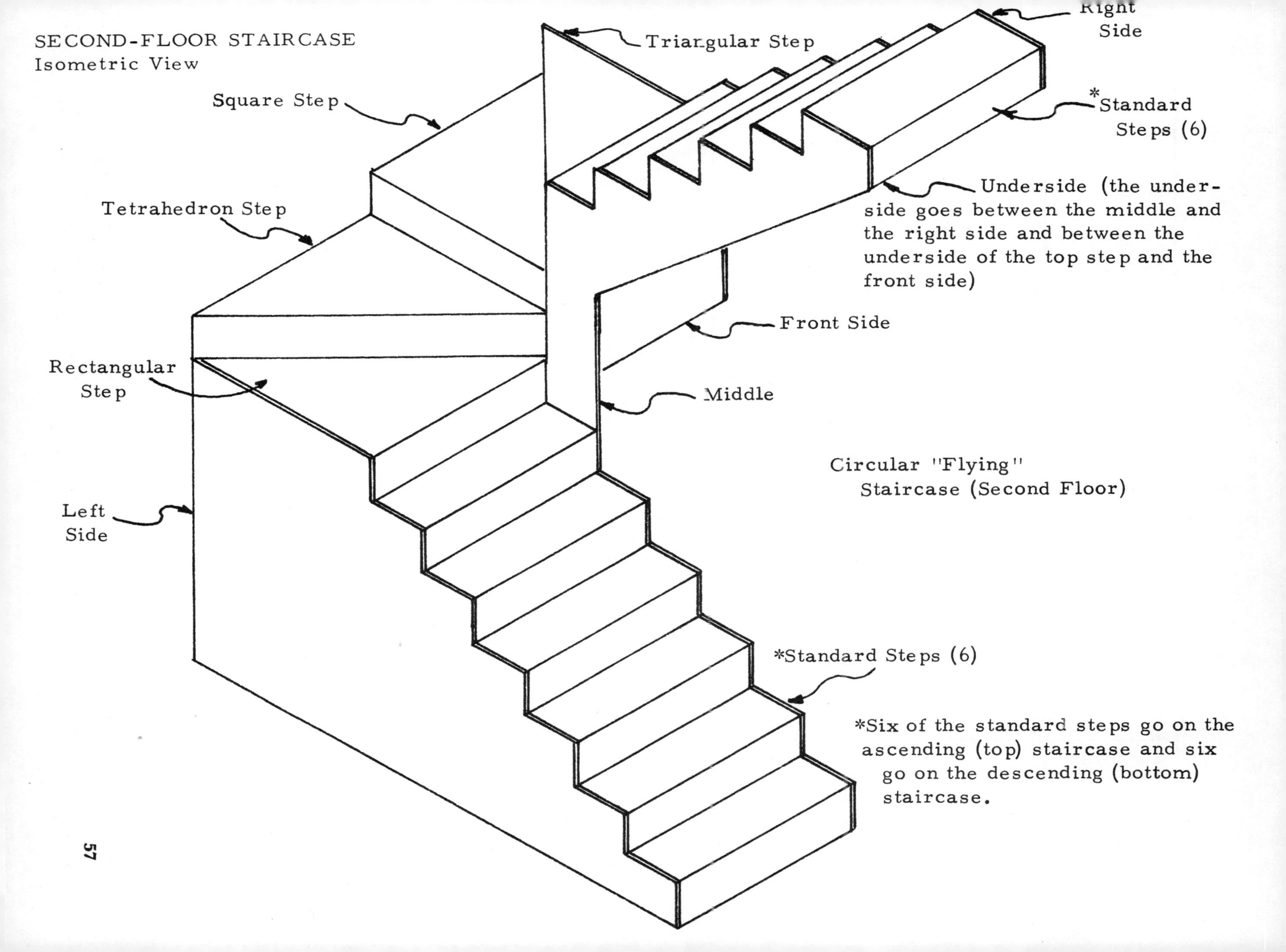
SECOND-FLOOR STAIRCASE
Isometric View
Triangular Step
Right Side
Square Step
*Standard Steps (6)
Tetrahedron Step
Underside (the underside goes between the middle and the right side and between the underside of the top step and the front side)
Front Side
Rectangular Step
Middle
Left Side
Circular "Flying" Staircase (Second Floor)
*Standard Steps (6)
*Six of the standard steps go on the ascending (top) staircase and six go on the descending (bottom) staircase.

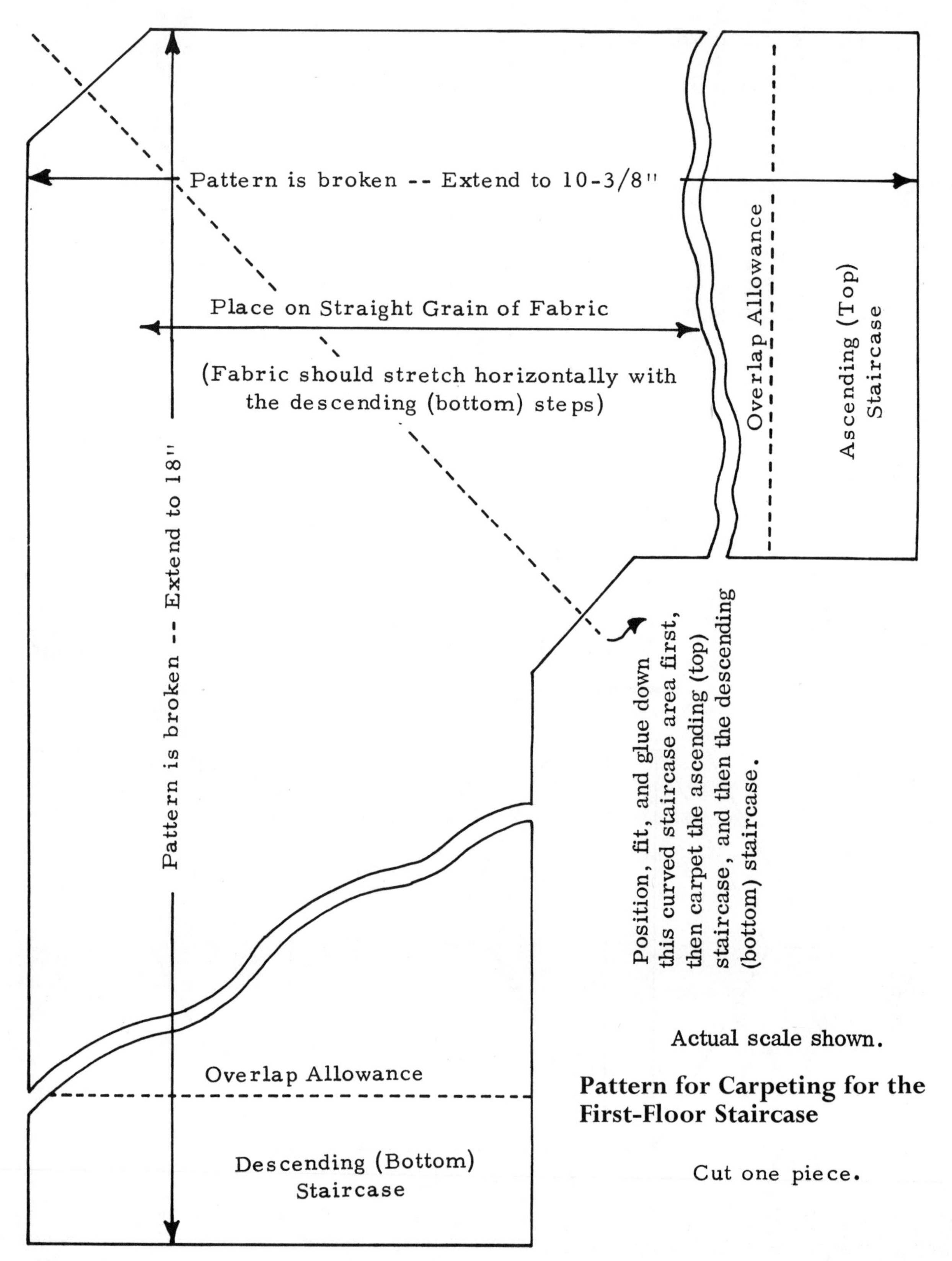

Actual scale shown.

Pattern for Carpeting for the First-Floor Staircase

Cut one piece.

Pattern for Carpeting for the Second-Floor Staircase

Cut one piece. Actual scale shown.

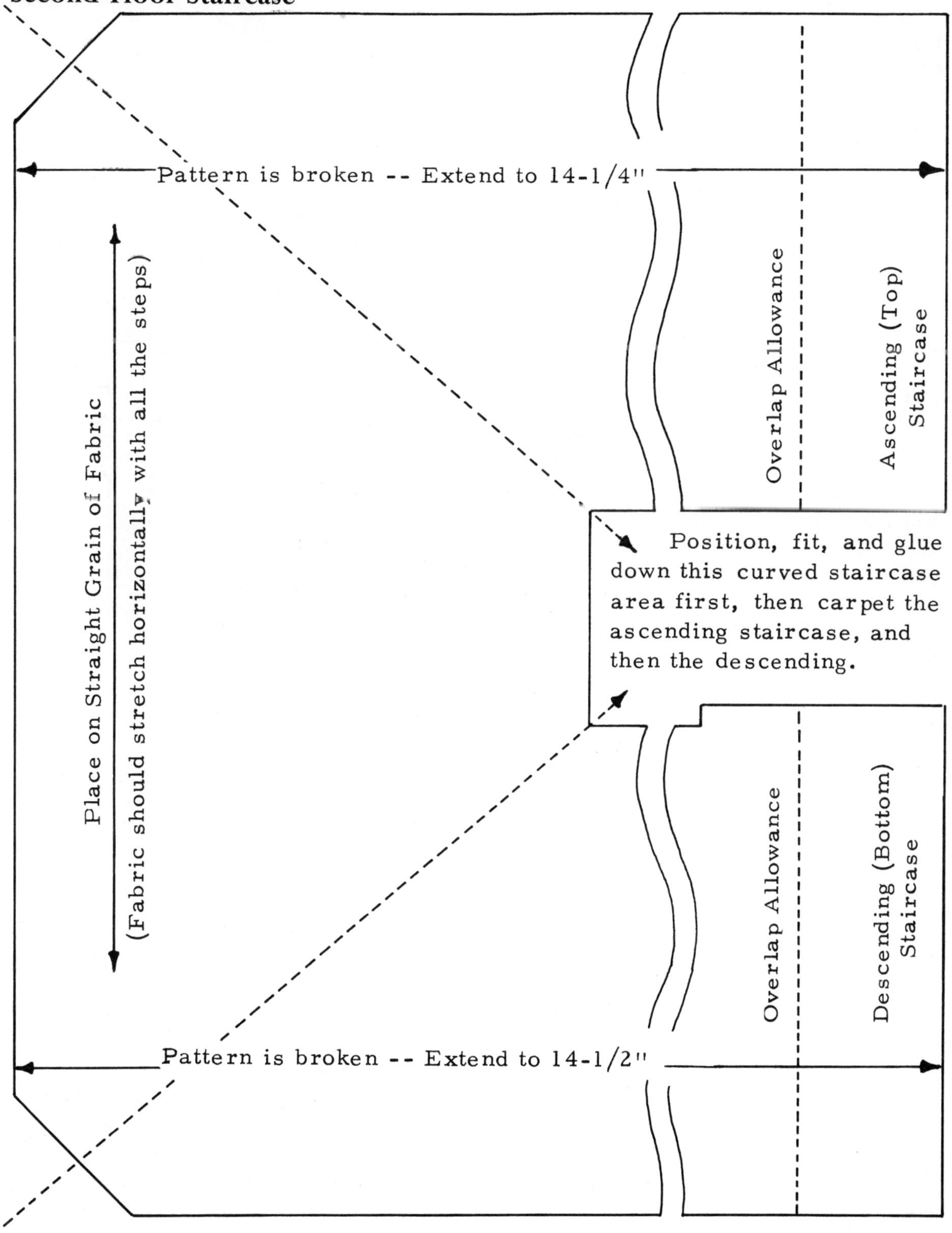

Pattern is broken -- Extend to 14-1/4"

Place on Straight Grain of Fabric

(Fabric should stretch horizontally with all the steps)

Overlap Allowance

Ascending (Top) Staircase

Position, fit, and glue down this curved staircase area first, then carpet the ascending staircase, and then the descending.

Overlap Allowance

Descending (Bottom) Staircase

Pattern is broken -- Extend to 14-1/2"

Instructions for the Balusters

In the Woodruff Dollhouse, white spindles joined with gold metallic thread were used to create the balusters on the stairways. However, these tend to break easily from even the slightest bumping, so you might want to leave them off entirely, unless your dollhouse is to be for show purposes only. If you do want balusters, you need about 50 $2\frac{1}{2}$-inch high, $\frac{1}{4}$-inch thick turned spindles (available at a lumberyard). Paint them white, and drill a hole through each, about $\frac{1}{4}$ inch from the top, for the metallic thread (to represent brass) to pass through and to join all the balusters. Glue the bottom tip of the spindles to the staircases and landings as applicable.

Carpeting the Staircase

To carpet the staircase, choose a fabric that will not ravel; there are no turning (hem) allowances in the pattern, except for the 1-inch overlap allowance at the top and the bottom staircase.

Suggested fabrics for carpeting are: fleece fabric, felt, antique velvet, or any other stretch fabric so you can "stretch" the fabric to fit the staircase. (The fabric should be cut to stretch width-wise, as in clothing.)

Instructions for the Grandfather Clock

1. Cut all pieces from $\frac{1}{8}$-inch plywood as follows:

a. one clock back;
b. one clock front (cut out an opening for the face);
c. two clock sides ($\frac{3}{4} \times 5\frac{1}{2}$ inches);
d. three clock bases: one base $1\frac{7}{8} \times 1\frac{1}{4}$ inches; one base $2\frac{1}{8} \times 1\frac{1}{2}$ inches; one base $2\frac{3}{8} \times 1\frac{3}{4}$ inches.

2. Sand all the pieces.

3. Position and glue the clock sides to the clock front and back along the dotted guidelines.

Close-up of the grandfather clock.

Patterns for the Tall-Case Grandfather Clock [c. 1760-1775]

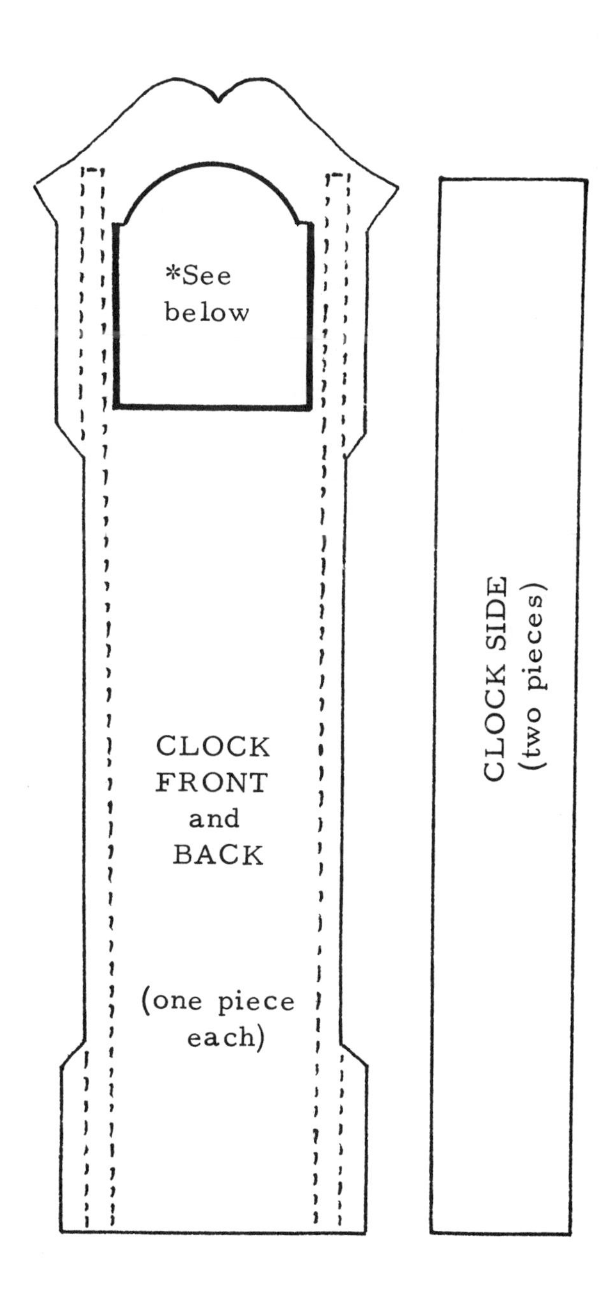

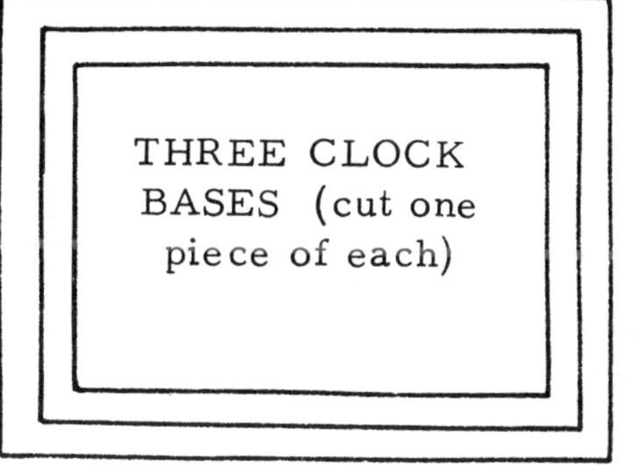

*Mount wristwatch
in this area.

4. Position and glue the smallest base onto the middle base, and the middle base onto the largest base.

5. Glue the bottom of the clock onto the three-step base.

6. Sand lightly, finish in the desired stain, and cover with two coats of shellac. Sand lightly between each coat. (See optional note below.)

7. Mount a large-sized wristwatch inside the opening. (If an old, inexpensive watch is not available, cut out a clock face from a magazine or make one, cover it with cellophane paper, and glue it inside the opening.)

OPTIONAL: This clock may also be japanned in the following manner:

a. Enamel the clock with high-gloss black paint.
b. Paint or decoupage small Oriental designs over the clock front.
c. Cover with several coats of varnish, sanding lightly between each coat.

Patterns for the French Louis XV Arm/Side Chair [c. 1723-1774]

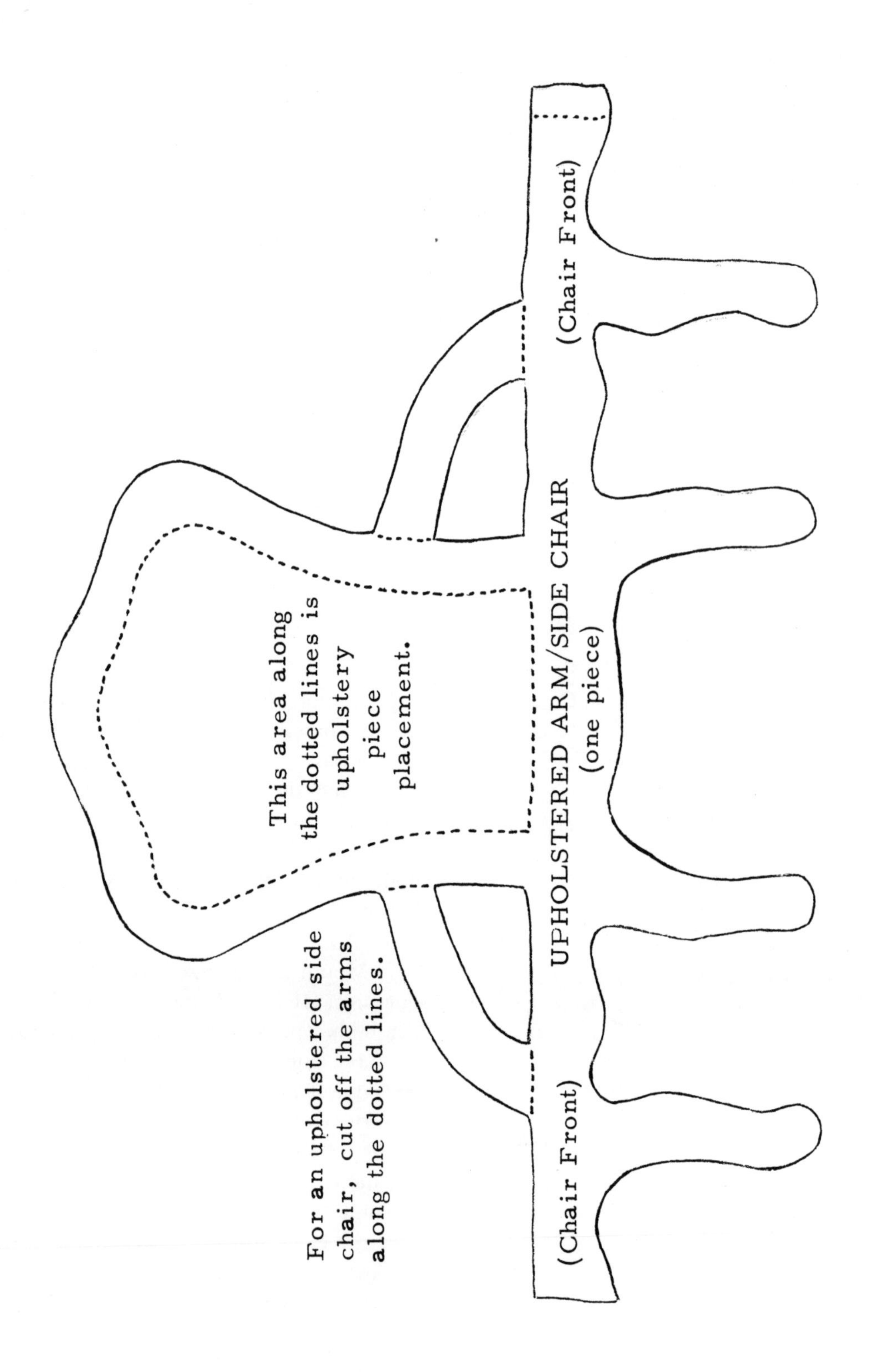

Outside notched circle is fabric upholstery piece.

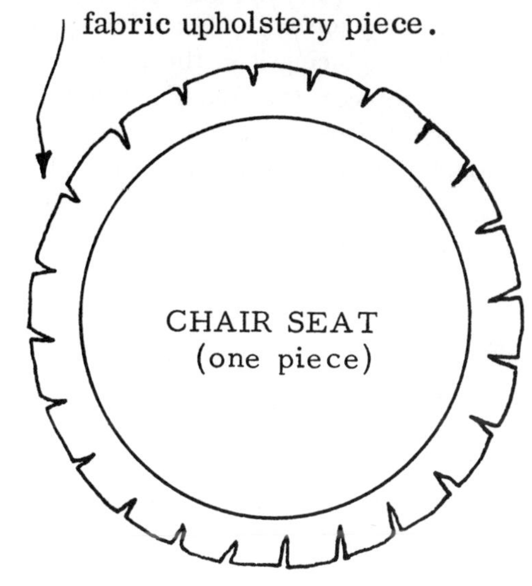

Cut one piece from plastic foam (or cardboard) and one piece from foam (for padding).

If you want to upholster the French chair on the outside back (as well as on the inside back), cut two upholstery pieces and position them on both sides of the chair back accordingly.

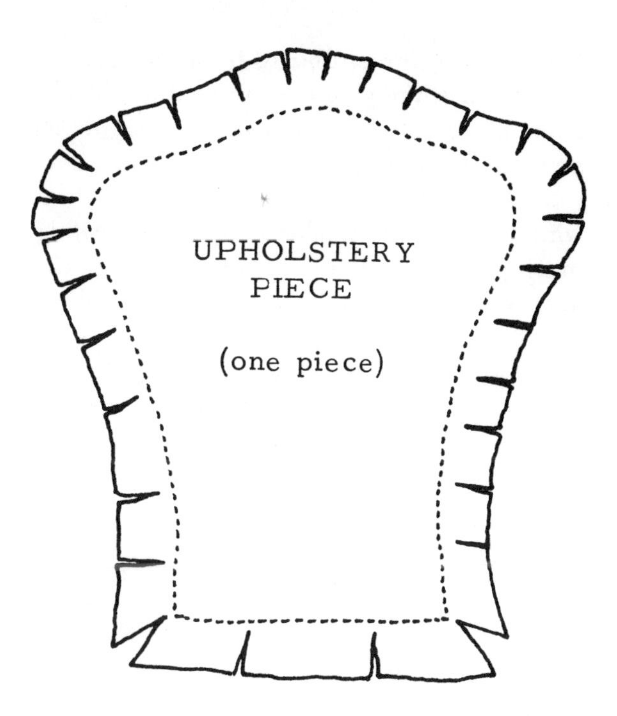

Illustration for step 7 showing how to cut the upholstery fabric to cover the upholstery piece (which is along the dotted lines).

Instructions for the French Louis XV Arm/Side Chair

1. Cut the following pattern pieces:
a. one armchair from thick cardboard;
b. one chair seat from plastic foam (approximately $\frac{1}{8}$ inch thick);
c. one chair seat from foam rubber (approximately $\frac{1}{4}$ inch thick);
d. one upholstery piece from bond paper, or the equivalent.

2. Wrap the cardboard chair (see step 1a) around an approximately 2-inch diameter cylinder. Join and glue the chair front ends together along the dotted line.

3. Wet the cardboard thoroughly, while it is still around the cylinder, with a sponge (to help mould the chair into a cylindrical shape). Let it dry thoroughly.

4. Remove the cardboard from the cylinder, and brush white glue over the entire chair to make it firm. Let the chair dry thoroughly for about 24 hours.

5. Gold leaf the chair or paint it with gold or white enamel and shellac it. For gold leafing, brush gold size over the area to be gold-leafed and, while it is still tacky, cover it with gold leaf paper. Work a small area at a time. This is a messy job, but the effect of gold leafing for this type of chair is well worth the time and effort.

6. Glue the foam rubber seat onto the plastic foam seat. Cover the seat with an upholstery fabric, such as silk, sateen, or velveteen.

7. Cover the upholstery piece in step 1d with the same upholstery fabric. Note: Cut the fabric approximately $\frac{1}{4}$ inch larger all around than the paper upholstery piece. Notch the fabric to facilitate glueing it to the wrong side of the upholstery piece. (See the illustration.)

8. Glue the upholstered piece, right-side-out, to the inside of the chair, and trim with cord, if you wish. (You can also use this same upholstered piece for the chair back.)

9. Glue the upholstered chair seat into position.

To imitate carved decorations on the Louis XV chair, glue on paper doily cut-outs before gold leafing or enamelling the cardboard.

In the Woodruff Dollhouse, this upholstered Louis XV armchair is used in the entrance hall, the sitting room, and the master bedroom.

Close-up of the gold-leafed Louis XV arm/side chair.

Illus. A 1 (above). This is an overall view of the inside of the dollhouse. From left to right, the first floor has the kitchen, entrance hall with the staircase and the dining room; the second floor has the parlor, sitting room and staircase and the library; the third floor has the child's bedroom, the dressing room and the master bedroom.

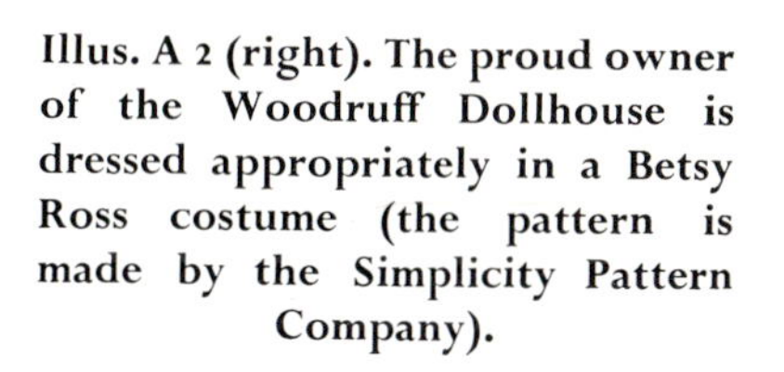

Illus. A 2 (right). The proud owner of the Woodruff Dollhouse is dressed appropriately in a Betsy Ross costume (the pattern is made by the Simplicity Pattern Company).

Illus. B 1. White-washed walls, intricate brickwork, and contrasting stained and painted furnishings give a warm, lived-in feeling to this charming kitchen.

Illus. B 2. This is a close-up view of the majestic fireplace-oven which is equipped with "wrought-iron" cookware and fireplace accessories.

Illus. B 3. This close-up shows the cozy eating corner of the kitchen, where cheerful red-and-white gingham curtains and tablecloth add special warmth to the room.

Illus. C 1. Pale pink and light green are the predominant colors in this elegant dining room. Although the room is mostly furnished in the Queen Anne style, the lovely side tea table is a Chippendale piece.

Illus. C 2. The fine, walnut-stained dining room table is set with "pewter" plates and is illuminated with a "pewter" chandelier. The light green sideboard in back holds several bottles of champagne to enhance the romantic atmosphere.

Illus. D 1. The lady of the house welcomes guests into her gracious home through this entrance hall. Family portraits adorn the white-washed walls and a gold-leafed Louis XV chair and working grandfather clock complete the setting.

Illus. D 2. Two plush, gold-leafed Louis XV chairs around a white enamelled gate-leg table form the seating area in this sitting room. Located on the second floor, this is actually the continuation of the family portrait gallery begun in the entrance hall.

Illus. E 1. Two Queen Anne settees and various other upholstered chairs can accommodate many guests in this richly panelled, wallpapered and painted parlor. The plush blue upholstery is particularly striking against the panelled fireplace wall. The elegant gold-leafed screen was an inexpensive plastic toy.

Illus. E 2. This close-up of the game area in the parlor features a mahogany Queen Anne card table and authentic playing cards. Notice the conveniently built-in candleholders to help the players see. The rest of the room is illuminated by a "crystal" chandelier which was a Christmas ornament.

Illus. F 1. Hand-worked Bargello upholstery, embroidery-trimmed draperies and an embroidered rug make the library one of the coziest rooms in the house. In addition, a filled newspaper rack and a Queen Anne secretary stacked with books add a literary atmosphere to the room.

Illus. F 2. This close-up of the library emphasizes the magnificent hand-worked upholstery and rug.

Illus. G 1. Dollhouse-size toys are especially enchanting in this simply decorated child's bedroom. The walnut pencil-post canopy bed is adorned with a hand-embroidered bedspread and canopy set trimmed with blue crocheted lace.

Illus. G 2. As beautiful as it is, this dainty dressing room is useful as well. Lacy ruffles and golden accents add elegance to the practical furnishings.

Illus. G 3. Masses of pink flowers bring a breath of spring to this 18th century French master bedroom. Predominantly pink and white, but accented with elegant gold and spots of orange and green, this luxurious room is highlighted by a stately Queen Anne canopy bed adorned with a colorful chintz coverette.

Illus. H 1 (left). The Christmas celebration is bound to be gay, judging by these colorful and festive costumes. A plastic foam Christmas tree, a beautiful wreath and lots of gift-wrapped presents ensure a fun time for all.

Illus. H 2 (right). Civilian dress for the men and beautiful, lacy opened overskirts for the women will make the New Year's Ball an elegant and unforgettable event. Beads, wire, pipe cleaners, curled ribbon and Christmas tree decorations adorn the ballroom.

Illus. H 3 (left). Fresh spring colors and cheerful ensembles characterize this Easter parade in the sitting room of the dollhouse. The Easter bunnies are cake decorations, and the eggs are beads.

Illus. H 4 (right). Colorful elegance is the theme at this romantic champagne party for two. The pink crocheted gown was ingeniously adapted from a piece of a knit pantyhose. The dashing red cutaway coat is made from felt.

Gracious dining is inevitable in this lovely, almost exclusively Queen Anne dining room.

The Dining Room

The main dining room is as intimate as it is formal, and as rustic as it is elegant. It has a romantic atmosphere that is conducive to many cozy hours of wining and dining with elegance. White, green, and pink are the colors predominately used in this Queen Anne room.

The two side walls are antiqued light green to harmonize with the white-stained, "worm-worn" wood panelling on the fireplace wall and the "white-washed" ceiling.

The maroon and beige velvet textured rug is a potholder and covers the walnut-stained, highly polished plank floor, both of which contrast to and harmonize with the old, rustic walls and ceiling.

Dinners are enhanced by watching sunsets from the west window. The draperies are pale pink organdy trimmed with green hand embroidery, and valanced with crisp, green, medallion-patterned fabric.

White, flat stones found at the beach in Mexico were used to stud the massive, quaint, white-stained, wood fireplace. Wood cut from real tree twigs "burns" in the fireplace. Red cellophane candy wrappers simulate the fire. On top of the mantel are a pair of "porcelain" birds from Moskatel's in Los Angeles, California (see page 175 for the address).

The gold, covered candy bowl is a cosmetic jar top. The authentic hurricane lamps are made from small mirror discs, birthday candles, and $\frac{1}{4}$-inch clear, plastic tubing. Coarse burlap, which was spray-glued to make it stiff and painted black to imitate wire mesh, makes a very convincing firescreen. Over the mantel hangs a portrait of an 18th century girl painted on silk and framed in gold filigree.

Queen Anne styling exclusively is used for all the furniture pieces in the formal dining room, with the exception of the side tea table, which is Chippendale.

The dark walnut-stained table is set to serve four. The pewter-like platters, salad dishes, and three-place setting flatware are from Shackman in New York (see page 175 for the address); the dessert bowls are self-cover buttons; the glass-blown tumblers are from Mexico; the bottle of champagne is from Solvang, California (see page 175 for the address). Tiny napkins were cut from light-weight cotton and pulled through napkin rings made from $\frac{1}{8}$-inch plastic tubing painted gold.

Pink upholstered dining room chairs are arranged around the dark walnut-stained dining room table, luxuriously set with "pewter" dishes. The atmosphere is completed with a bottle of champagne for the dinner guests.

Arranged around the table are four walnut-stained chairs upholstered in pink "brocaded" fabric.

On the Chippendale tea table is a four-piece carving set (from Shackman in New York) which is "pewter" with "staghorn" handles. It is a replica of a museum set that was actually used in 18th century colonial America. The fruits in the bowl are magnetic memo holders and beads. Over the tea table hang two silver-framed paintings, which are costume jewelry pins, depicting romantic 18th century scenes. Plastic doily cut-outs adorn the claw-and-ball feet on the tea table.

The cherrywood highboy is from Shackman in New York. It has 11 drawers, all of which open and close. (This highboy is the only piece of furniture in the entire Woodruff Dollhouse that was not handcrafted by the Woodruffs.)

In the sitting area, popularly used by the dolls for serving beverages and enjoying conversation after dinner, are two chairs, cushion-padded and fully upholstered in crisp green, medallion-patterned silk that matches the swag-style valance over the draperies.

The portable corner cabinet is used for displaying fine miniature china, silver, and crystal. The cabinet has a cherrywood finish with matching open shelves. Paper-thin veneer strips were wrapped around the cabinet edges in front to give a rounded, carved look. A real sea shell was glued against the wall of the top shelf and painted to reproduce a carved shell design. Bric-a-brac "porcelain" figurines are actually cake decorations. The brass beakers are sample lipstick holders. Other dinnerware pieces are bottle caps, buttons, and hardware discs that were painted to simulate the various metals and enamelwares that were popular in colonial America.

To the left of the fireplace is a sideboard enamelled light green to tie in with the other light green features in this room. The walnut drawer really pulls out. On top of the sideboard is a crystal, covered candy dish which is a replica of a museum piece. Two more bottles of champagne indicate a big forthcoming party. The three-candle gold candelabra is from the German handcrafted Spielwaren collection of museum quality furnishings in the International Christmas Castle also designed by the author (see page 4). The framed cameo silhouette over the sideboard is a costume jewelry brooch.

A "pewter" chandelier, made from a metal can lid, fine costume jewelry chain, and birthday candles, hangs directly over the dining area. Its design is a version of the chandelier in the dollhouse kitchen.

Patterns and Instructions for the Dining Room

Patterns for the Queen Anne Upholstered Straight Back Chair [c. 1740-1760] and the Queen Anne Side Chair [c. 1730-1750]

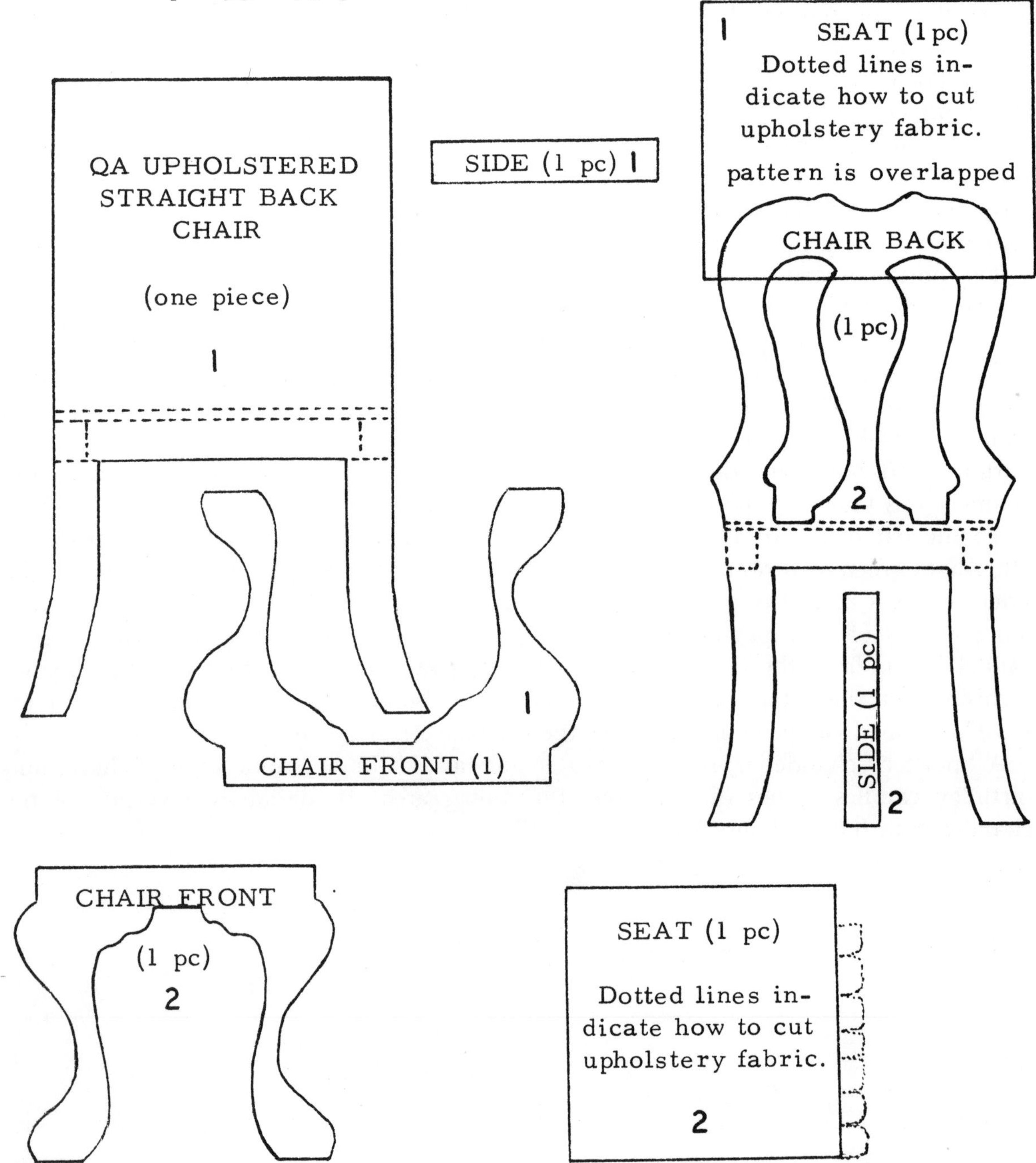

Instructions for the Queen Anne Upholstered Straight Back and/or Side Chair

1. For either chair, cut the following from $\frac{3}{16}$-inch plywood (following the applicable pattern pieces marked "1" for the upholstered straight back chair and "2" for the side chair):
a. one chair back;
b. one chair front;
c. two chair sides ($\frac{1}{4} \times 1\frac{3}{8}$ inches).

2. Sand all the pieces to fit.

3. Assemble and glue the side pieces at the back ends to the inside back of the chair and the front ends to the inside chair front. (See the illustration.)

4. Sand, finish, and shellac as desired.

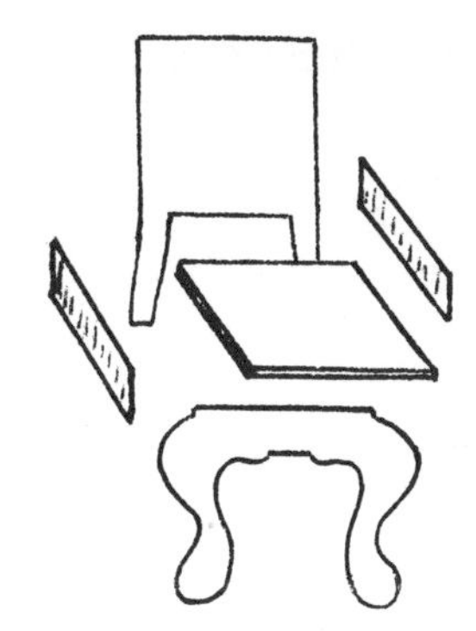

Illustration showing standard chair assembly.

UPHOLSTERY

1. Cut one upholstery seat from light-weight cardboard and one from foam rubber (approximately $\frac{1}{8}$-inch thick). Glue both pieces together.

2. Cover the seat with upholstery fabric (note on the pattern piece how to cut the upholstery fabric), and position in place.

For the full upholstered straight back chair, use the chair back (without the legs) as the pattern piece for the back upholstery. Cut one piece from cardboard, and cover it with the upholstery fabric. Glue in position.

OPTIONAL: You can use fleece padding for the back upholstery and the seat, and quilt it for interest. You can also make wool "rush" seat upholstery for either chair (see page 152 in the chapter "Needlecrafts").

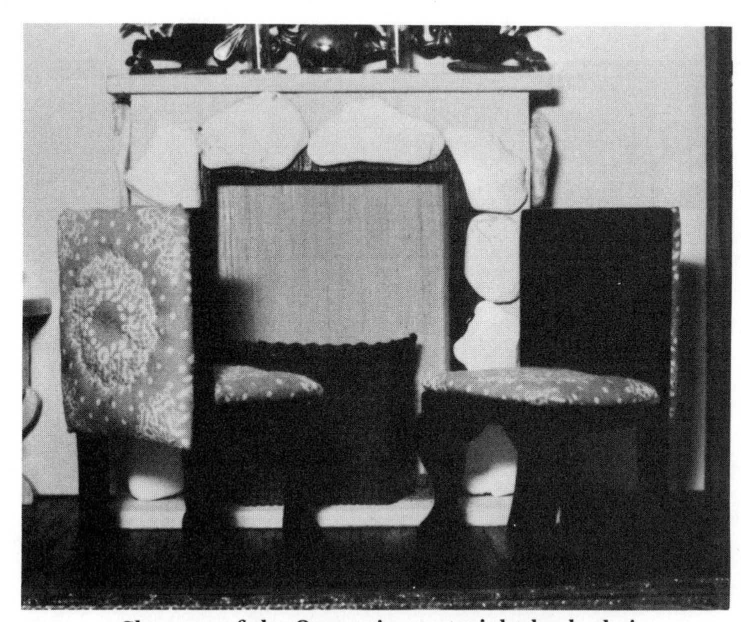

Close-up of the Queen Anne straight back chair.

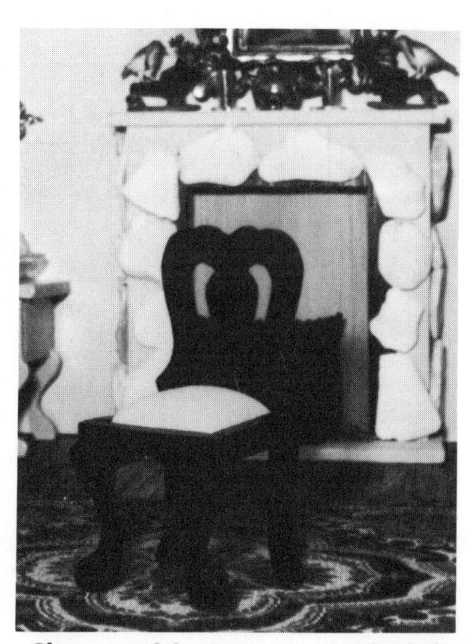

Close-up of the Queen Anne side chair.

Patterns for the 18th Century Fireplace

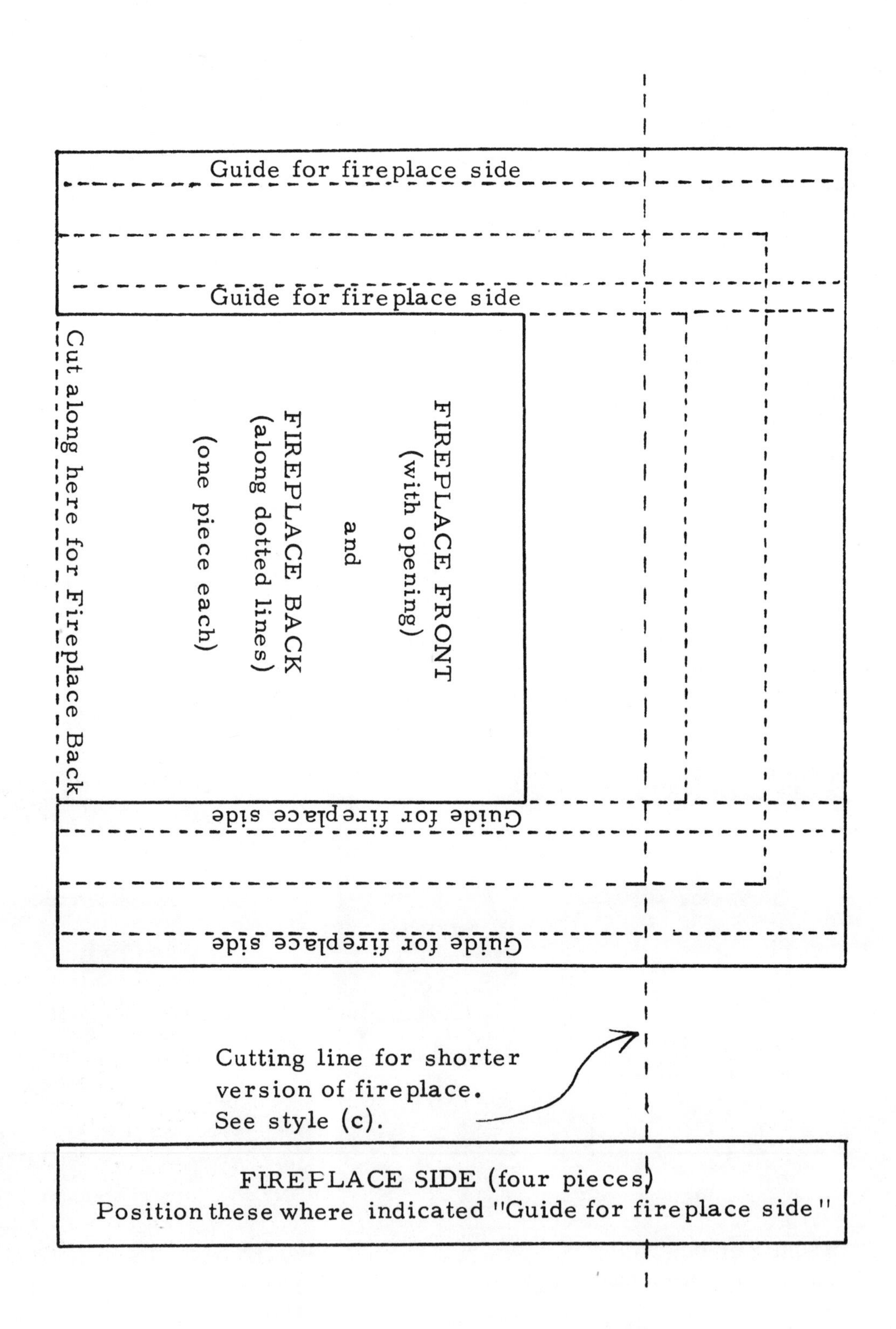

HEARTH (one piece)

MANTEL (one piece)

The following fireplace styles are possible from this pattern:

(a) 5"x5" fireplace with 3"x4" opening;
(b) 5"x5" fireplace with 3"x3" opening;
(c) 5"x3-3/4" fireplace with 3"x3" opening;
(d) 4"x4-1/2" fireplace with 3"x3" opening;
(e) 4"x4-1/2" fireplace with 3"x4" opening.

Instructions for the Fireplace (Standard for All Fireplaces)

1. Cut the following pieces from $\frac{3}{16}$-inch plywood:
a. one fireplace back;
b. one fireplace front with opening;
c. four sides;
d. one mantel;
e. one hearth.

2. Sand all the pieces to fit.

3. Position and glue, on the inside (wrong side) of the fireplace front, the four sides (along the dotted lines indicated "Guide for fireplace side"). Line them up with the inside fireplace back. Add the mantel on the top and the hearth on the bottom.

4. Sand any overlapping edges with coarse sandpaper, and finish with fine.

Suggested finishes for the fireplace:
a. Stain the fireplace mahogany, walnut, teakwood, or cherrywood.
b. Paint $\frac{1}{2}$-inch wide veneer strips to simulate marble (white, black, or green) and trim around the stained fireplace opening.

c. Paint the entire fireplace to simulate marble.
d. Cover the fireplace with tiny sandpaper "bricks" inside and/or outside (see the fireplace-oven instructions on page 34). Leave the "bricks" natural or paint them white.
e. Cover the fireplace with small, white, flat stones (for the 5 × 5 inch fireplace with the 3 × 3 inch opening).
f. Stud the fireplace with tiny garden-landscaping pebbles.
g. "White-wash" the fireplace by adding very fine white sand to the acrylic or flat paint.

Pattern for the 18th Century Over-Mantel

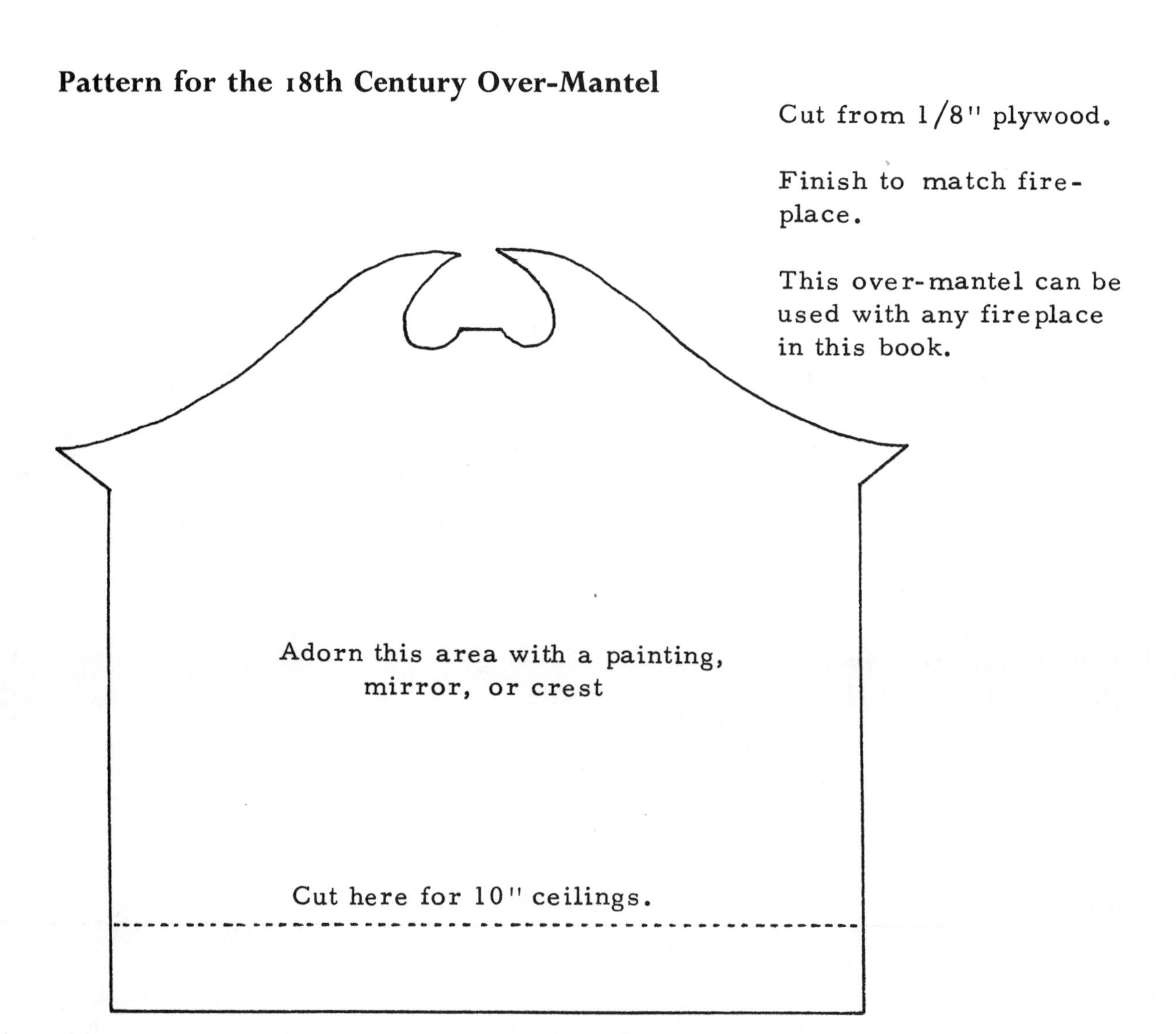

Patterns for the Queen Anne Corner Cabinet [c. 1700-1775]

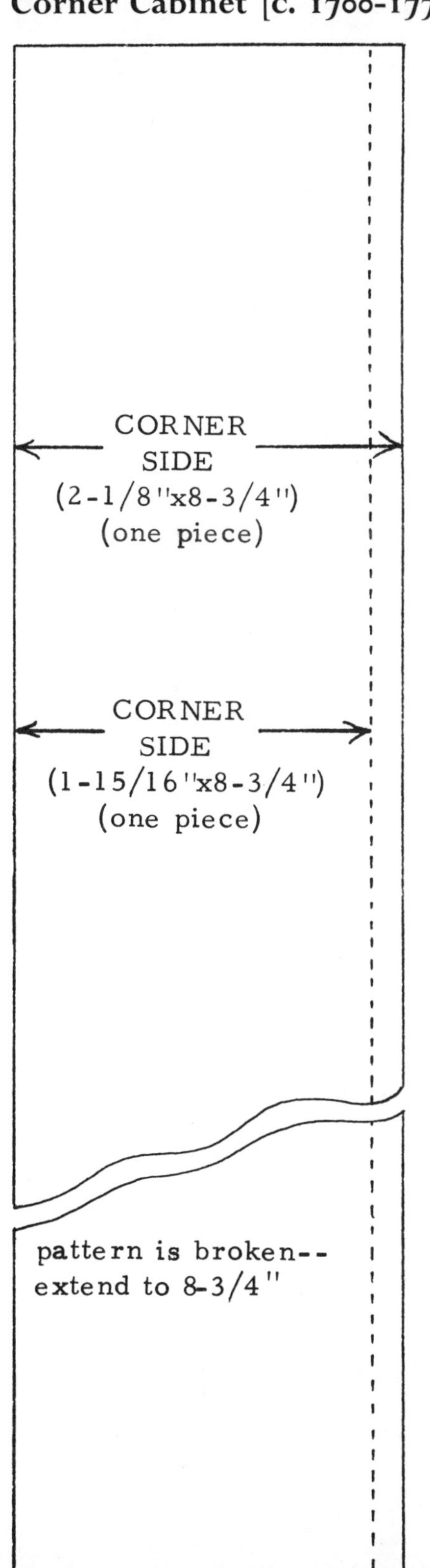

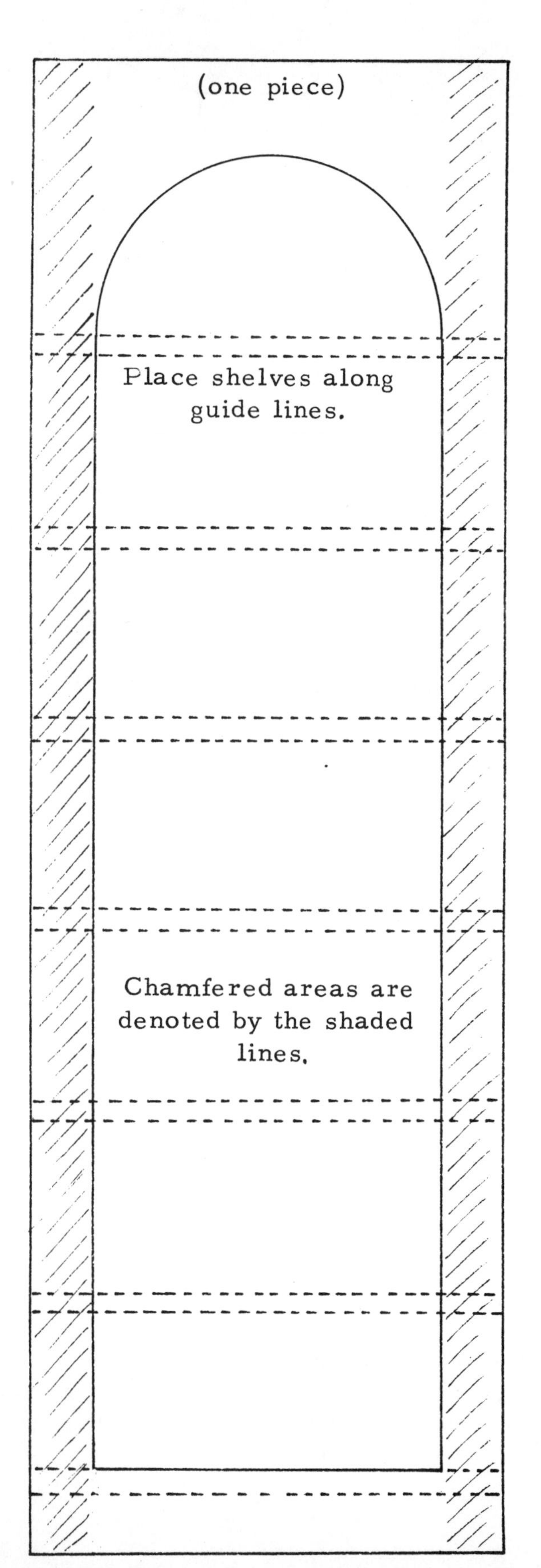

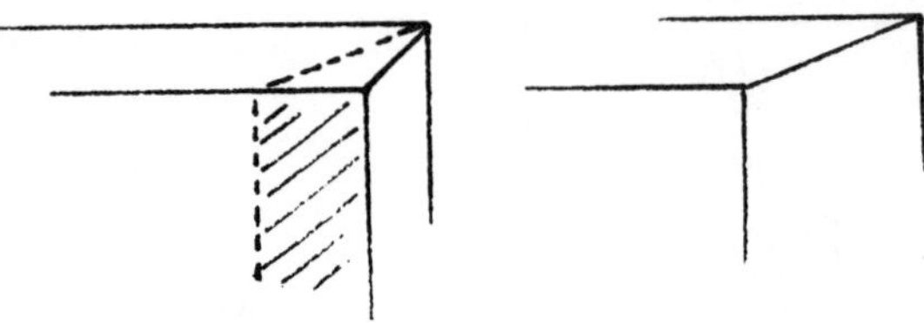

Illustration showing how to chamfer the corner cabinet front (in the shaded areas).

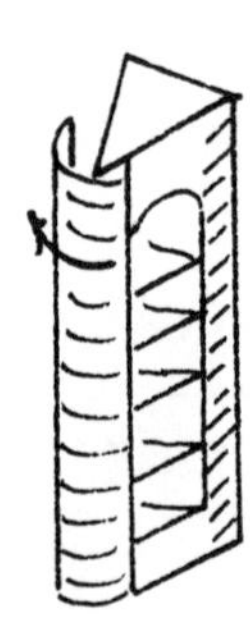

Wrap veneer strips over chamfered area in front and over to the two corner sides like this.

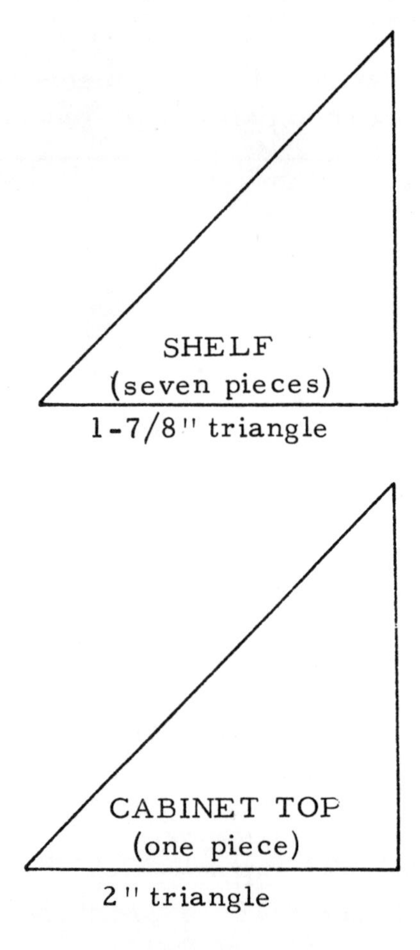

Instructions for the Queen Anne Corner Cabinet

1. Cut the following from $\frac{3}{16}$-inch plywood:
a. one corner side ($2\frac{1}{8} \times 8\frac{3}{4}$ inches);
b. one corner side ($1\frac{15}{16} \times 8\frac{3}{4}$ inches);
c. one cabinet front ($2\frac{7}{8} \times 8\frac{3}{4}$ inches);
d. one cabinet top (right triangle 2×2 inches).

2. Cut from $\frac{1}{8}$-inch plywood seven shelves (right triangle $1\frac{7}{8} \times 1\frac{7}{8}$ inches).

3. Sand all the pieces.

4. Chamfer (cut off at the angle shown in the illustration) the cabinet front slightly towards the outer edges in the shaded area of the pattern.

5. Position and glue the two corner sides at a 45° angle.

6. Paint the inside cabinet sides white, or the color of the dining room walls.

7. Stain the shelves. Position and glue them as indicated along the dotted guide lines.

8. Add the cabinet front. Stain it and the outside corner cabinet walls (even though the outside corner walls will not show) to match the shelves.

9. Wrap 1-inch wide veneer stripping (stained the same as the rest of the cabinet) as indicated in the illustration, over the chamfered area and around to the corner side walls. This gives the cabinet a rounded, carved look.

10. Sand lightly. (This piece of furniture was not shellacked, although this is optional, of course.)

11. Glue a white sea shell in the top shelf to illustrate the carved shell design that was popular on Queen Anne corner cabinets of this period.

Close-up of the Queen Anne corner cabinet.

Patterns for the Queen Anne Sideboard [c. 1720-1740]

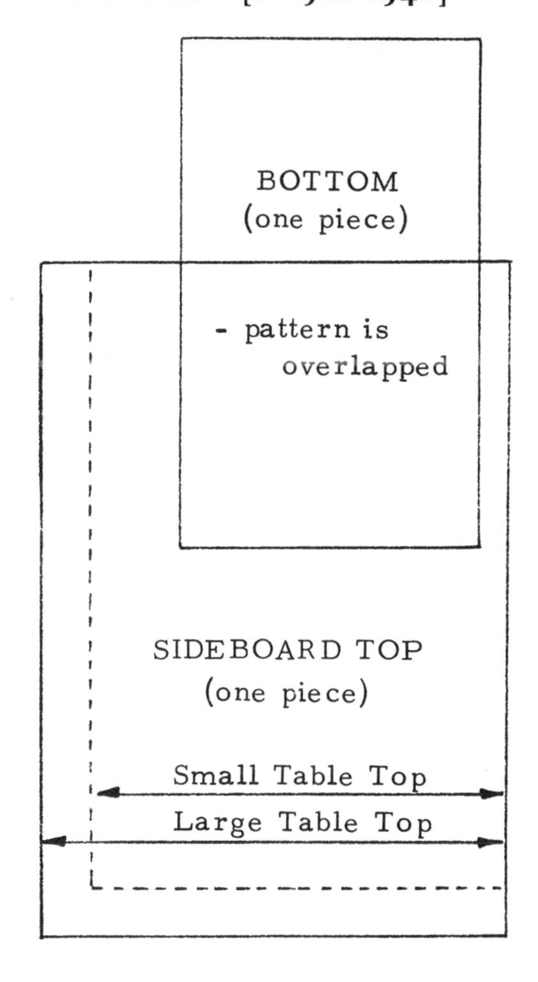

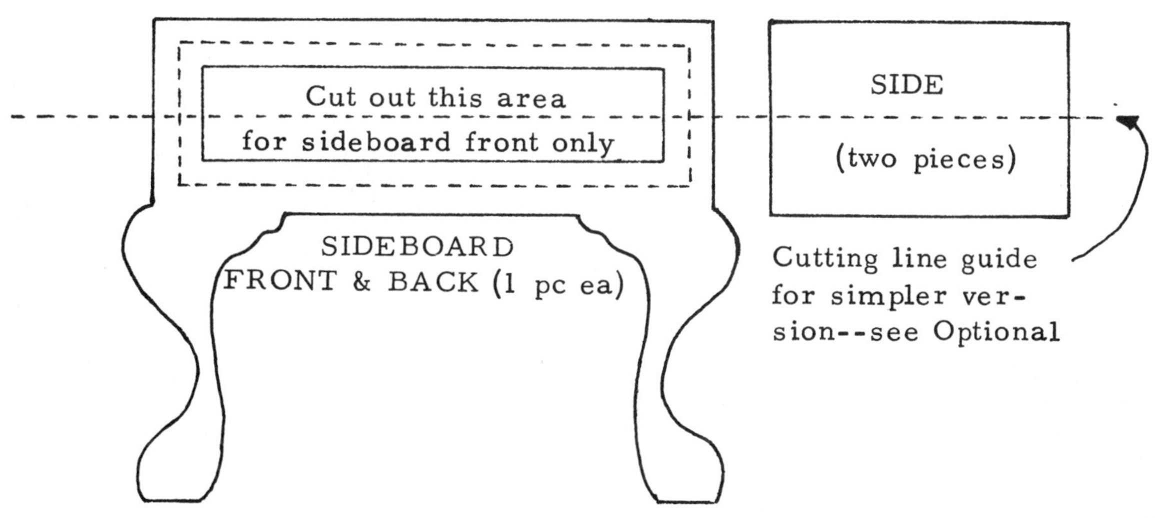

Instructions for the Queen Anne Sideboard

1. Cut from $\frac{3}{16}$-inch plywood:
a. one table front with an opening for the drawer;
b. one table back (the same as the front, but without the opening for the drawer);
c. two table sides ($1 \times 1\frac{5}{8}$ inches);
d. one table bottom ($1\frac{5}{8} \times 2\frac{5}{8}$ inches);
e. one small table top ($2\frac{1}{4} \times 3\frac{1}{4}$ inches).

2. Cut the drawer parts from $\frac{1}{8}$-inch plywood (see the highboy/lowboy drawer parts on page 124 in the section "Patterns and Instructions for the Master Bedroom" to trace the patterns):
a. one each of drawer pattern piece B ($1\frac{3}{4} \times 2\frac{1}{4}$ inches); E ($\frac{3}{4} \times 2\frac{3}{4}$ inches); and G ($\frac{3}{8} \times 2\frac{1}{4}$ inches).
b. two each of pattern piece C ($\frac{1}{2} \times 1\frac{3}{4}$ inches).

3. Sand all the pieces.

4. Assemble and glue the two table sides to the inside table front (on the wrong side) and the inside back. Line up the table bottom immediately below the cut-out drawer opening, so the drawer can slide in and out along this bottom. Add the table top.

5. Construct the drawer (see the highboy/lowboy drawer parts on page 124 in the section "Patterns and Instructions for the Master Bedroom").

6. Sand everything again, and finish as desired.

7. Use a costume jewelry bead for the drawer pull.

OPTIONAL: For a simpler version, cut out the table front, back, and sides along the dotted lines, but omit the drawer. Add the larger table top ($2\frac{1}{2} \times 3\frac{1}{2}$ inches). You can also glue a dummy drawer front onto the table front and add a bead for the pull. This will not be as detailed as the sideboard with the pull-out drawer, but it will be equally convincing.

Either way, this table can be used in virtually any room.

Close-up of the Queen Anne sideboard.

Close-up of the Queen Anne dining room table.

Patterns for the Queen Anne Dining Room Table [c. 1725-1750] and the Chippendale Side Table [c. 1730-1750]

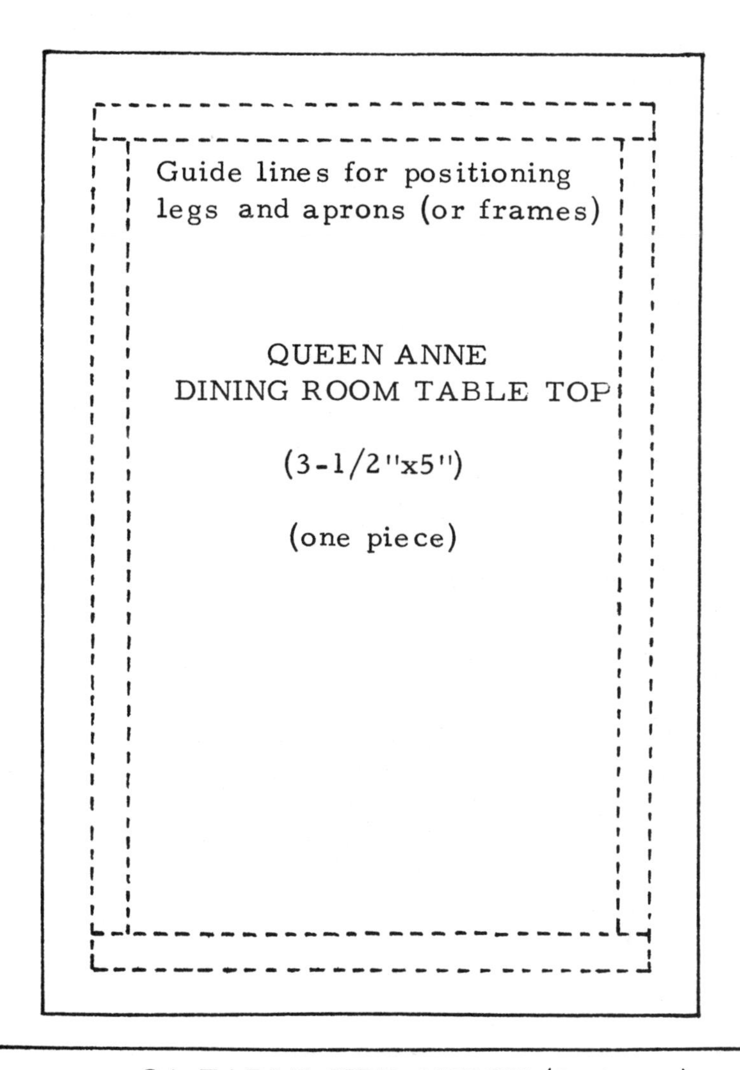

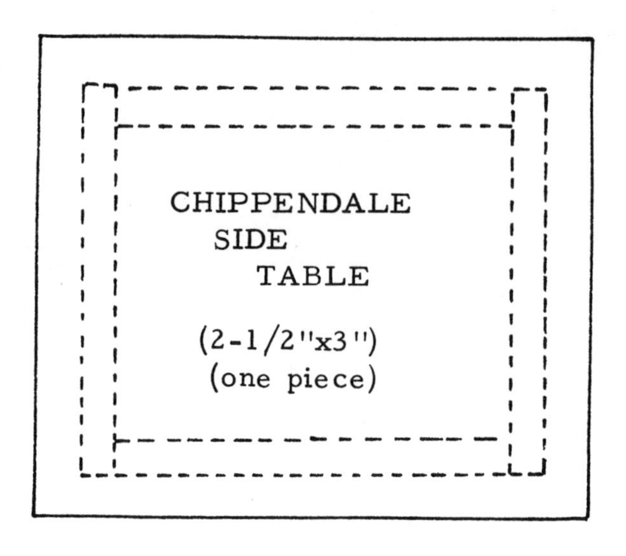
CHIPPENDALE
SIDE
TABLE
(2-1/2"x3")
(one piece)

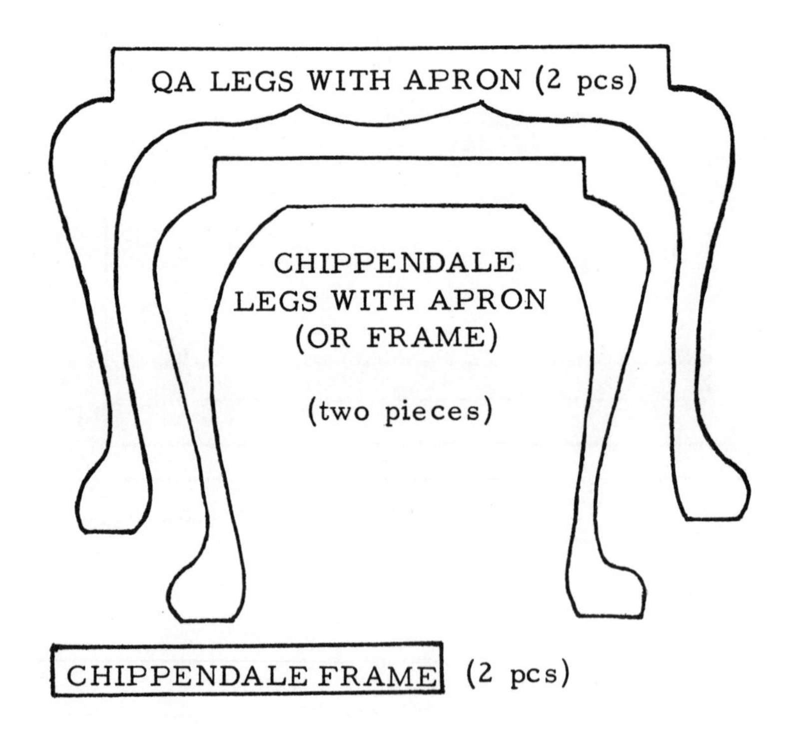
QA LEGS WITH APRON (2 pcs)
CHIPPENDALE
LEGS WITH APRON
(OR FRAME)
(two pieces)
CHIPPENDALE FRAME (2 pcs)

Instructions for the Queen Anne Dining Room Table and the Chippendale Side Table

1. For either table, cut the following from $\frac{3}{16}$-inch plywood:
a. two legs with apron (or frame) pieces;
b. two table side aprons (or frames);
c. one table top.

2. Sand all the pieces.

3. Position and glue the legs with the apron pieces and the side aprons on the underside of the table top along the dotted guide lines.

4. Sand, finish with mahogany stain, and shellac twice. Sand lightly between each coat.

For a Chippendale décor, cut out designs from plastic doilies, and glue them on the ends of the "ball" feet. Paint or stain them the same as the rest of the table. This will give the feet a carved, Chippendale look.

For particular detail, a fine crocheted doily is especially nice for the dining room tablecloth. To make placemats and napkins, see the chapter "Patterns and Instructions for the Linens" on page 143. To make napkin rings, cut pieces of $\frac{1}{8}$-inch diameter plastic tubing and paint them.

Close-up of the Chippendale side table.

Formal, but friendly, is the parlor in the Woodruff Dollhouse. As you can see, there is plenty of seating, for those interested in conversation, as well as a game area for those who wish to play cards.

The Parlor

The Georgian parlor is the most richly and elegantly decorated room in the dollhouse. Cool, sky blues and rich, warm browns provide a very formal, yet friendly, atmosphere that lends itself to graceful and relaxed entertaining. The parlor expresses a sense of family.

A French architectural touch was achieved on the richly panelled fireplace wall by glueing artist's wood plaques right onto the wall and staining everything cherrywood. Flat veneer strips cut to illustrate a dentilled cornice with running fretwork were glued along the ceiling on the cherrywood panelled wall. This makes the room distinctly Georgian. The middle Queen Anne style panel was cut from $\frac{1}{8}$-inch plywood and is part of the fireplace.

Roman ruins wallpaper, from Tiny Line in El Monte, California (see page 175 for the address), on the right wall, and wainscoting on the left highlight the international interest prevalent in colonial America. Use of this wallpaper was inspired by the Pannini wallpaper in the drawing room of the Jeremiah Lee Mansion in Marblehead, Massachusetts.

The "Oriental" rug on the plank floor is a beige linen placemat embroidered with a brown cross-stitch design.

Lacework cut from plastic doilies was glued onto the ceiling and painted white to imitate a decorated Adam-style plaster ceiling. This parlor ceiling was inspired by the decorated plaster ceiling in the drawing room of Mount Pleasant, in Philadelphia, Pennsylvania, built in 1761.

The 18-panel window has lace and velvet ribbon draperies which were cut from the hem of an old slip. Light-weight cardboard covered with matching drapery fabric was used to make the padded valance.

The cherrywood fireplace, with its Queen Anne over-mantel panel, was inspired by the fireplace in the west parlor of George Washington's Mount Vernon colonial mansion. Veneer strips were oil-painted to represent marble around the opening of the "wood-burning" fireplace. Each of the "hobnail" lamps on the mantel was made from a toothpaste cap, cotton swab stick, bead, and filigree cap. Flowers were oil-painted on the base (the bead) of each lamp.

This shows a slightly different arrangement of the furniture in the parlor. Remember that a dollhouse is a home, too—you can certainly re-arrange the furniture from time to time, just as you would in your own home.

Avid card players will be especially interested in the Queen Anne mahogany card table. Notice that the corners are specially shaped to hold candles to illuminate the playing area.

The coal bucket near the fireplace is a cosmetic jar top and holds real coal that came from a fish aquarium filter. The hearth brush and shovel are a mascara brush and coffee stirrer respectively, both painted gold. The handsome, curved firescreen was cut out from an ornate, plastic basket and painted gold.

Over the fireplace is a portrait of the dollhouse's owner dressed in the 18th century costume that she wore to celebrate her fourth birthday (see page 5). On the other two wood panels flanking the fireplace over-mantel are portraits of her mother and father.

On each side of the east window is a painting depicting Roman ruins. The "swan neck" pediment frames were cut from plywood and painted to look like silver.

To the right of the fireplace is a Queen Anne side chair stained walnut and fully upholstered in light blue velveteen; on the left is a winged easy chair stained walnut, fully upholstered in royal blue velvet and trimmed with light blue wool cording. A pair of matching, elegant Queen Anne settees stained mahogany and upholstered in light blue velveteen complete the fireplace seating arrangement.

The folding screen is on loan from the owner's International Christmas Castle (see page 4). The screen is an inexpensive plastic toy turned into an heirloom by gold-leafing it and glueing on tiny round mirrors on each panel.

The Queen Anne coffee table in the middle of the room holds a "Lowestoft" tea service which was found in Santa Claus, a novelty town in northern California.

In the game area against the window wall is a Queen Anne mahogany card table with corners shaped to hold four candles. The miniature playing cards and score sheet are authentic in every detail. The brass candleholders are made from gold filigrees and birthday candles. The elegant, French armchairs at the card table are stained mahogany and are fully upholstered in light blue velveteen to match the upholstery of the pair of Queen Anne settees and the side chair.

Facing the inside wall are a pair of Queen Anne side chairs antique-stained light walnut and upholstered with light blue wool "rush" seat cushions. The cross-base candle table between the chairs holds a genuine French Limoges vase with hand-painted 18th century costumes and designs.

The grandiose "French crystal" chandelier, which is a Christmas-tree ornament, is the focal point in this spacious parlor. It towers gracefully from a rosette ceiling moulding made from a plastic doily.

Patterns and Instructions for the Parlor (see also page 95)

Patterns for the Queen Anne Card Table [c. 1735]

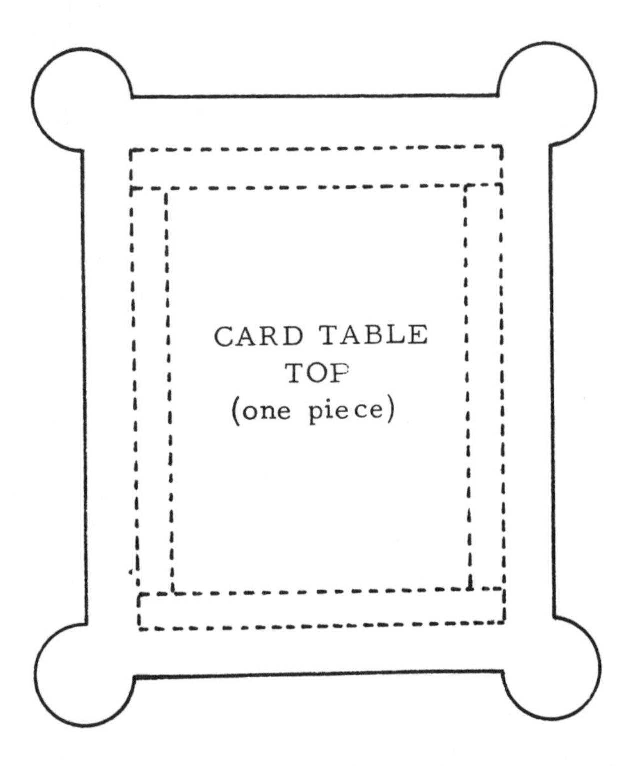

TABLE SKIRT (2 pcs)

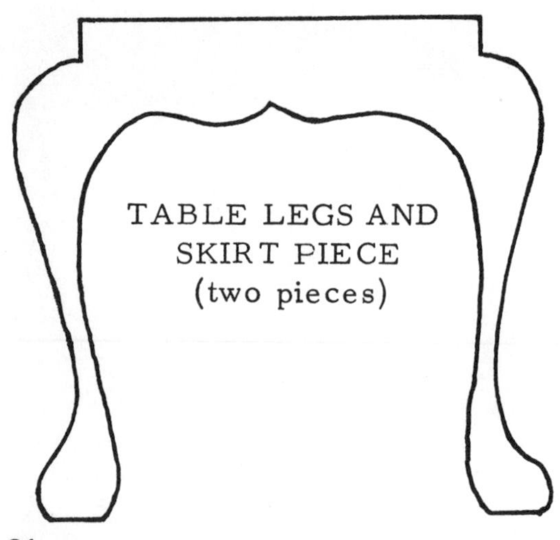

Instructions for the Queen Anne Card Table

1. Cut the following from $\frac{3}{16}$-inch plywood:
a. one table top;
b. two table legs and skirt pieces;
c. two table skirts.
2. Sand all the pieces.
3. Position and glue the table legs and the skirt pieces and the skirts to the underside of the table along the dotted guide lines.
4. Sand, finish, and shellac twice. Sand lightly between all coats.

Shape the rounded corners to hold candles. (See the chapter "Accessories" on page 132 for how to make the candleholders.)

Close-up of the Queen Anne card table.

Patterns for Tables with a Cross-Base Stand [c. early 1700's]

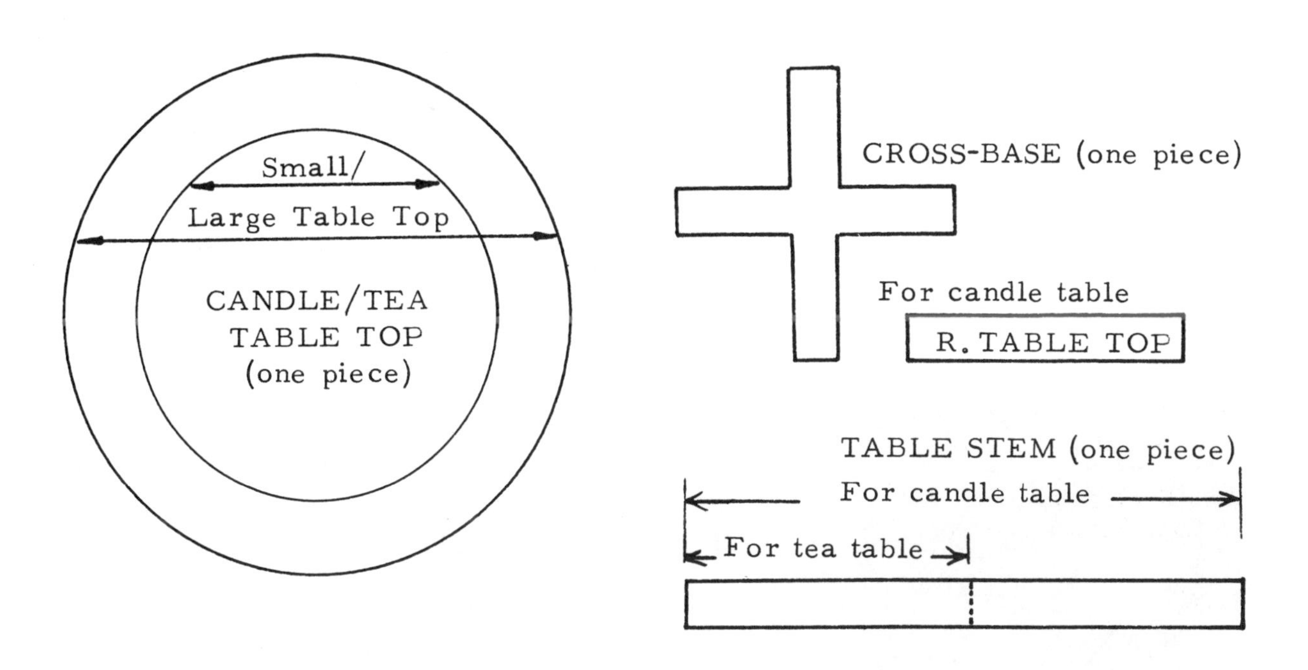

Instructions for Tables with a Cross-Base Stand

You can cut the table tops from either $\frac{1}{8}$-inch or $\frac{3}{16}$-inch plywood. Cut the cross-base and stem from $\frac{3}{16}$-inch plywood. (Dowelling is also good for the stem.)

For a candle table, use the 3-inch stem, and either the small round or the narrow rectangular top.

For a tea table, use the $1\frac{1}{2}$-inch stem, and the larger round top.

For a night table or dressing table, use the round table tops and mount them on top of a cylinder (approximately 2 inches high). Cover with a velvet or lace tablecloth.

Close-up of a table with a cross-base stand.

Pattern for the Folding Screen

Instructions for the Folding Screen

1. Cut four panels from ⅛-inch or $\frac{3}{16}$-inch plywood.
2. Sand and paint with enamel.
3. Glue a printed fabric or paper across the four front panels. (The print "hinges" the panels together.)

You may paint or decoupage the screen with pastoral or Oriental scenes. Use clear upholstery mending tape in the back to "hinge" the panels together. You can paint the edges gold for interest. Boutique mirrors glued on each of the panels are especially decorative too.

Close-up of the folding screen.

A secretary shelved with books and lots of comfortably upholstered seats make the library a perfect place to retire for some enlightening and relaxing reading.

The Library

Color, pattern and texture are the outstanding features in the cheerful library. Soft, warm yellows and muted earth colors are dominant. A large collection of needlework completes the total effect of this retreat. The library is the most peaceful and romantic room in the dollhouse. It is also the cultural center of the home.

Soft yellow, medallion-patterned Con-Tact paper was used to wallpaper all the 12-inch high walls of the spacious and light library.

The Jacobean crewel-embroidered rug depicts a proud fabled bird and flowers worked on Belgian linen. The arrangement was inspired by a full-scale throw pillow, whose design came from a kit.* The assortment of colors in the rug is repeated throughout the library.

Pale yellow valanced draperies trimmed with blue wool hand-embroidery cover the 18-panel window. The solid yellow color does not compete with, but rather complements, the patterned wallpaper, rug, and upholstery.

* The embroidery kit from which the rug was adapted is Columbia - Minerva's "Fabled Bird."

The hand-embroidered rug is a beautiful focal point in the library. The Bargello upholstered Chippendale armchair at the secretary adds a stately feeling to the literary corner of the room.

The massive, "wood-burning," teakwood-stained fireplace is the focal point upon entering the room. Veneer strips were oil-painted to simulate green marble and were arranged around the opening of the fireplace. The two swords on the fireplace are cocktail stirrers painted to look like brass. On top of the mantel are two oil lamps, each of which was made from a bead, a cotton swab stick, and filigrees. The Oriental ornament is from Solvang in California (see page 175 for the address). Over the mantel hangs a gold filigree-framed painting on silk of an 18th century little girl. The imposing painting over the massive fireplace emphasizes the fireplace's dominance in the library.

For the fireplace accessories: the coal bucket is a bottle cap, the hearth brush and shovel set are a mascara brush and coffee stirrer respectively, and the firescreen is a shoe buckle. All pieces are painted silver. Red cellophane simulates fire that "burns" wood cut from real tree twigs.

The delicate Chippendale settee is mahogany-colored, and padded and upholstered in soft beige, metallic thread brocade. On the sofa is a copy of Captain William Bradford's *Log of the Mayflower.*

To the left of the settee is a cross-base table covered with a very fine, hand-made white lace doily. It is topped with an Oriental ornament that was found at the Japanese Village in Buena Park, California.

On the other side of the fireplace is a Chippendale wingback easy chair stained walnut, padded and fully upholstered with blue antique velvet, and trimmed with corded wool in soft yellow. The mass of blue color in the easy chair is repeated in the rug. Over the chair on the back wall is an oblong, two-candle "pewter" sconce, hand-cast and hand-finished by Shackman in New York (see page 175 for the address). It is a metal replica of an antique original.

The newspaper rack is a dishwasher soap dispenser painted brown to simulate wood. Tiny hand-printed newspapers of the 18th century include, in alphabetical order: *Boston Gazette, New England Courant, New England Weekly Journal, Pennsylvania Gazette,* and *The Spectator.*

At the window is a Queen Anne, walnut-stained daybed upholstered in a popular 18th century flame-stitch worked in flaming colors of rust, salmon, tan, and yellow.

The handsome mahogany secretary is Queen Anne. It is shelved with books by American authors of the 17th and 18th centuries. Four of these are early children's books. The books are made from tiny, thin sheets of plastic foam covered with bond paper for the pages, and covered with cardboard for the book binding. The literary collection includes history, philosophy, and poetry books. On the secretary for ready reference is Benjamin Franklin's *Poor Richard's Almanack,* printed in 1770.

The desk lamp is made from a piece of filigree weighted down with modelling clay, beads, and cotton swab stick. The double-orb lamp is oil-painted with dainty floral nosegays. The inkwell and pen are the top of a liquid soap detergent container and a feather. The desk blotter is made from real blotter paper and cornered with snap-shot picture corners.

At the secretary is a Chippendale armchair, also stained mahogany-color and fully upholstered in hand-worked Bargello needlework in Persian wools of yellow, tan, and salmon. Its complementary side chair is fully upholstered in the same Bargello pattern, and has a matching upholstered footstool.

High in the ceiling from a rosette moulding hangs a crystal and gold chandelier made from half a plastic foam ball, clear tear-drop beads, a string of crystal pearls, gold metallic sparkle, pins, and green birthday candles. The "wedding cake" design for the chandelier was influenced by the multi-prism chandelier in the dining room of Hampton House in Towson, Maryland, built in 1783.

Patterns and Instructions for the Library (see also page 95)

Patterns for the Queen Anne Daybed [c. 1730-1740]

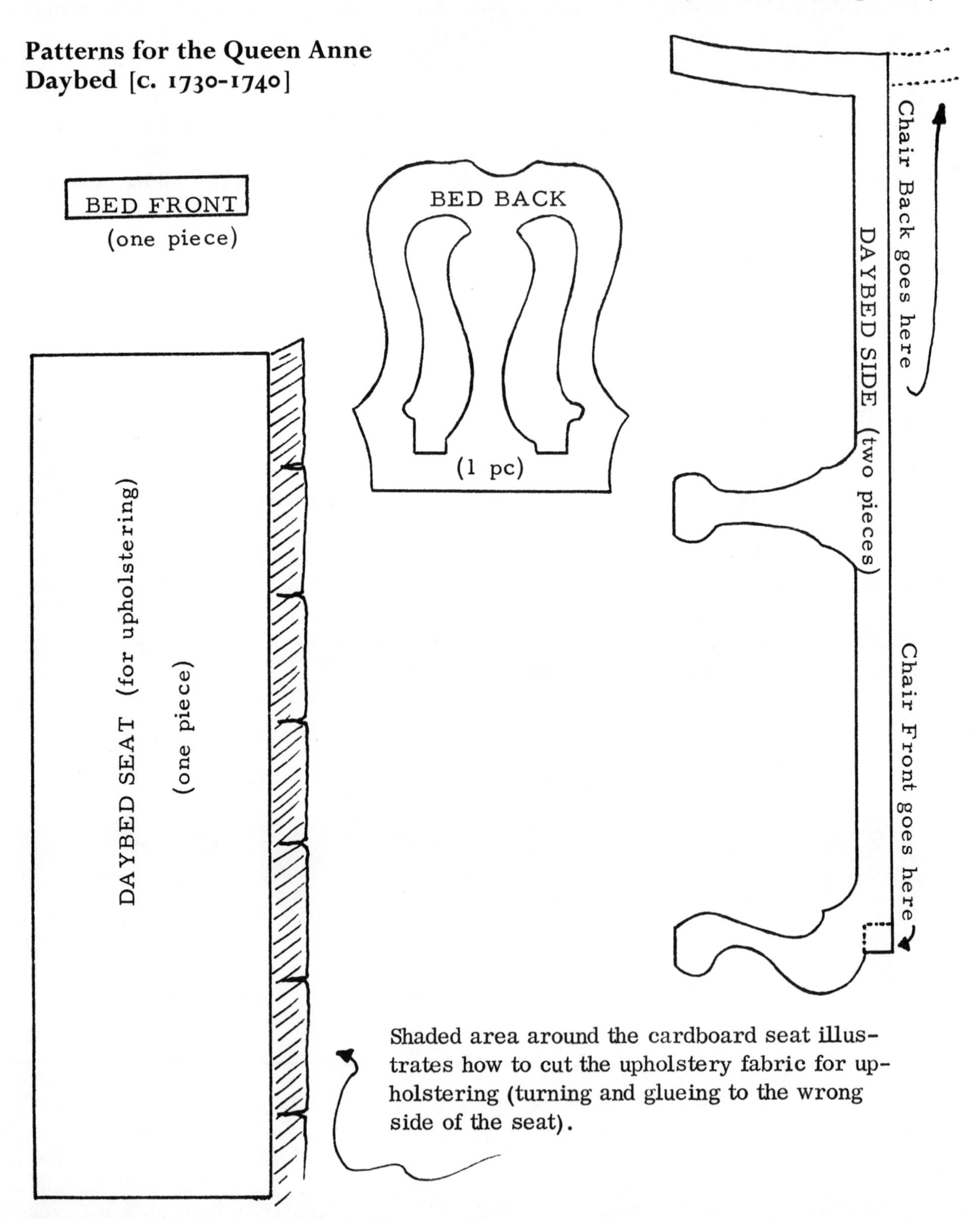

Instructions for the Queen Anne Daybed

1. Cut the following parts from $\frac{3}{16}$-inch plywood:

a. one bed back;

b. one bed front ($\frac{1}{4} \times 1\frac{1}{4}$ inches);

c. two bed sides.

2. Sand all the pieces.

3. Position and glue the bed back and front to the sides, as shown by the dotted lines in the pattern.

4. Sand, stain as desired, and shellac twice, sanding lightly between each coat.

UPHOLSTERY FOR THE DAYBED

1. Cut one seat from cardboard ($1\frac{5}{8} \times 5\frac{5}{8}$ inches).

2. Cover the seat with upholstery fabric (cut $\frac{1}{4}$ inch larger all around than the seat), and glue the upholstered seat into position.

NOTE: A pattern for the Bargello stitchery for this upholstered piece is illustrated on pages 152 to 153 in the chapter "Needlecrafts."

You can use this daybed in any room of the dollhouse.

Close-up of the Queen Anne daybed.

Patterns for the Queen Anne Secretary [c. 1730-1750]

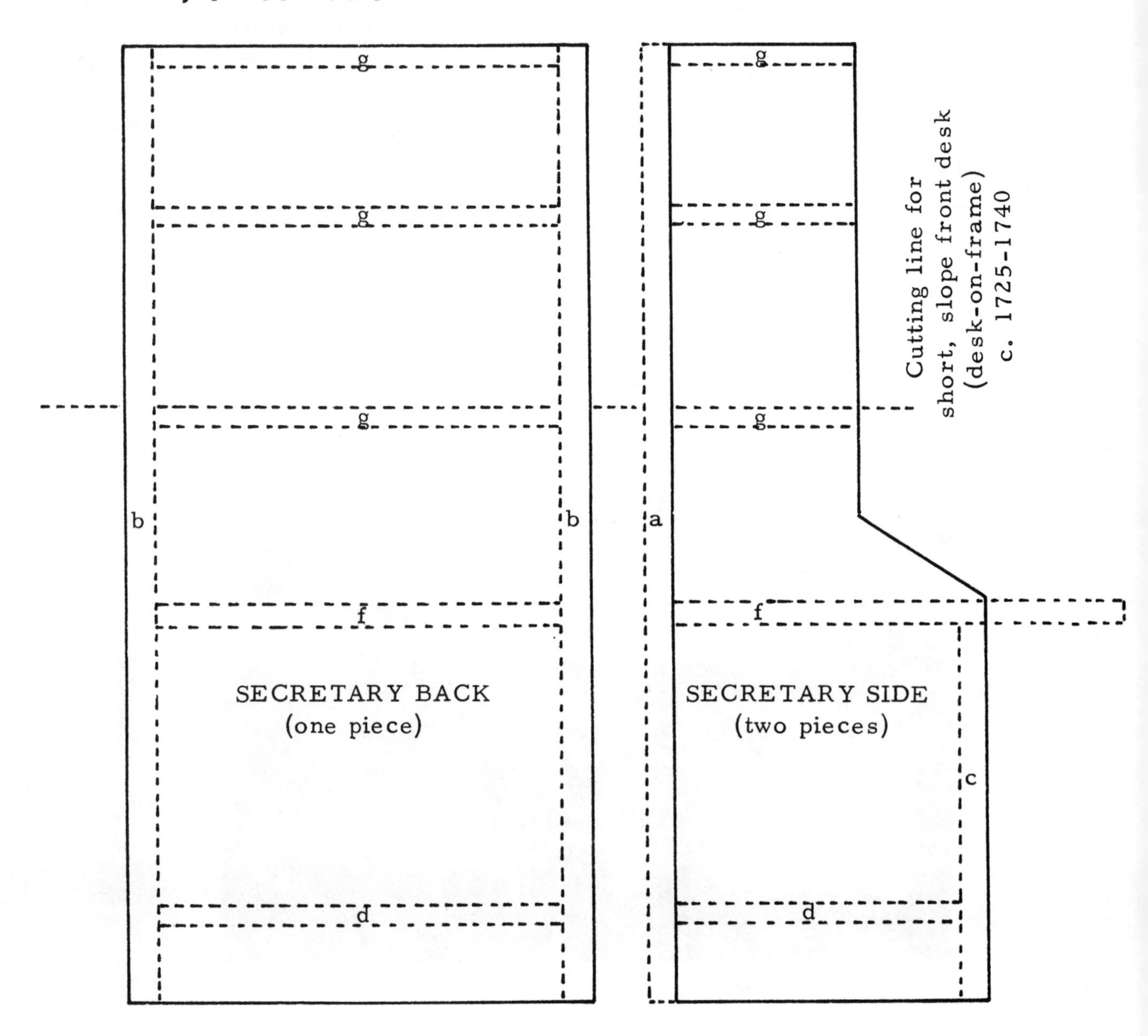

Instructions for the Queen Anne Secretary

1. Cut from $\frac{3}{16}$-inch plywood:
a. one secretary back (3 × 6 inches);
b. two secretary sides;
c. one secretary front ($2\frac{3}{8}$ × $2\frac{5}{8}$ inches);

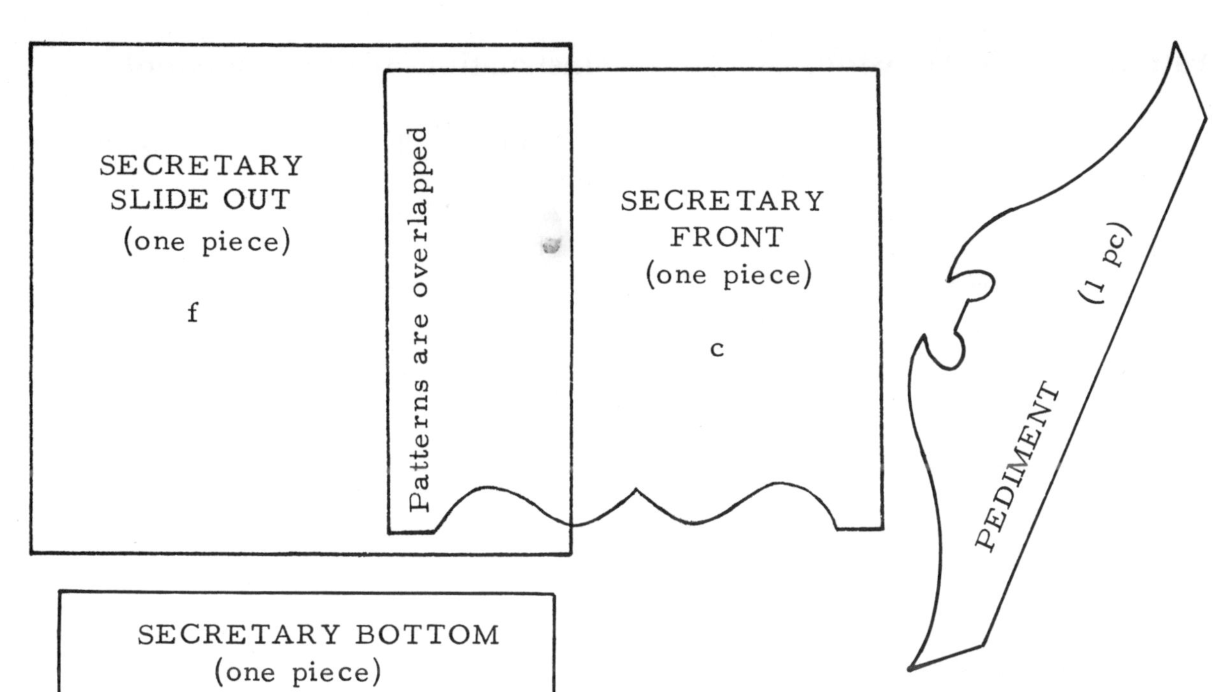

d. one secretary bottom ($1\frac{13}{16} \times 2\frac{5}{8}$ inches);
e. one pediment.

NOTE: The letters for all parts indicated here correspond to the placement position drawn schematically by dotted lines on the applicable pattern pieces.

2. Cut from $\frac{1}{8}$-inch plywood:
f. one secretary slide-out ($2\frac{5}{8} \times 2\frac{7}{8}$ inches);
g. three book shelves ($1\frac{3}{16} \times 2\frac{5}{8}$ inches).

3. Sand all the pieces to fit.

4. Center and glue the three book shelves (one will be the top), the slide-out, and the secretary bottom to the secretary back along the dotted guide lines. Top with the pediment.

5. Sand any overlapping edges, and finish.

6. Fill with books (including children's books). Write in each book the title, its author, and the publishing date for authenticity. (You will have to do some research on 18th century literature for this.) Top the secretary slide-out with an inkwell (liquid soap detergent container top), a quill feather pen, and desk blotter.

Close-up of the Queen Anne secretary.

Patterns for the Footstool

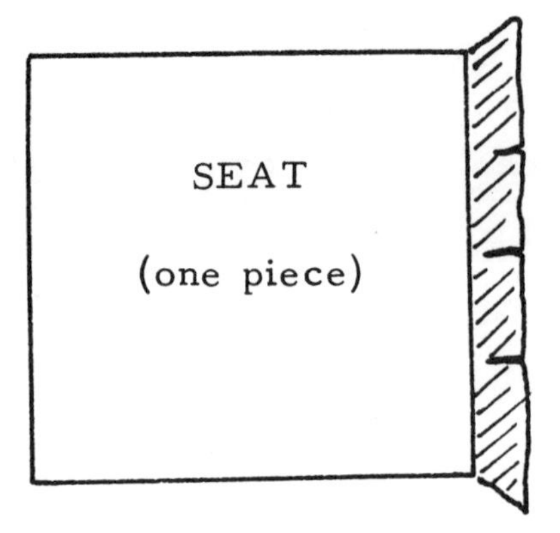

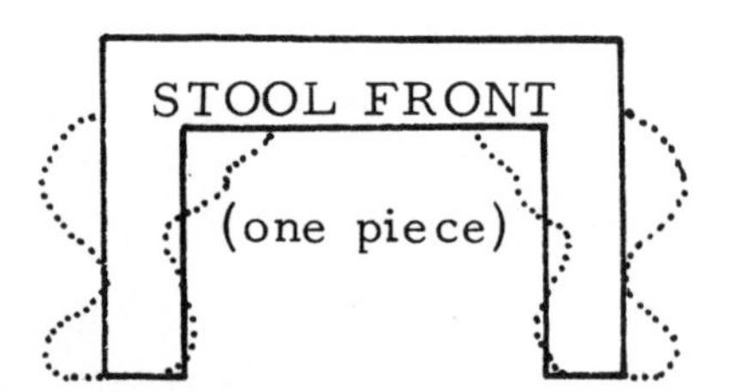

Instructions for the Footstool

1. Cut two stool fronts and two stool bars from $\frac{3}{16}$-inch plywood.
2. Sand. Glue the stool bars to line up with the bars in the stool front.
3. Sand again. Finish with any stain you want.
4. Cut the seat ($1\frac{3}{8} \times 1\frac{3}{4}$ inches) from cardboard and cover with fabric.
5. Glue the upholstered seat into position.

Use either style footstool with any easy chair, side chair, or rocking chair. It may also be used as a dressing table bench (see the Dressing Room on page 127).

BAR (1 pc)

Close-up of the upholstered Chippendale side chair and matching footstool.

Patterns and Instructions for the Parlor and Library

Patterns for the Late Queen Anne [Parlor] [c. 1750] and Chippendale [Library] [c. 1760-1775] Settee

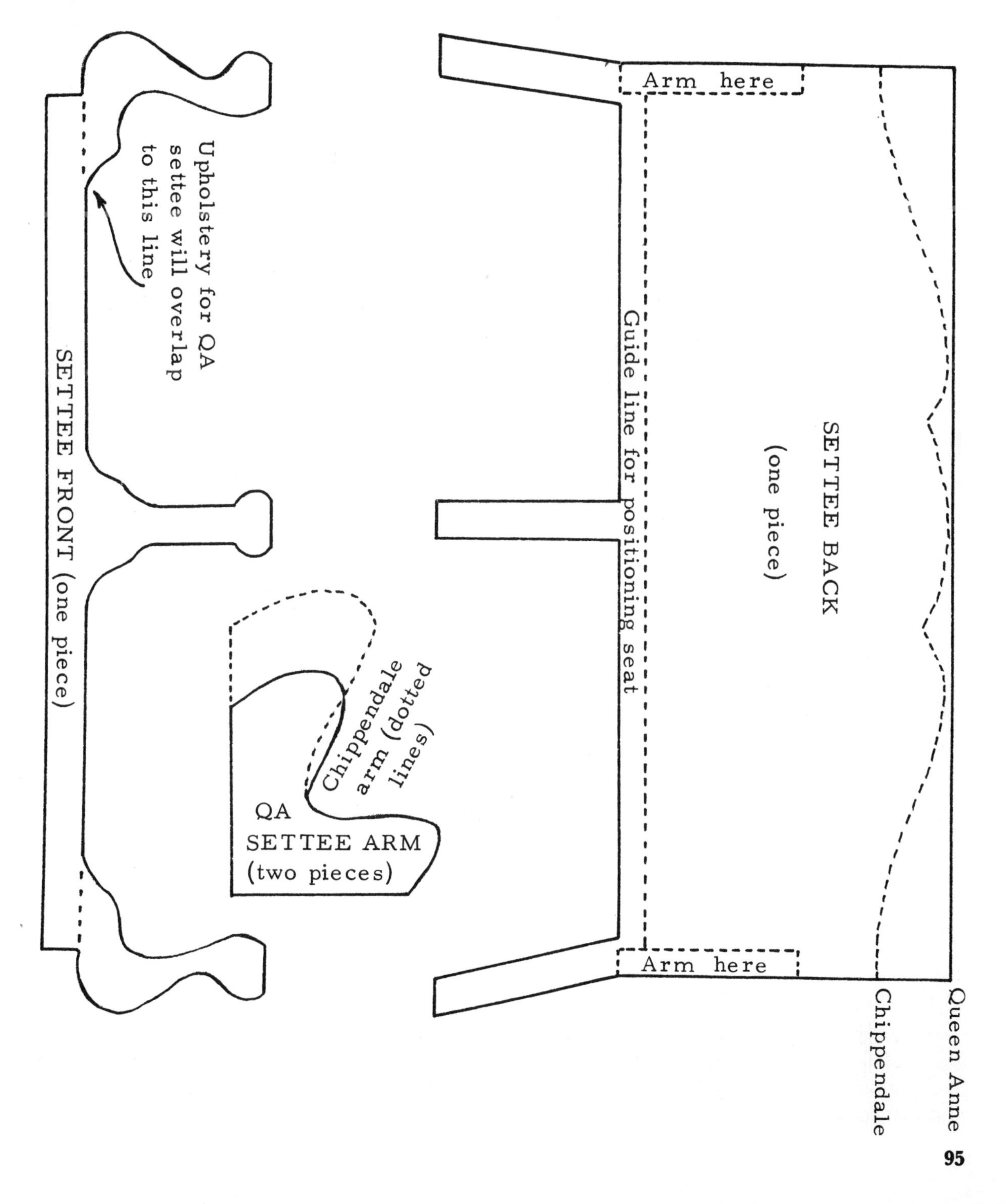

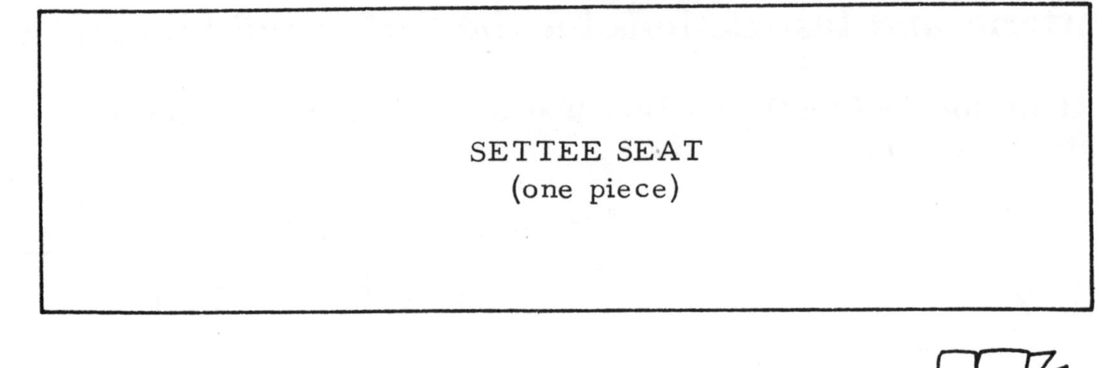

Pattern is broken. Extend vertically to 6-5/8".

UPHOLSTERY PIECE to be upholstered
for Queen Anne settee.

(one piece)

Extend to 6-5/8"

Instructions for the Queen Anne (Parlor) and Chippendale (Library) Settee

1. Cut the following from $\frac{3}{16}$-inch plywood for either the Queen Anne or Chippendale settee:

a. one settee back (this piece determines the style);
b. one front (with legs);
c. two arms;
d. one seat ($1\frac{9}{16} \times 5\frac{5}{8}$ inches).

2. Sand all the pieces to fit.

3. Position and glue the seat to the back along the guide lines. Glue the arms to the back and the seat sides along the guide lines. Add the three-legged front.

4. Sand to fit smoothly. Stain mahogany-color and shellac twice, sanding lightly between all coats.

UPHOLSTERY FOR THE QUEEN ANNE SETTEE

1. Cut from white bond paper one upholstery piece ($5\frac{5}{8} \times 6\frac{5}{8}$ inches) and one seat ($1\frac{3}{4} \times 5\frac{1}{2}$ inches). Cover both pieces with fabric. (Pad the seat with fleece or a very thin sheet of foam rubber.)

2. Upholster the settee with the above upholstered piece ($5\frac{5}{8} \times 6\frac{5}{8}$ inches) by starting at the outside back. Then go over to the inside front, across the seat, and over to overlap the settee front ($\frac{1}{4}$ inch), just before the legs begin to curve (see the guide line on the pattern).

3. Glue the upholstered seat into position.

Close-up of the Queen Anne settee in the parlor.

Close-up of the Chippendale settee in the library.

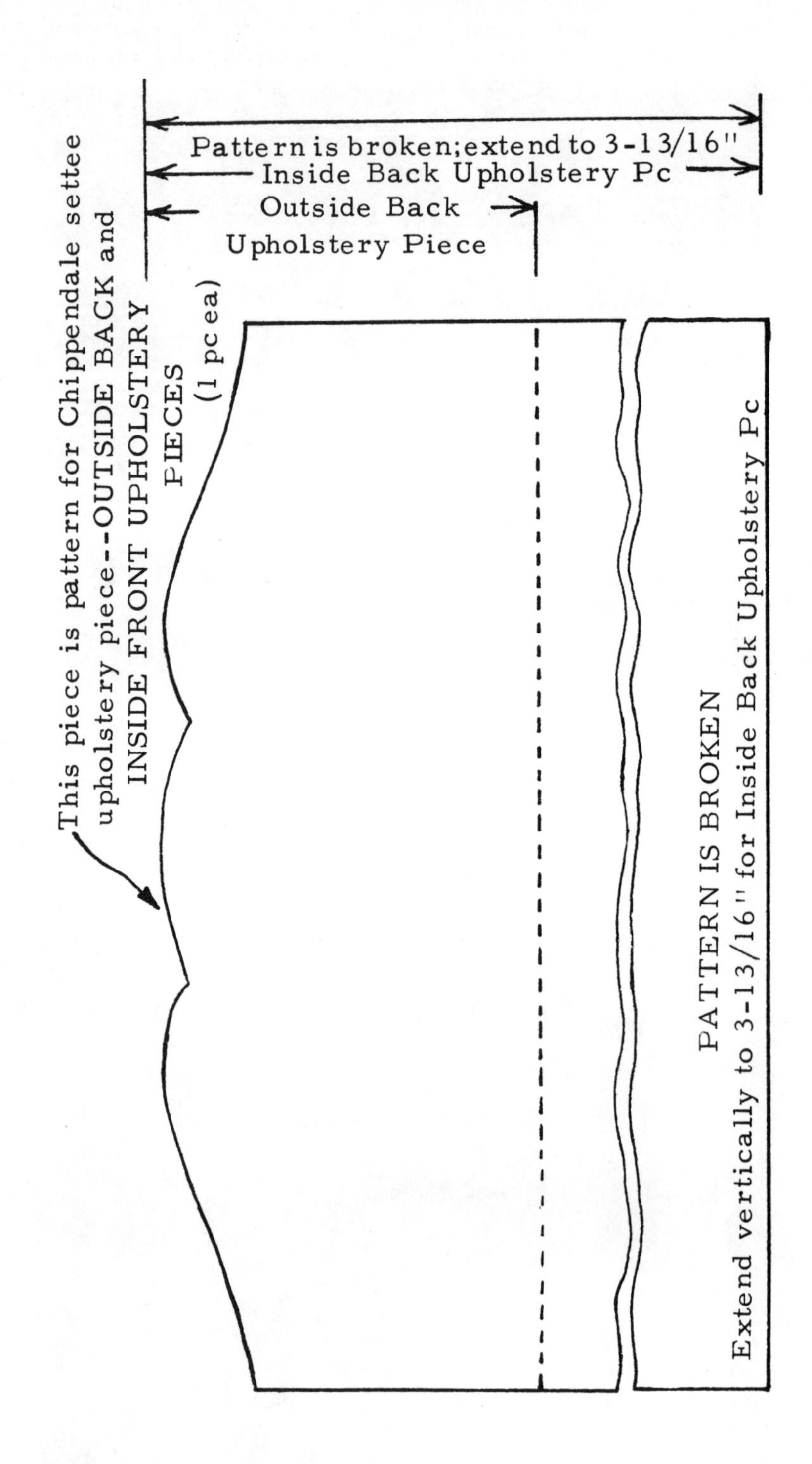

UPHOLSTERY FOR THE CHIPPENDALE SETTEE (STYLE 1)

1. Cut from white bond paper one settee back upholstery pattern piece along the three curves as indicated, one seat ($1\frac{3}{4} \times 5\frac{1}{2}$ inches), and one outside back piece. Cover all three pieces with fabric. (Pad the seat with fleece or a very thin sheet of foam rubber.)

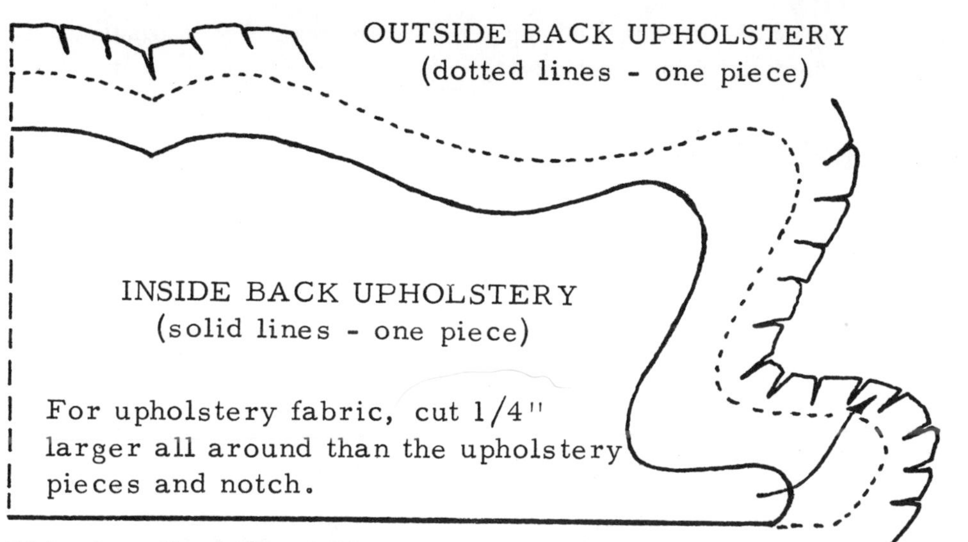

This is only half of the pattern. Be sure to trace the mirror image for the other half of the settee upholstery.

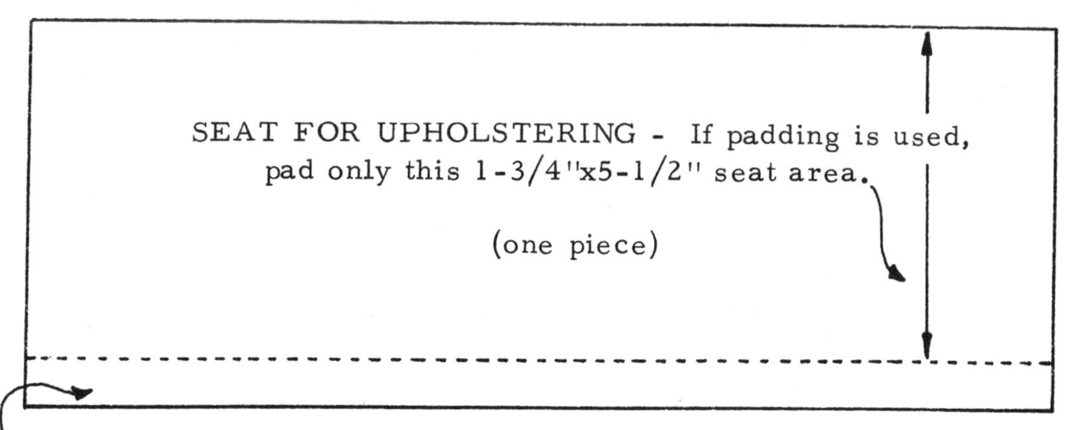

This area will fold over to overlap the settee front (as indicated along the dotted lines on pattern) just before the three legs begin to curve. This area should not be padded.

Suggested fabrics: Tapestry, brocade, velveteen, pinwale corduroy, sateen. Decorative trims may also be used to enhance the upholstery.

2. Start upholstering on the inside back, about $\frac{1}{4}$ inch below the edge. Continue across the seat in the same manner as for the Queen Anne settee.

3. Position and glue the upholstered, padded settee seat.

4. Add the back upholstered piece to the outside back.

UPHOLSTERY FOR THE CHIPPENDALE SETTEE (STYLE 2)

1. Cut from white bond paper one outside upholstery piece (along the dotted lines), and one inside upholstery piece (along the solid lines). Cover these pieces with elegant fabric.

2. Cut from white bond paper one seat ($2 \times 5\frac{1}{2}$ inches). Cover this piece with matching fabric. (If you use padding, pad only the $1\frac{3}{4} \times 5\frac{1}{2}$ inch seat area.)

3. Position and glue the outside back upholstery, then the inside back upholstery, and then the seat. (See instructions on the pattern for how to position the seat on the settee.)

Patterns for the Chippendale French Chair [c. 1764-1775]

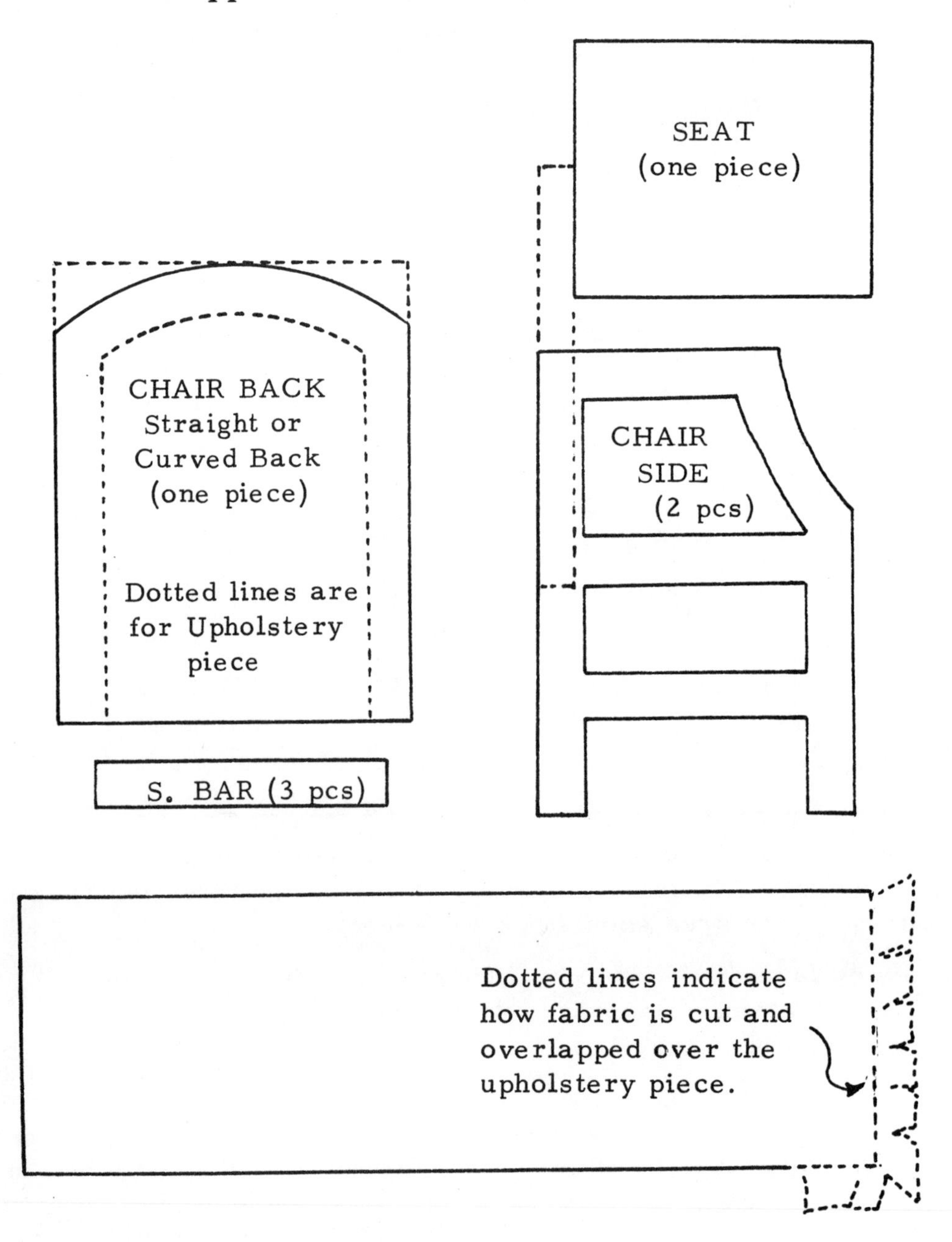

Instructions for the Chippendale French Chair

1. Cut the following from $\frac{3}{16}$-inch plywood:
a. one chair back;
b. three stretcher bars (with sides $\frac{1}{4} \times 1\frac{5}{8}$ inches);
c. two chair sides.
2. Sand all the pieces to fit.
3. Position and glue the chair sides to the back along the dotted guide lines as shown.
4. Add stretcher bars, two in front and one in back, to line up with the existing stretcher bars in the chair sides.
5. Sand, stain, and cover with two coats of shellac. Sand lightly between all coats.

UPHOLSTERY

Cut from cardboard or heavy bond paper two upholstery back pieces and one seat. Cut the fabric $\frac{1}{4}$ inch larger all around than the paper upholstery pieces, and notch the seams as illustrated to facilitate overlapping to the wrong side.

Cover both back pieces with fabric. Glue one on the inside back and one on the outside back of the chair. Suggested fabrics are: light-weight velveteen, sateen, and pinwale corduroy.

Pad the cardboard seat with fleece or $\frac{1}{8}$-inch foam rubber, cover with fabric, and glue in position.

CHIPPENDALE SETTEE: This chair pattern can very easily be incorporated into a Chippendale settee by widening the back, seat, stretcher bars, and upholstery pieces to approximately 4 to 5 inches *longer* than the existing patterns for the chair.

OPTIONAL: If you are using a straight-cut back chair (cut along the dotted lines), cut the cardboard $1\frac{1}{2} \times 4\frac{3}{4}$ inches, cover with fabric, and upholster onto the chair in one continuous piece from the outside back to the inside front. Add the upholstered seat.

Close-up of the Chippendale French chairs.

Patterns for the Chippendale Winged Easy Chair

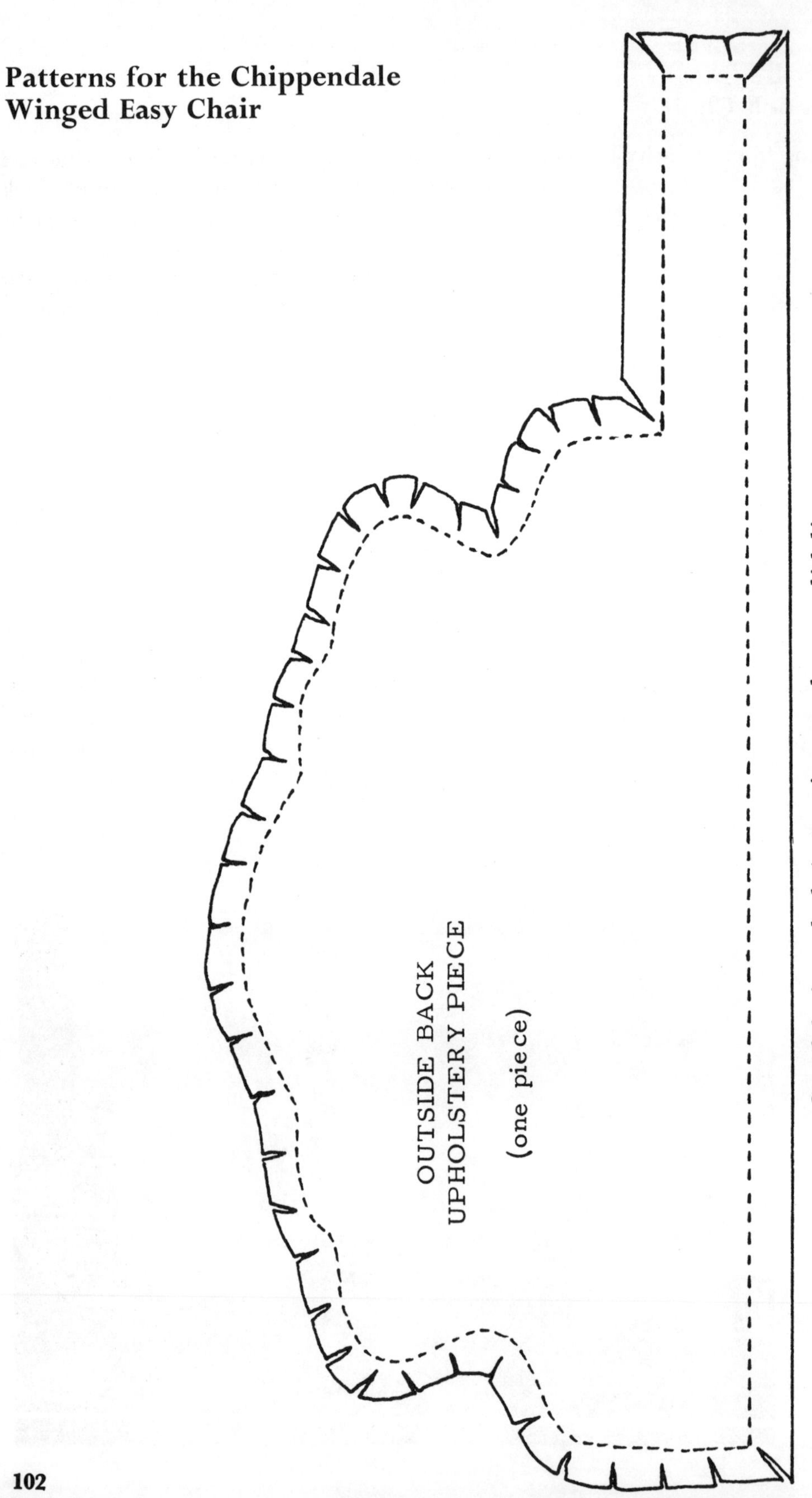

Cut fabric upholstery pieces along solid lines.
(Dotted lines indicate actual chair area that will be upholstered.)

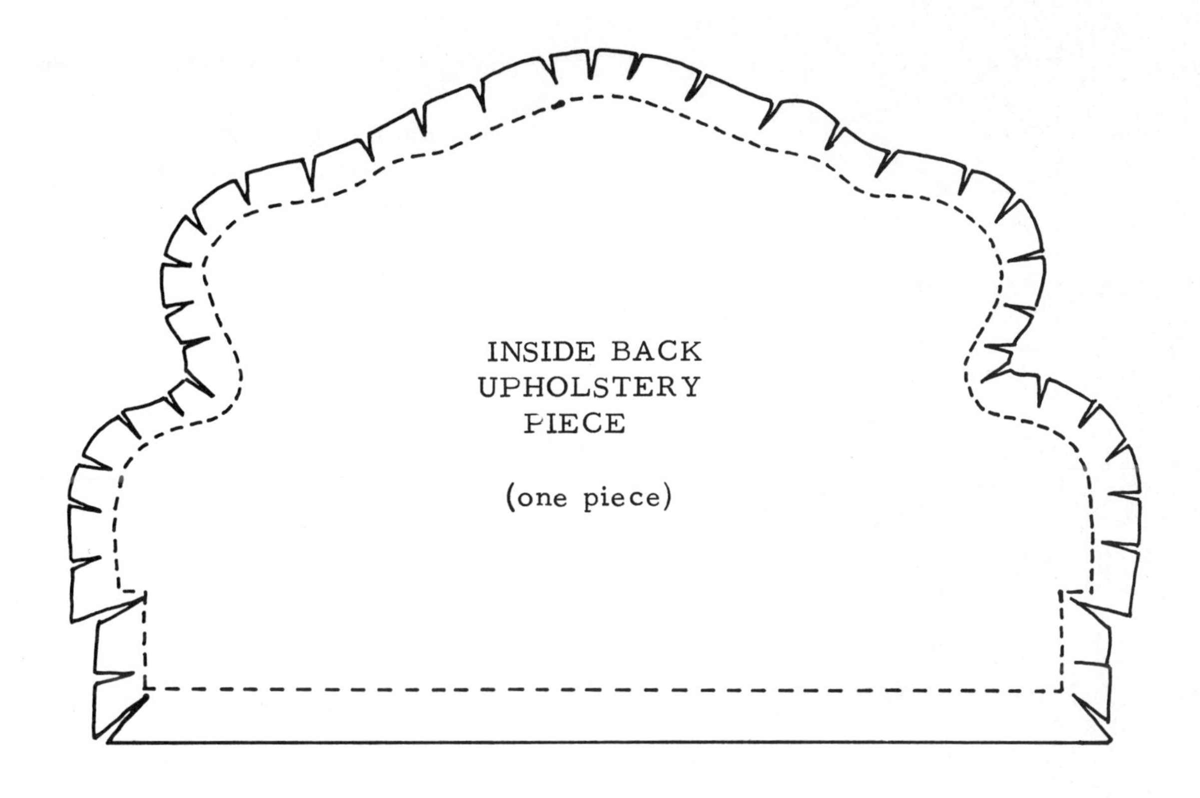

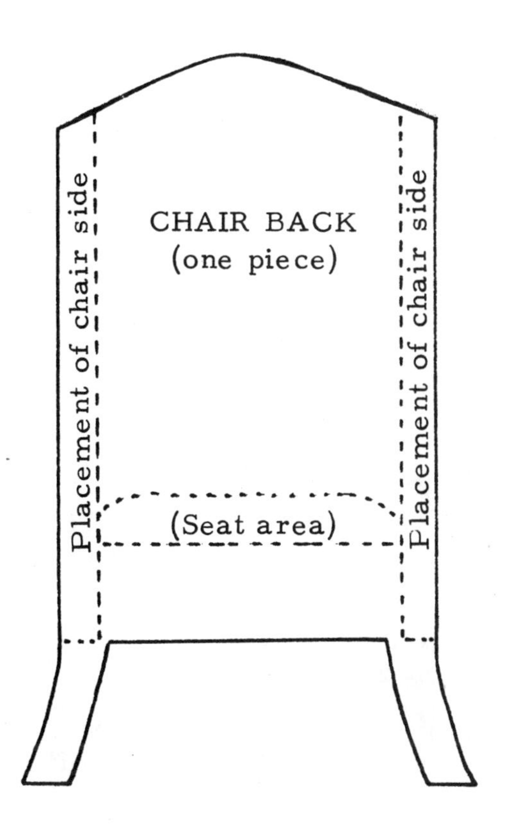

Instructions for the Chippendale Winged Easy Chair

1. Cut from $\frac{3}{16}$-inch plywood:
a. one chair back;
b. two chair sides;
c. one chair front.

2. Sand all the pieces.

3. Position and glue the chair sides to the back as indicated along the dotted lines. Add the chair front as indicated in the pattern.

4. Sand again. Finish the legs in a stain you choose, and shellac them. Sand between each coat of stain and shellac.

UPHOLSTERY

1. Cut two seats ($1\frac{5}{8} \times 1\frac{9}{16}$ inches), one from $\frac{1}{8}$-inch cardboard or plywood, and one from $\frac{1}{8}$-inch foam rubber. Glue the two pieces together and cover with upholstery fabric. Note on the pattern how to cut the fabric upholstery. A suggested fabric to use is a stretch print, which is especially good for covering an entire chair such as this, the stretch to "stretch" the fabric

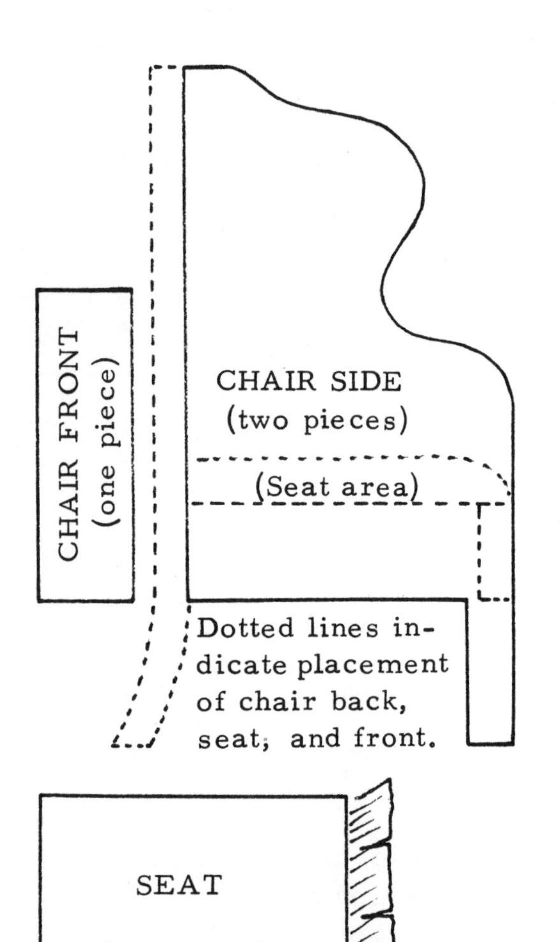

to the chair, and the print to hide any possible errors.

2. From fabric, cut one outside back and one inside front upholstery piece along the solid and notched outside edges. (It is a good idea to cut mock-up upholstery pieces from paper or inexpensive fabric scraps first to ensure a proper fit.)

3. Spread a thin layer of white glue over the entire chair to be upholstered. Position the inside front upholstery piece, then the outside back piece in place. The $\frac{3}{16}$-inch notched edges will be overlapped along the thickness (also $\frac{3}{16}$ inch) of the chair (see the illustration). The notches in the pattern are $\frac{1}{4}$ inch to allow for an approximate $\frac{1}{16}$-inch crease overlap allowance.

4. Position and glue firmly the upholstered, padded chair seat.

5. Trim with matching or contrasting cord or ribbing to hide the notched, overlapped edges of the upholstery fabric. A $\frac{1}{2}$-inch flounce of the same fabric or a fringe would be nice for this type of chair.

Cut all pattern pieces around only the solid lines.

Shaded area on right indicates the fabric upholstery piece and how it covers the chair.

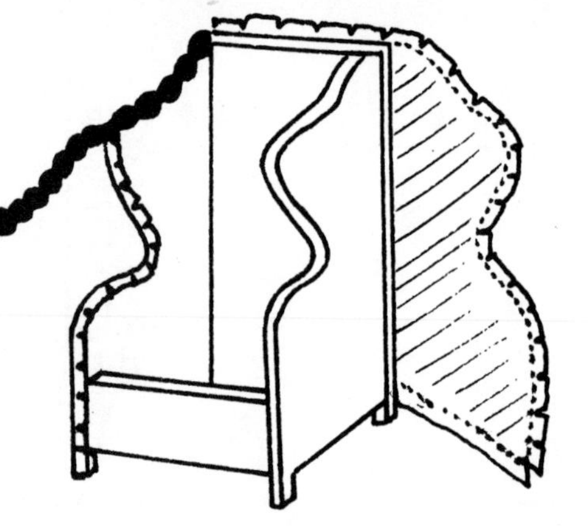

Illustration showing how fabric upholstery piece is applied to the chair. Notches fold over along edge (3/16")of chair (as shown on the right-hand arm), and are then concealed by use of trim (indicated by dark cord). A stretch, print fabric is best to use for this type of chair.

The sitting room is actually the second floor landing. A cozy corner, it is the continuation of the "flying" family portrait gallery begun in the entrance hall on the first floor.

The Sitting Room

The sitting room is actually the second-storey landing as the continuation of the circular staircase and the "flying" portrait gallery, both of which began in the entrance hall on the first floor.

One side wall is panelled in dark walnut; the other is "white-washed plaster," as is the back wall. As on the parlor fireplace wall, veneer strips were cut to imitate a dentilled cornice with fretwork projecting along the ceiling on the white back wall.

The gate-leg table is an antique from the late 17th century. The table top is made from an artist's plaque and $\frac{1}{4}$-inch turned rods form the carved gate-legs. The table is painted with white enamel. The pink cups and saucers and coffee pot are inexpensive cake decorations.

Two French Louis XV chairs are arranged around the gate-leg table. They are papier-mâchéd, gold-leafed, shellacked, upholstered in pink silk, and trimmed with pink wool cording.

The chandelier is constructed from half a plastic foam ball, a chain of pearls, crystal tear-drops, costume jewelry beads, hairpins, push pins, pink and gold glitter, and pink birthday candles. It was copied from a chandelier in the Boscobel Mansion in Garrison, New York.

Simple white-washed walls in this child's bedroom create a pleasant background for the fun toys that fill the room. Although this room was done mostly in pinks, with linens appropriate for a little girl, you can easily change it to suit a little boy!

The Child's Bedroom

Jacobean crewel embroidery, velvet ribbon, and loads of toys—all mostly blue, pink, red, and white—make up a little girl's bedroom. The room is whimsical and charming—a wonderful hideaway for any child.

All the walls and ceiling are "white-washed" and simple so they do not interfere with the busy play area in the rest of the room. The walnut-stained floor is highly polished with shellac. In front of the fireplace is a blue and navy fringed wool rug that was hand-woven on a mini-loom.

The white sheer drapes are trimmed with blue velvet ribbon and navy wool embroidery. Alongside the window are some pictures (which are really postage stamps glued on wood plaques) depicting government scenes and famous quotes celebrating the United States' Bicentennial.

The walnut-stained, pencil-post canopy bed is Queen Anne style. The Jacobean design bedspread and canopy set are hand-embroidered with pink and blue embroidery floss, and trimmed in blue crocheted lace. Blue velvet ribbon holds the canopy on the frame. Bedding includes a mattress made from cardboard, foam rubber, and muslin, and two tiny pillows stuffed with cotton batting and covered with percale pillowcases. At the foot of the bed is a blue and white hand-quilted coverette made of fleece fabric for the lining and covered with a soft cotton print. The print designs are quilted. The pink chamber pot underneath the bed is a bottle cap.

The William and Mary wardrobe and lowboy set are mahogany-colored. The wardrobe has hinged doors that really open and close. It is filled with the little girl's dresses and accessories which are described in a later chapter (see page 164). The lowboy, with two large drawers that open and shut, is filled with extra bed linens, clothing and accessories, and more toys. Costume jewelry beads were used for the drawer pulls, door knobs, and feet on both the wardrobe and the lowboy. Over the lowboy are hung the baby's first rattle and shoes which are cake decorations bought at a variety store.

The toy chest against the window is actually a plastic foam container. The decorations on the toy chest were cut out from magazines. The "child-scale" rocking horse is an interesting contrast to the "toy" rocking horse which is a prize from a box of popcorn. Other toys scattered about the room are either cake decorations or popcorn charm prizes. Some of the toys that looked too much like plastic were enamelled to look like painted wood toys. The Chinese checkers are set upon a thread spool for a game table appearance. The Chinese checkers were a very inexpensive find at a pet supply house. The charming three-bears-having-tea ensemble was found in Solvang, California (see page 175 for the address). This "toy" furniture is certainly dwarfed in comparison to its "full-scale" counterpart pieces!

Next to the bed is a child-scale, walnut-stained, "wood-burning" fireplace. The blue English horn on the mantel is a gift wrap decoration. The firescreen was made from burlap. The fireplace brush is a mascara brush.

Two white enamelled Pennsylvania-German chairs are used for the seating arrangement in front of the fire.

The chandelier is made from half a plastic foam ball, some gold filigree that was a Christmas ball discard, blue velvet ribbon, navy dress pins, costume jewelry chain and beads, and blue birthday candles.

Of course, by changing the colors in this room slightly, and altering the bed coverings appropriately, you can easily turn this room into a boy's room rather than the girl's room it is here.

Patterns and Instructions for the Child's Bedroom (see also page 119)

Patterns for the Fireplace in the Child's Bedroom [c. 18th century]

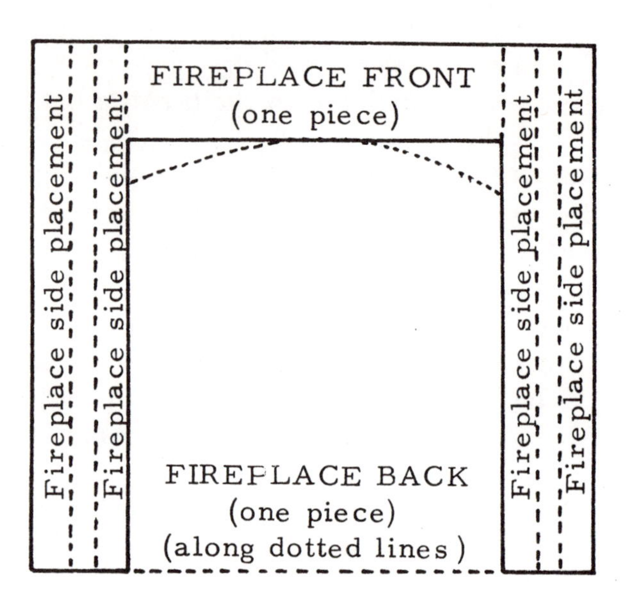

Instructions for the Fireplace

1. Cut the following from $\frac{3}{16}$-inch plywood and follow the *standard* fireplace assembly instructions on page 71:
a. one fireplace back ($2\frac{1}{2} \times 2\frac{3}{4}$ inches);
b. one fireplace front (the same as the back but with a $2 \times 2\frac{1}{4}$ inch opening);
c. four sides ($\frac{5}{8} \times 2\frac{3}{4}$ inches);
d. one mantel ($1\frac{1}{4} \times 3\frac{1}{2}$ inches);
e. one hearth ($1\frac{3}{4} \times 3$ inches).

FIREPLACE SIDE (4 pcs)

MANTEL (one piece)

--patterns are overlapped--

HEARTH (one piece)

As you can see, there are several points of interest in this fresh and charming master bedroom. The Queen Anne canopy bed is one special area, as is the sitting area highlighted by two Chippendale winged rocking chairs.

The Master Bedroom

The master bedroom gives a feeling of romance, gaiety, and freshness. White and various shades of pinks are the dominant colors, with a hint of orange, green, and gold for accent and interest. Although most of the furniture pieces are Queen Anne, the mood is definitely 18th century French.

A field of pink spring flowers on Con-Tact paper covers the massive back wall. The two side walls and ceiling are "white-washed" with flat acrylic paint. The portrait gallery on the stairwell wall is a continuation of the gallery that began in the entrance hall, and continued through the sitting room on the second storey. White, turned spindles, joined with brass-colored metallic thread, enclose the staircase landing. Decorative gold lace trim borders all the walls at the ceiling.

The sheer, shirred draperies match the pink canopy hanging on the bed. The bedroom window is flanked by a pair of gold-colored English mirrors with sconces made from earrings, mirror discs, and birthday candles.

The popular oval-braid colonial rugs covering the walnut-stained floor are hand-crocheted pink and white doilies.

The stately Queen Anne canopy bed is enamelled white, which dramatically contrasts with the walnut floors and stained furniture, and blends well with the graceful whites and dainty pinks in the bedroom. Pink lace edges the canopy cover, duster, and pillow shams. The coverette is made from flowered and striped pink, orange, and pale gold chintz. The mattress is made from cardboard and foam rubber, and is covered with pink and white candy-stripe percale. Underneath the bed is a porcelain chamber pot decorated with pink flowers and gold trim.

At the foot of the bed is a pine baby cradle that can rock the baby doll to sleep. The baby doll is a shower gift ornament. Flannelette was used to make the receiving blanket. A tiny pillow is stuffed with sheep wool and is covered with a tiny pillow case.

The elegant, gold-leafed, pink silk-upholstered Louis XV chair has been described in an earlier chapter (see page 62), and is very much a natural piece of furniture in this bedroom setting.

The "wood-burning" fireplace is stained mahogany-color. Veneer strips, oil-painted to simulate white marble, were used to trim the fireplace openings. The fireplace brush is a cosmetic brush; the bellows were made from old, leather garden gloves; the andirons were cut from an ornate, plastic basket; the firescreen is a shoe buckle. Real wood cut from tree twigs "burns" in the fire, simulated with red crumpled cellophane paper. A brass-colored pillbox and tongue depressor made the bedwarmer that has real coal in it. On the mantel are a pair of boudoir lamps, each of which was made from some gold filigree

This close-up features the luxurious Queen Anne canopy bed, the Queen Anne highboy and wardrobe set, the "marble" trimmed fireplace, and even a baby cradle with a baby in it.

Under the elegant French chandelier is a tavern table, set for tea, and surrounded by two lovely, upholstered Chippendale winged rocking chairs.

weighted down with modelling clay, and a bead oil-painted with a floral design, a cotton swab stick, and a toothpaste cap for the lamp shade. The gold wishing well ornament is a bracelet charm. Hanging over the mantel, the gold-framed painting was found at Knott's Berry Farm, Buena Park, California (see page 174 for the address).

The Queen Anne highboy and wardrobe set are mahogany-colored and authentic in every detail. The wardrobe has hinged doors that swing open and shut. A wide selection of clothes hangs from a rod in the closet. All five drawers in the highboy pull out for storing the dolls' accessories, lingerie and underwear, and extra bed linens. Brown beads were used for the drawer pulls on the highboy and the door knobs on the wardrobe. Brass eagle ornaments, originally decorative picture hooks from Nevco Products Inc., Yonkers, New York (see page 175 for the address), were mounted on the swan-neck pediment for a late 18th century colonial look. The hat box on top of the wardrobe is a bottle cap covered with wide ribbon and tied with very narrow ribbonette. The straw basket on the floor is from The Last Straw in Solvang, California (see page 175 for the address).

Under the French chandelier is an 18th century tavern table (*c.* 1725). The fine lace tablecloth is a hand-crocheted doily. The knitting needles are decorator pins which are stuck through a ball of yarn.

The Chippendale, winged rocking chairs are fully upholstered in white, pink, and green pinwale, striped knit. Foam rubber padding was used for the seats.

The grand chandelier is made from half a plastic foam ball, a garlic bottle cap sprayed gold, crystal tear-drops, beads, and pink birthday candles. Its design was influenced by the chandelier in the Green Drawing Room of the Nathaniel Russell House in Charleston, South Carolina.

Patterns and Instructions for the Master Bedroom

Patterns for the Fireplace in the Master Bedroom [c. 18th century]

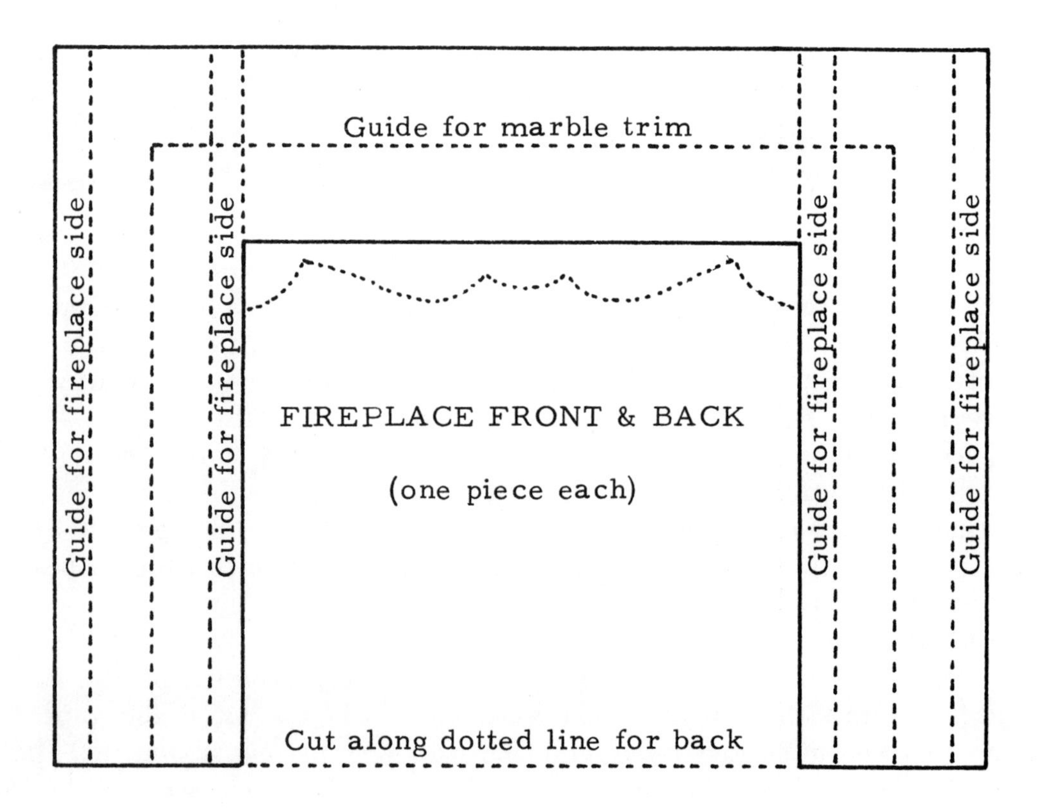

FIREPLACE SIDE (four pieces)

HEARTH
(one piece)

MANTEL (one piece)

--patterns are overlapped--

Instructions for the Fireplace

1. Cut the following pieces from $\frac{3}{16}$-inch plywood:

a. one back ($3\frac{3}{4} \times 5$ inches);
b. one front (the same as the back, but with $2\frac{3}{4} \times 3$ inch opening);
c. four sides ($\frac{5}{8} \times 3\frac{3}{4}$ inches);
d. one mantel ($1\frac{1}{4} \times 5\frac{1}{2}$ inches);
e. one hearth ($2 \times 5\frac{1}{2}$ inches).

2. Follow the guide lines in the pattern pieces and refer to the *standard* fireplace assembly instructions on page 71.

Close-up of the fireplace in the master bedroom.

Patterns for the Baby Cradle [c. early 18th century]

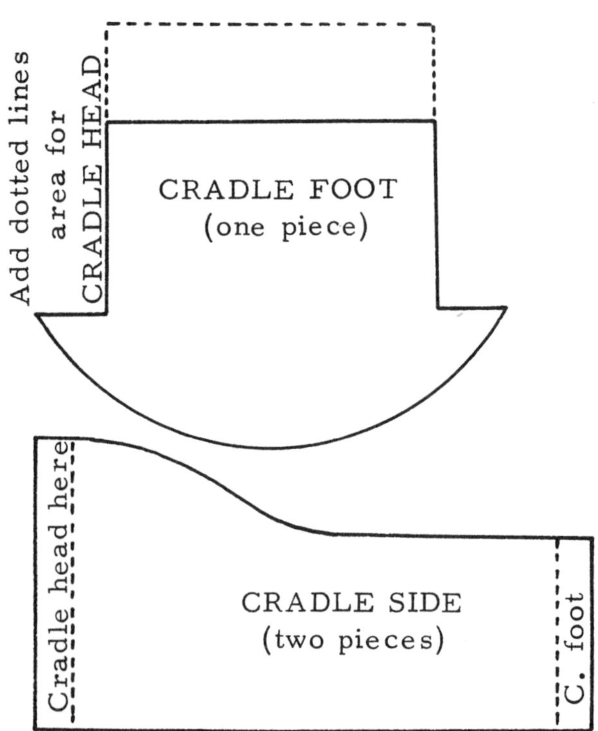

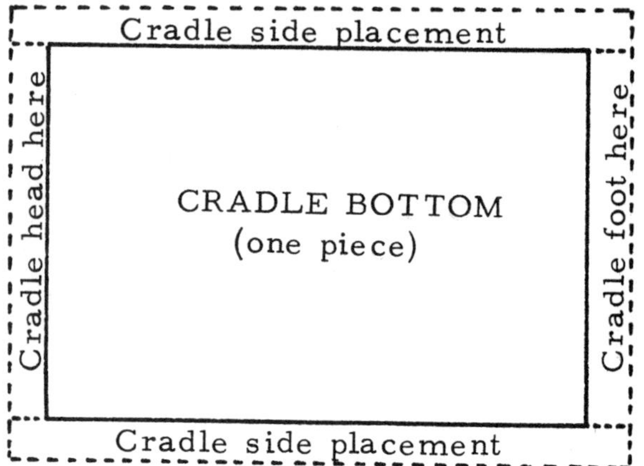

Instructions for the Baby Cradle

1. Cut all the pieces from $\frac{3}{16}$-inch plywood:
a. one cradle foot (along the solid lines);
b. one cradle head (the same as the foot plus the dotted lines);
c. one bottom (along the solid lines only);
d. two sides.

2. Sand all the pieces to fit.

3. Glue all the pieces to the cradle bottom, as illustrated in the pattern.

4. Sand again, and stain as desired.

Close-up of the baby cradle.

Patterns for the Chippendale Rocking Chair [c. 1760-1775]

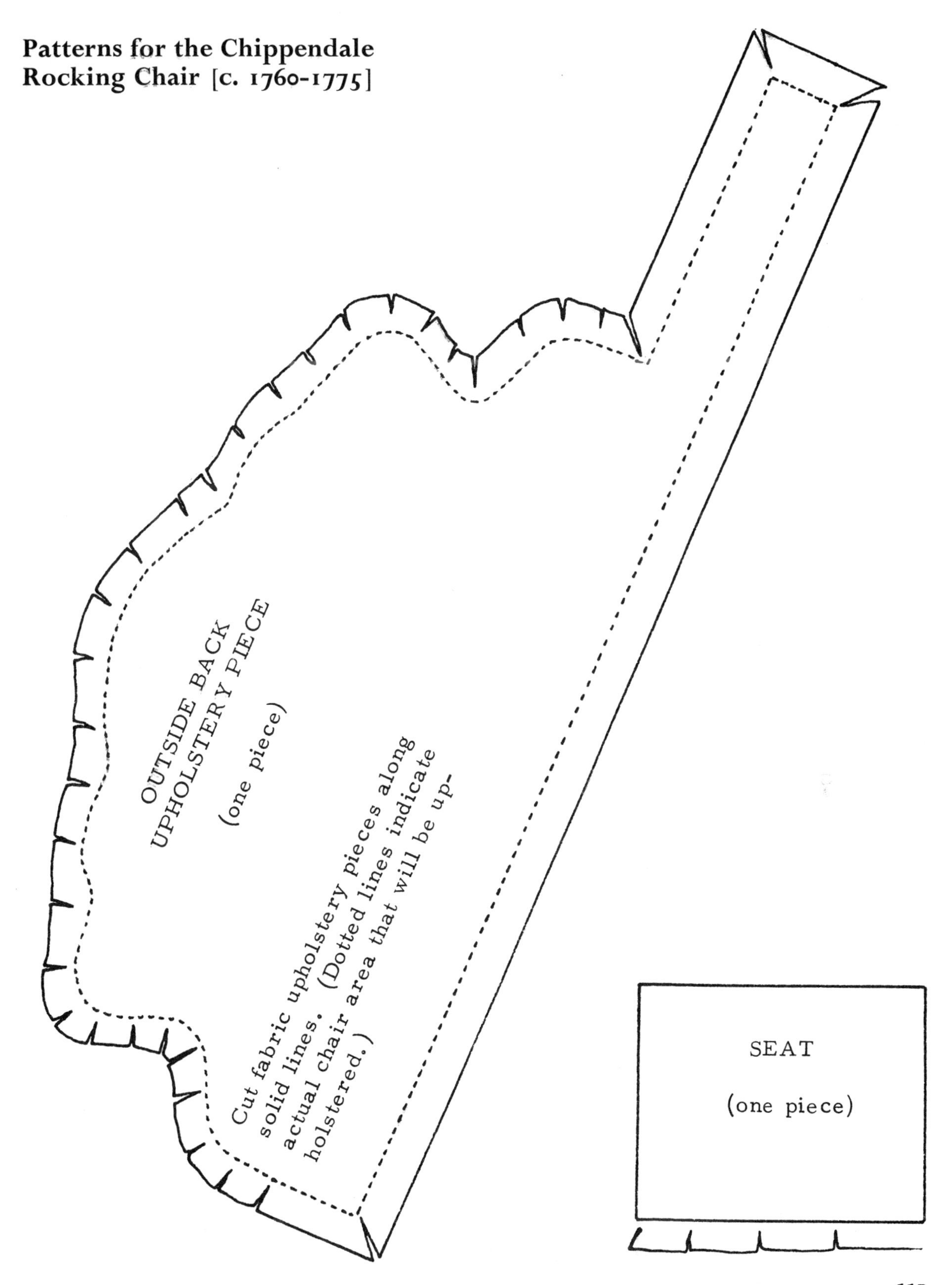

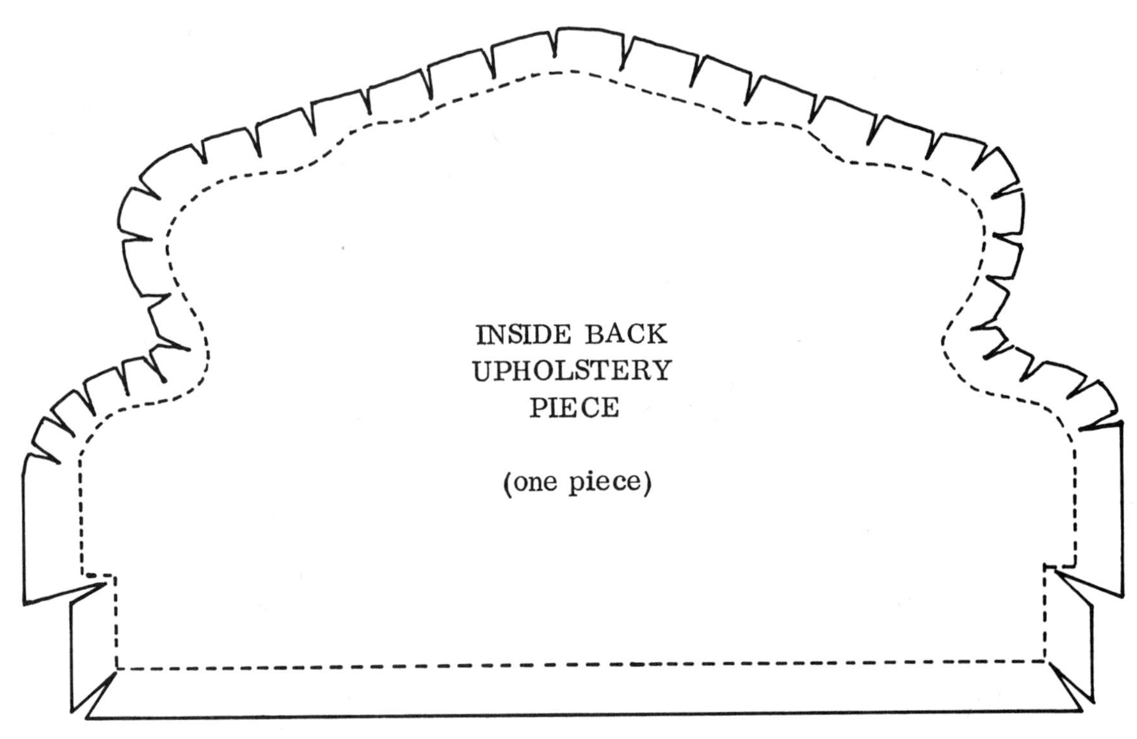

Placement of rocker side

ROCKER BACK
(one piece)

(Seat area)

Placement of rocker side

For easy chair, cut legs around dotted lines.
CUT ALL PATTERN PIECES AROUND SOLID/NOTCHED LINES.

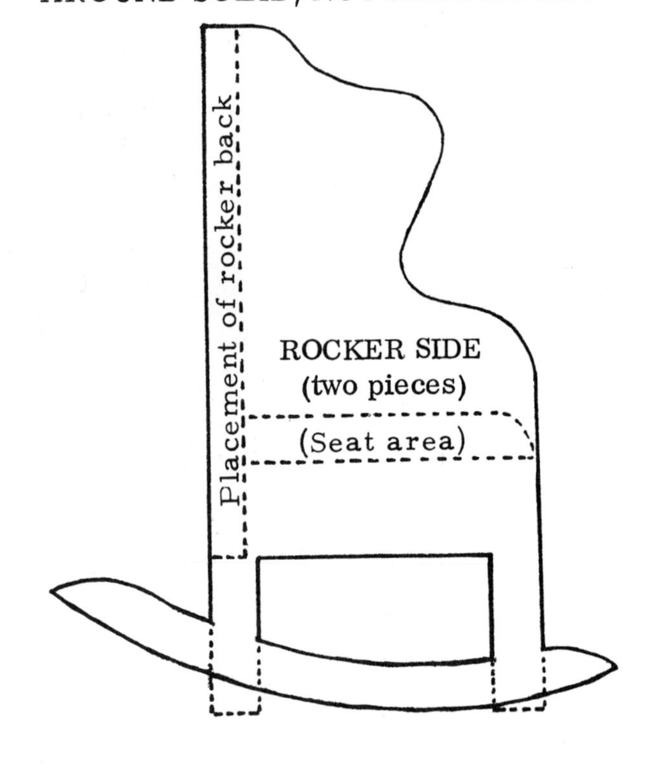

ROCKER FRONT
(one piece)

Instructions for the Chippendale Rocking Chair

1. Cut the following pieces from $\frac{3}{16}$-inch plywood:

a. one rocker back;
b. two rocker sides;
c. one rocker front.

2. Sand all the pieces to fit.

3. Position and glue the sides to the back as indicated by the dotted lines in the pattern pieces.

4. Sand again. Finish the rocker in any stain you wish and shellac. Sand between each coat of stain and shellac.

UPHOLSTERY

1. Cut two seats ($1\frac{9}{16} \times 2$ inches), one from cardboard and one from approximately $\frac{1}{8}$-inch thick foam rubber. Glue the two pieces together, cover with upholstery fabric, and follow the upholstery instructions for the Chippendale Easy Chair on page 103.

NOTE: Stretch prints are especially good for fully upholstering a rocking chair such as this, the stretch to "stretch" the fabric to the chair, and the print to hide any possible mistakes.

Close-up of two Chippendale rocking chairs with a tavern table between them.

Patterns for the Tavern Table [c. 1725]

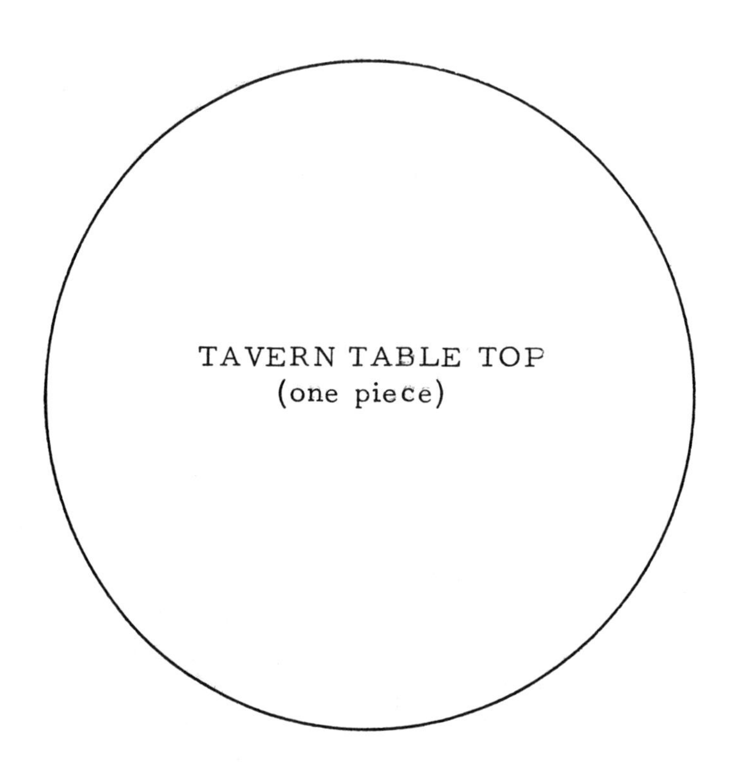

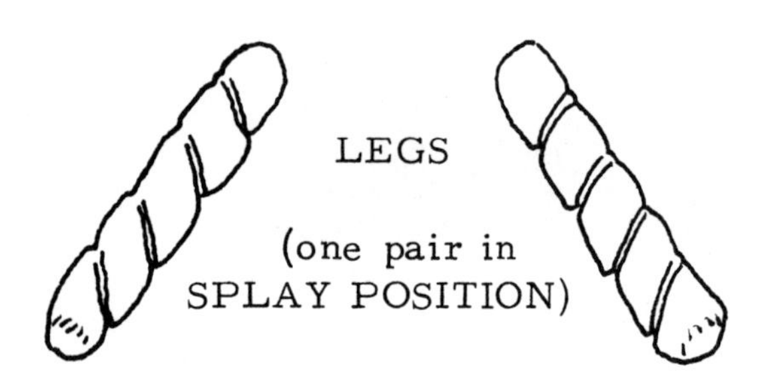

Instructions for the Tavern Table

1. Cut from $\frac{3}{16}$-inch plywood one round table top, approximately 3½ inches in diameter. Add the turned dowels, approximately 1½ inches long, to the underside of the table in splay position (see the illustration). (Dowels are available at any lumberyard or hobby shop.)

Patterns and Instructions for the Child's Bedroom and Master Bedroom

Patterns for the Queen Anne Pencil-Post Bed [Child's Bedroom] [c. 1760's] and the Queen Anne Canopy Bed [Master Bedroom] [c. 1735-1750]

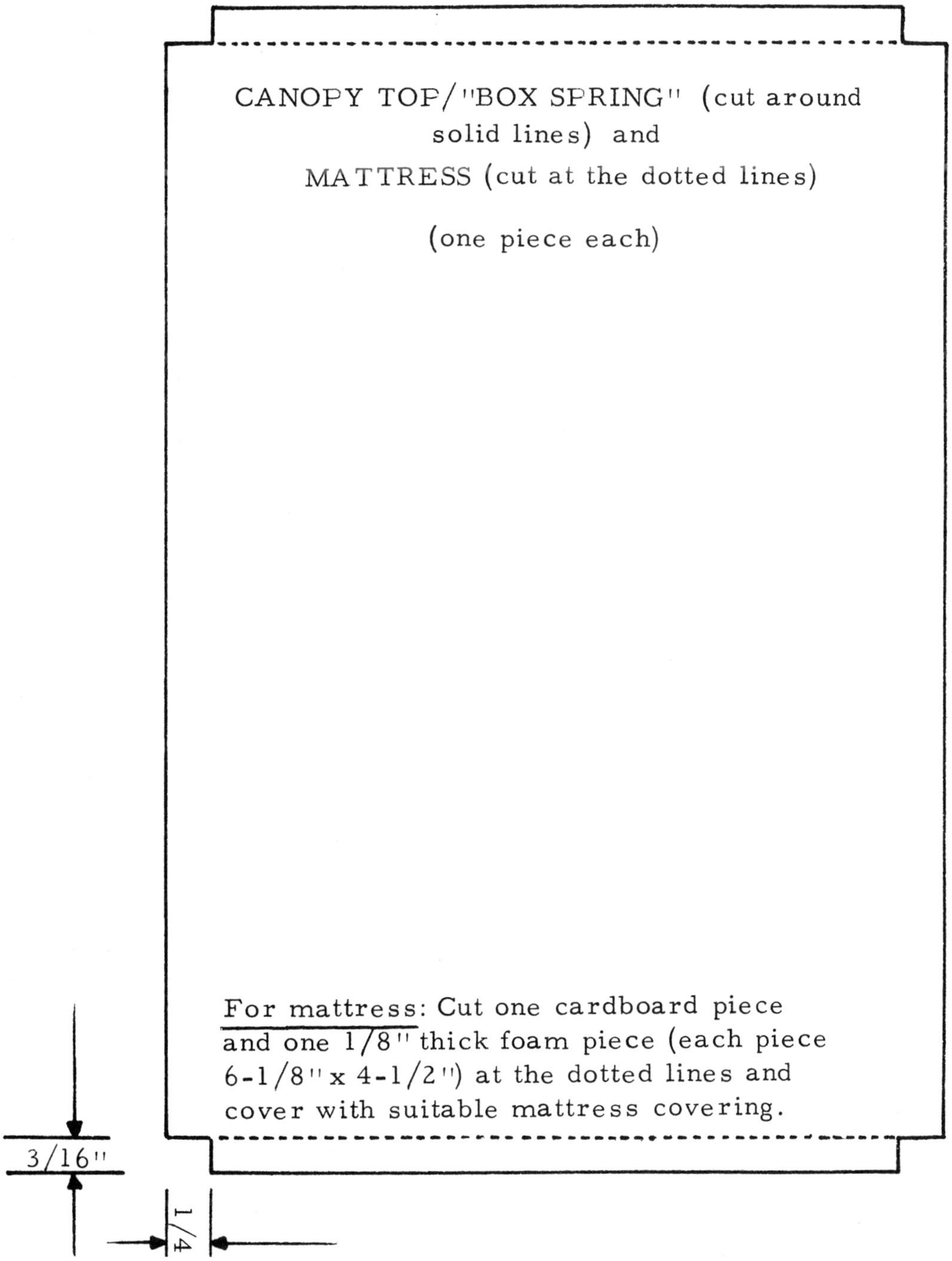

CANOPY TOP/"BOX SPRING" (cut around solid lines) and
MATTRESS (cut at the dotted lines)

(one piece each)

For mattress: Cut one cardboard piece and one 1/8" thick foam piece (each piece 6-1/8" x 4-1/2") at the dotted lines and cover with suitable mattress covering.

3/16"

1/4

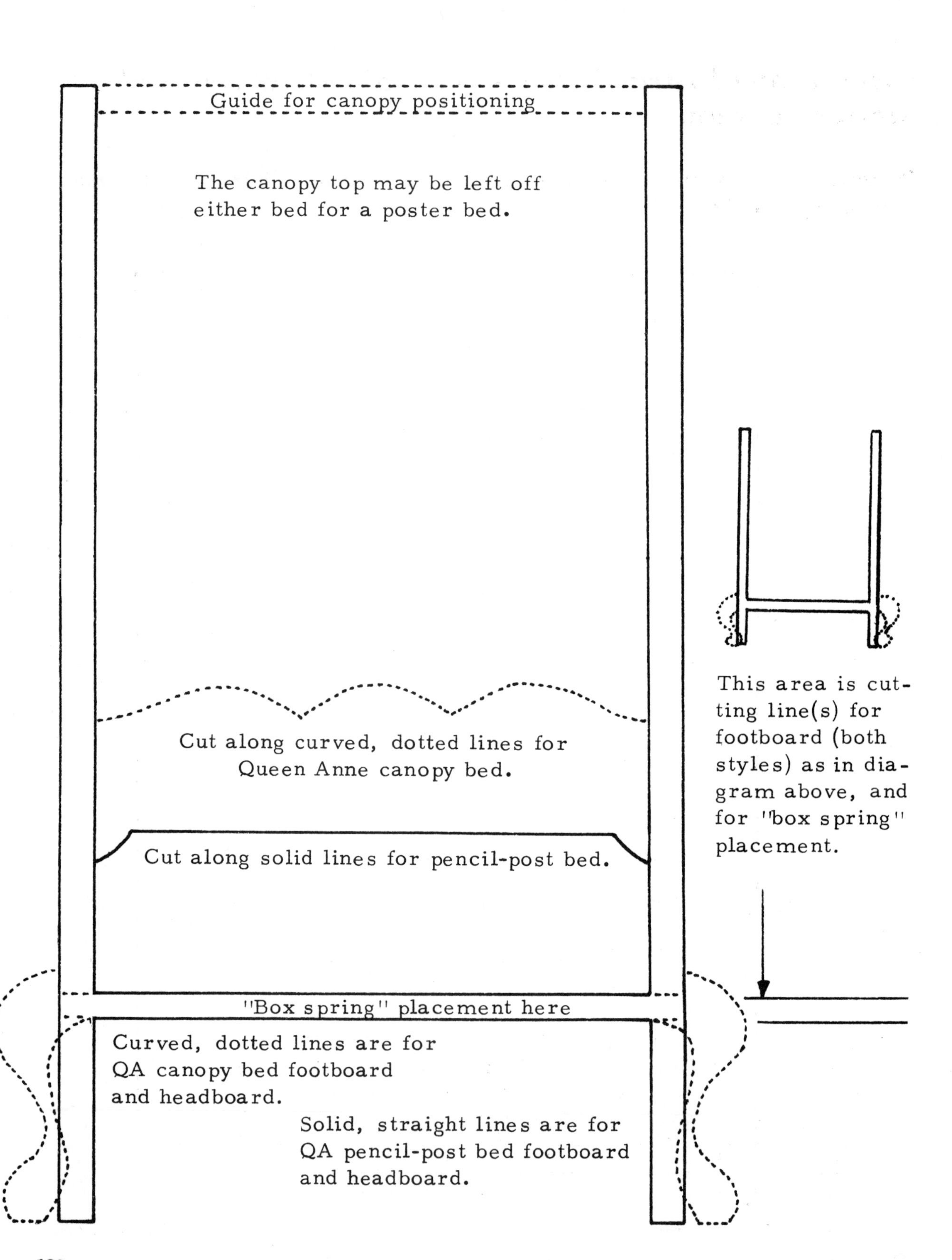

Guide for canopy positioning
The canopy top may be left off either bed for a poster bed.
Cut along curved, dotted lines for Queen Anne canopy bed.
Cut along solid lines for pencil-post bed.
"Box spring" placement here
Curved, dotted lines are for QA canopy bed footboard and headboard.
Solid, straight lines are for QA pencil-post bed footboard and headboard.
This area is cutting line(s) for footboard (both styles) as in diagram above, and for "box spring" placement.

Instructions for the Queen Anne Pencil-Post and Canopy Beds

1. For either bed, cut from $\frac{3}{16}$-inch plywood:

a. one headboard; } These pieces determine
b. one footboard; } the style of bed.
c. one canopy top; }
d. one box spring.

2. Sand all the pieces to fit.

3. Position and glue the canopy top and box spring as illustrated by the dotted lines in the pattern.

4. Sand and finish as desired.

See the chapter "Patterns and Instructions for the Linens" on page 143 for how to make bedspreads, quilts, and pillows for the beds.

Close-up of the pencil-post bed in the child's bedroom.

Close-up of the canopy bed in the master bedroom.

Patterns for the Queen Anne/William and Mary Highboy/ Lowboy [c. 1730-1760 and 1689-1702 respectively] and for the Child's and Adults' Wardrobes

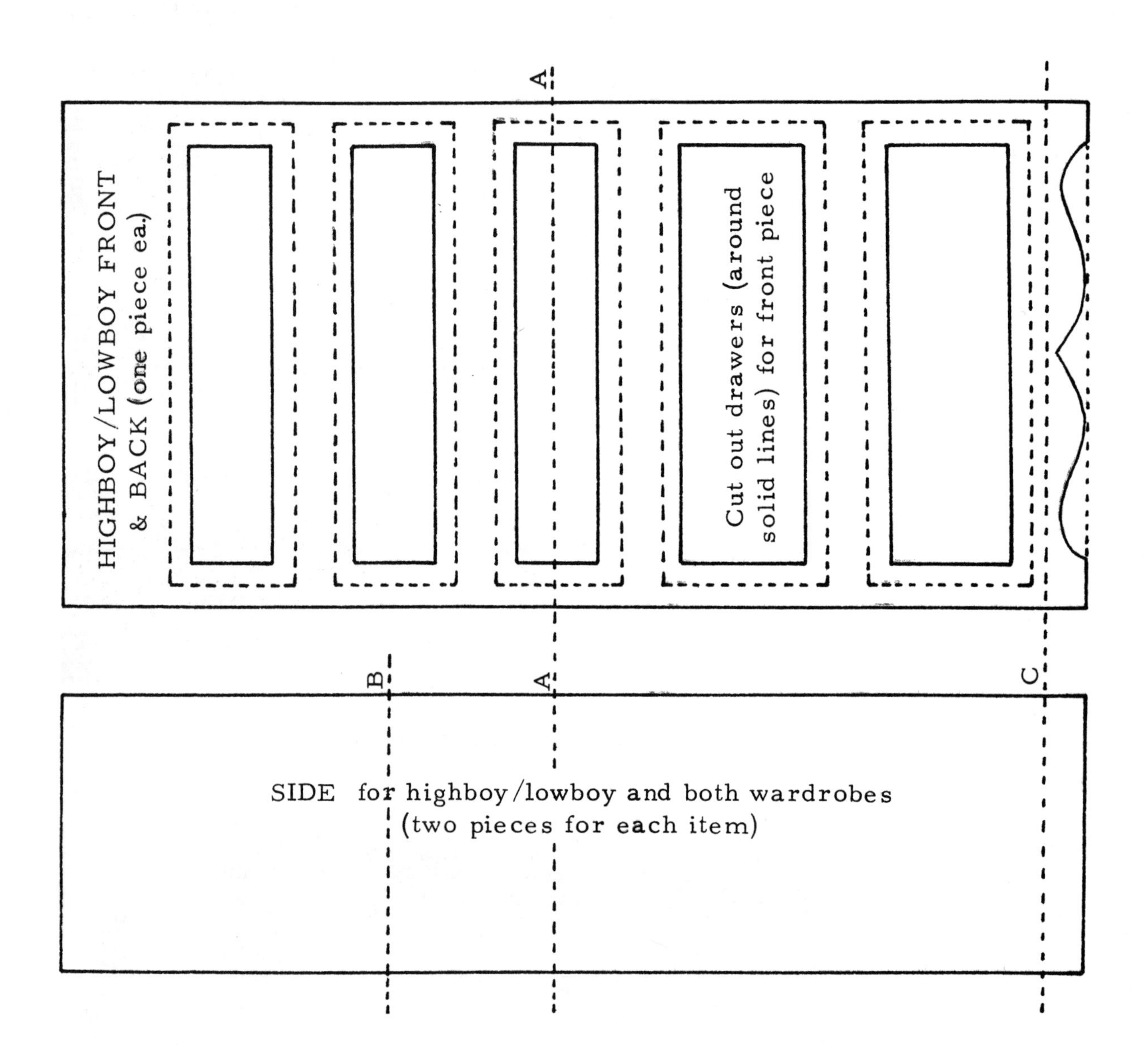

A: Cutting line for child's lowboy (front, back, and sides with two large drawer openings).

B: Cutting line for child's wardrobe (front, back, and sides).

C: Cutting line for William and Mary style (with ball feet).

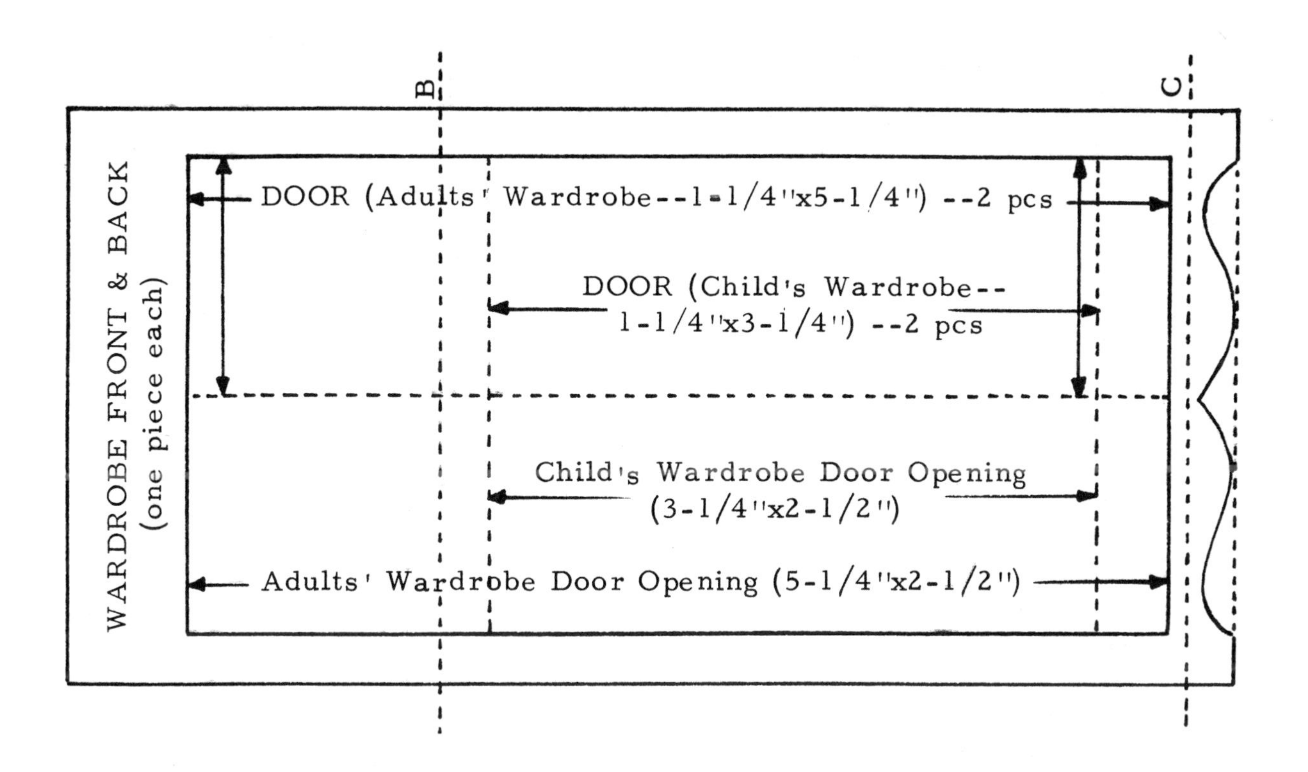

TOP
for W&M lowboy/highboy or
either wardrobe

2-1/4"x3-1/4" (one pc ea item)

A

DRAWER RAIL
1-5/8"x2-5/8"
(one piece)

B

DRAWER BOTTOM
1-3/4"x2-1/4"
(one piece)

TOP
for adults' highboy or
wardrobe
1-5/8"x2-5/8"
(one piece)

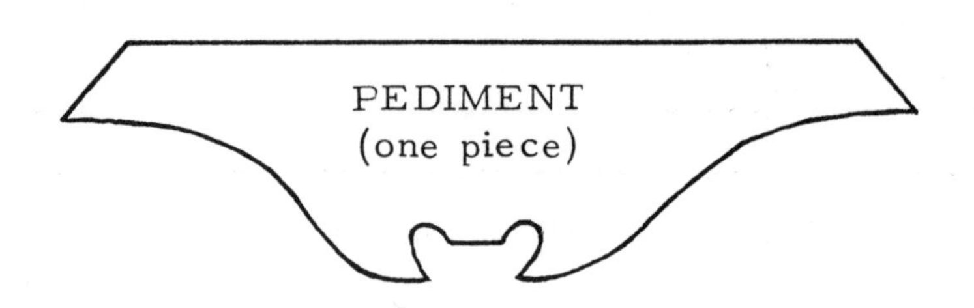

C — SMALL DWR SIDE
1/2"x1-3/4" (2 pcs)

F — LARGE DWR FRONT FACE
1"x2-3/4" (one piece)

D — LARGE DWR SIDE
3/4"x1-3/4"
(2 pcs)

G — SMALL DWR REAR
3/8"x2-1/4" (1 pc)

E — SMALL DWR FRONT FACE
3/4"x2-3/4" (one piece)

H — LARGE DWR REAR
5/8"x2-1/4" (1 pc)

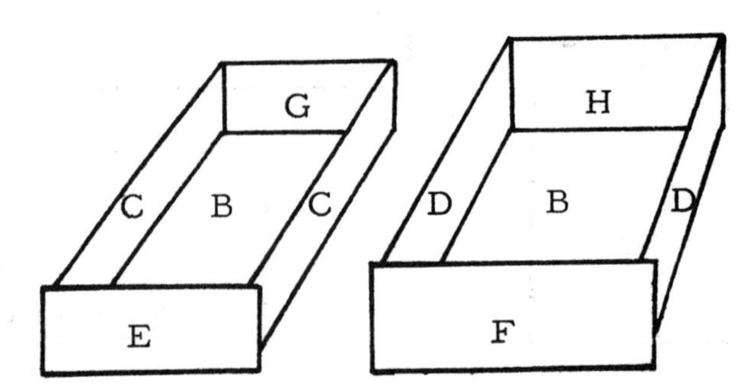

Small Drawer Parts   Large Drawer Parts
(representative scale)

Instructions for the William and Mary Lowboy in the Child's Bedroom

1. Cut the following from $\frac{3}{16}$-inch plywood:
a. one chest back without drawer openings (3×3 inches);
b. one chest front the same as the back, but with the drawer openings;
c. two chest sides ($1\frac{5}{8} \times 3$ inches);
d. one chest top ($2\frac{1}{4} \times 3\frac{1}{4}$ inches);
e. two drawer rails ($1\frac{5}{8} \times 2\frac{5}{8}$ inches).

2. From $\frac{1}{8}$-inch plywood, cut, *on the inside of the cutting line**, the following drawer parts for *two* large drawers:
pattern piece B: two pieces for the drawer bottom;
pattern piece D: four pieces for the drawer sides;
pattern piece F: two pieces for the drawer front face;
pattern piece H: two pieces for the drawer rear.

3. Sand all the pieces to fit.

4. Center and glue the two drawer rails to the inside lowboy front (on the wrong side) just below the bottom openings for the drawers. The drawers slide in and out along these rails. Add the chest sides, back and top.

5. Assemble the two large drawers (see the illustration) and position them into the drawer openings.

6. Sand everything again, stain and shellac twice. Sand lightly between all coats.

7. Add beads for William and Mary ball feet and for the drawer pulls.

*The drawers are designed to fit *exactly* into the drawer openings. However, sometimes glue alone adds slightly to the overall dimensions of the drawer itself and causes the drawer not to fit properly into the drawer opening. Cutting inside the cutting line and/or sanding the cut edge down to fit can solve the problem (see the illustration opposite).

Close-up of the William and Mary lowboy (left) and child's wardrobe.

Close-up of the Queen Anne highboy.

Inside of cutting line

Outside of cutting line

Instructions for the Queen Anne Highboy in the Master Bedroom

1. Cut the following from $\frac{3}{16}$-inch plywood:
a. one chest back without the drawer openings (3 × $6\frac{1}{4}$ inches);
b. one chest front, the same as the back except with the drawer openings, and with the Queen Anne scallop cut out on the bottom;
c. two chest sides ($1\frac{5}{8}$ × $6\frac{1}{4}$ inches);
d. one chest top ($1\frac{5}{8}$ × $2\frac{5}{8}$ inches);
e. five drawer rails ($1\frac{5}{8}$ × $2\frac{5}{8}$ inches);
f. one pediment.

2. From $\frac{1}{8}$-inch plywood, cut on the *inside cutting line* the following drawer parts for *two large* drawers and *three small* drawers.
Large drawers (2): Cut the same as for the two lowboy drawers (see the William and Mary Lowboy instructions on page 125).
Small drawers (3): pattern piece B: 3 pieces for the drawer bottom; pattern piece C: 6 pieces for the drawer sides; pattern piece E: 3 pieces for the drawer front face; pattern piece G: 3 pieces for the drawer rear.

3. Sand all the pieces.

4. Center and glue the five drawer rails to the inside highboy front (on the wrong side) just below the bottom openings for the drawers. Add the chest sides, back, top, and the pediment.

5. Assemble all the drawers indicated in the illustration and fit into the drawer openings.

6. Sand, and finish as desired.

7. Add beads for drawer pulls on each drawer, and an eagle (from a piece of costume jewelry or a decal, or decoupage one cut from a magazine) on the pediment for interest.

Instructions for the Queen Anne Wardrobe in the Master Bedroom

1. Cut the following pieces from $\frac{3}{16}$-inch plywood:
a. one wardrobe back, along the dotted lines at the bottom (3 × $6\frac{1}{4}$ inches);
b. one wardrobe front, the same as the back except cut along the scalloped solid line, and cut out a $2\frac{1}{2}$ × $5\frac{1}{4}$ inch opening for the doors;
c. two sides ($1\frac{5}{8}$ × $6\frac{1}{4}$ inches);
d. one top ($1\frac{5}{8}$ × $2\frac{5}{8}$ inches);
e. one drawer rail ($1\frac{5}{8}$ × $2\frac{5}{8}$ inches);
f. two doors ($1\frac{1}{4}$ × $5\frac{1}{4}$ inches);
g. one pediment.

2. Sand all the pieces to fit.

3. To the inside back, position and glue the top, the drawer rail for the bottom, and the two sides. Add the front and the pediment.

4. Sand lightly again. Finish the wardrobe and the loose doors in any desired finish.

5. Hinge the doors with miniature hinges. Add a clothes rod (a $\frac{1}{8}$-inch-diameter dowel that is $2\frac{5}{8}$ inches long). Glue beads onto the doors for pulls.

For a WILLIAM AND MARY STYLE WARDROBE, cut the wardrobe front, back, and sides at the C cutting line, use the William and Mary $2\frac{1}{4}$ × $3\frac{1}{4}$ inch top, leave off the pediment, and glue on beads for the ball feet.

For a CHILD'S WARDROBE IN EITHER STYLE, follow the B cutting line instructions and all directions indicated on the pattern for the child's wardrobe.

Close-up of the Queen Anne wardrobe.

The Dressing Room

Both bedrooms upstairs join the dressing room, which is as useful as it is elegant. Its color scheme consists of delicate pinks and cool blues. "Imported" laces and exotic perfumes add to its grandeur.

The walls and ceiling are all "white-washed." The floor is walnut-stained and shellacked.

The main dressing table is 18th century French in style. It is crafted from a cardboard box covered with pink sateen cotton and several layers of beautiful ruffles. It has an overhead oval mirror mounted on a blue wood plaque which contrasts with the pinks, yet coordinates with the rest of the blues in the room.

Dainty laces and lots of frilly ruffles decorate the dressing room which adjoins both the child's bedroom and the master bedroom on the third floor.

Pieces of gold filigree and some old beads form the beautiful perfume bottles that adorn this elegant dressing table. A "pewter" dresser set completes the arrangement.

Dainty perfume bottles are made from pieces of filigrees weighted down with modelling clay, and costume jewelry beads oil-painted with country flowers. The three-piece dresser set is English "pewter" handcrafted by Colonial Craftsmen in Cape May, New Jersey (see page 174 for the address). The raised tray is a cosmetic jar cap.

On the dressing table are several wigs. On the swinging wall hanger is an elegant "undress" jacket. The wigs and the "undress" jacket are made for a contemporary doll, but are quite appropriate for an 18th century lady's wardrobe.

The Queen Anne dressing bench is fruitwood-colored, upholstered with a pink and blue wool "rush" seat cushion, and trimmed with embroidered pink-flowered lace. The wastebasket is a three-dimensional "weaving" made from a dishwashing soap dispenser and blue velvet ribbon.

The smaller, round dressing table in the corner is similar to the large one, except that a cardboard drum and wood top were used for the base. Above it hangs a gold filigree-framed painting of flowers on silk, and a gold filigree-framed mirror made from a piece of costume jewelry and a mirror disc.

The Japanese folding screen is made from four pieces of wood that were painted with white enamel, gold-leaf trimmed, and hinged by a Japanese scene cut out from a magazine. The screen is decorative as well as functional; it has a pair of mirror discs on each panel.

The Queen Anne dry sink is enamelled blue on the outside and navy on the inside. It is filled with towels made from thin terrycloth, and cosmetic jars and perfume bottles made from pieces of filigrees and costume jewelry beads. The ceramic water pitcher and basin set were bought in Mexico. The towel rack is a juice can snap ring painted brass-color. Additional toiletry supplies are on the bracketed shelf over the dry sink. The blue jar with the rubber stopper holds an additional supply of water.

A crown-domed, "crystal"-studded, gold-filigree chandelier completes the décor. It is crafted from a plastic foam ball, rhinestone necklace, dishwashing soap dispenser sprayed gold, costume jewelry crystal tear-drop beads, and white birthday candles. It was fashioned after the chandelier in the Red Room of the White House.

Patterns and Instructions for the Dressing Room

Instructions for the Dressing Tables

One of the dressing (or vanity) tables in the dollhouse is made from a cardboard drum and the other from a cheesebox, both about $2\frac{1}{2}$ inches high. Cover the base lavishly with cotton sateen and several layers of ruffled lace.

Patterns for the Dry Sink [c. 18th century]

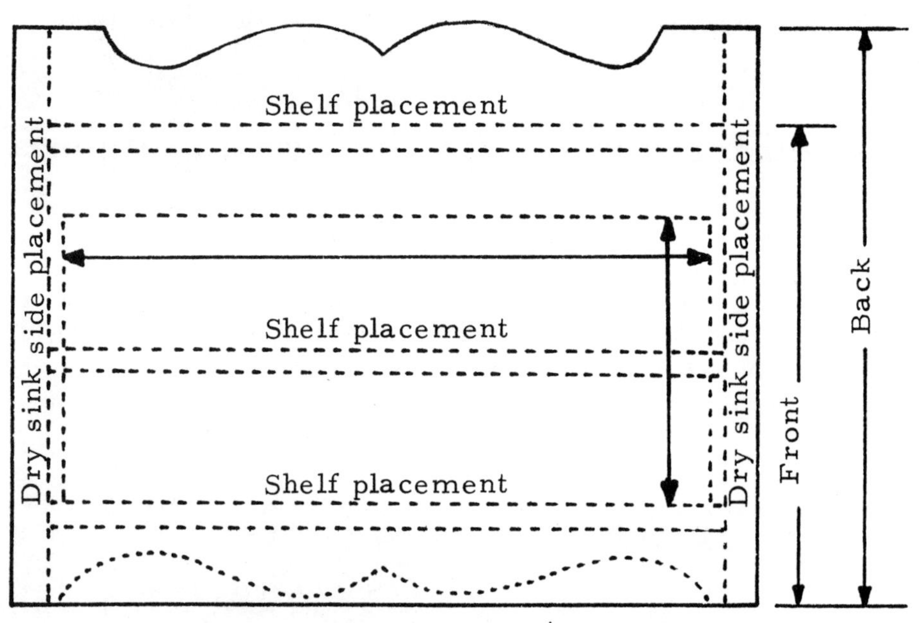

DRY SINK FRONT (4" wide x 2-1/2" high)
and DRY SINK BACK (4" wide x 3" high) -- one piece each

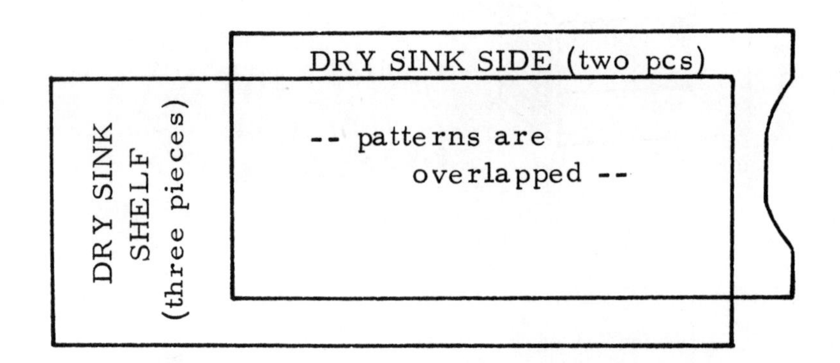

Instructions for the Dry Sink

1. From $\frac{3}{16}$-inch plywood, cut the following pieces:
a. one dry sink back (overall 3 × 4 inches);
b. one dry sink front (overall $2\frac{1}{2}$ × 4 inches with a $1\frac{1}{2}$ × $3\frac{1}{2}$ inch opening);
c. two sides (overall $1\frac{3}{8}$ × 3 inches);
d. three shelves ($1\frac{3}{8}$ × $3\frac{5}{8}$ inches; you can use $\frac{1}{8}$-inch plywood for the shelves).

2. Sand all the pieces to fit.

3. Align and glue the two sides to the inside front (on the wrong side) and the inside back, as illustrated in the pattern. Add the three shelves along the dotted guide lines (one of the shelves is the sink top, and the other is the sink bottom).

4. Sand again, and enamel.

Close-up of the dry sink.

Close-up of the folding screen in the dressing room.

Accessories

Just as Michelangelo saw beautiful art forms in a piece of marble while others saw a mere slab of stone, so does an astute craftsperson see innumerable possibilities for valuable miniature accessories in everyday discards that others throw out as junk.

In a dollhouse, it is the collection of accessories that makes the dollhouse a dolls' home. The cost of miniature accessories has become exorbitant, yet there is almost nothing in miniatures sold on the market that most novice craftspeople cannot make from everyday household items and discards. Experiment with such simple things as modelling clay, baker's clay, and papier-mâché for crafting miniature accessories and food items. There is a vast selection of paints available to simulate wood, metals, porcelains, and even the "wet look" to help you create "professional"-looking items. Try oil painting, decoupaging designs cut out from magazines, or decorating with fabric, ribbon, trims, decals, or decorative paper on your miniature accessories. And, always look for miniature accessories from such sources as cake decorations, jewelry, bracelet charms, and confectionery and cereal prizes. If you find an inexpensive plastic tea pot prize in a cereal box, paint it silver to look like sterling, or paint it with enamel to look like porcelain! This is a good way to collect some very valuable and one-of-a-kind accessory items very easily and, best of all, very inexpensively. Being on the look-out for bargains is part of the fun.

Some accessory items, such as plates, firescreens, and picture frames, can be cut out from paper, hardened with white glue, and painted to simulate their authentic, full-scale counterparts.

An entire book could be written and illustrated on crafting miniature accessories from everyday household items and discards. Therefore, this chapter is limited to the mere bottle/can cap that you throw out every day, but which has dozens of uses in a miniature 18th century household. Note that the size and shape of the bottle cap can very easily be changed, if necessary. If you do not have a barrel-shaped bottle cap, for example, consider sculpturing one from modelling clay, baker's clay, or papier-mâché, using a regular-shaped bottle cap(s) for the framework (see illustration below). To do this, fill

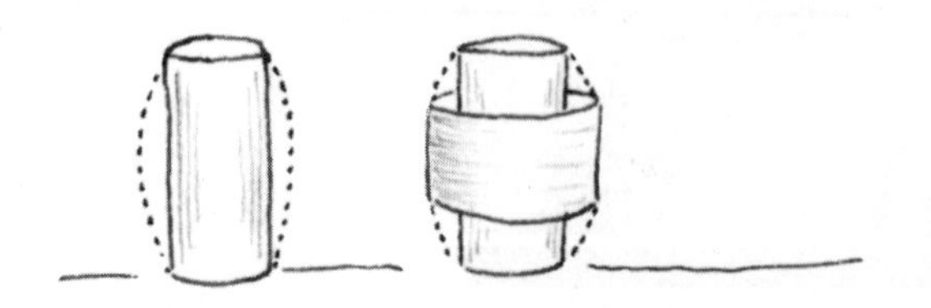

with clay inside the dotted lines until the barrel shape results. You can carve the wood grain right into the clay. When the clay is dry, stain as you would any wood.

1. Bowl/tureen: Can be used as is (hereafter referred to as CBUAI). Glue handle(s) from thread. For a tureen, use a small bottle cap or piece of filigree for the base.

2. Covered candy dish: Make a lid from cardboard, and add a small tapioca pearl on the lid.

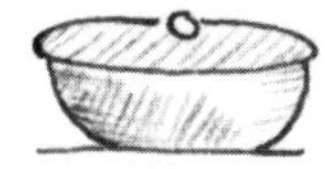

3. Compote: Use two bottle caps and join them with a bead or a stem made from a cotton swab stick.

4. Gelatin (or copper) mould: CBUAI or paint copper-colored.

5. Plates and saucers: Use very small, shallow bottle caps.

6. Kitchen canister: Make a lid from cardboard and top with a small tapioca pearl.

7. Cake cover: Add a small tapioca pearl on the cover (the bottle cap) and place on a plate made from cardboard, a metal washer, or a disc.

8. Cake: Cover the cap with real sugar icing and place on a plate. Decorate with real confectionery decorations.

9. Cookie jar: Cut cookies from sliced, dried apples or from cereal flakes.

10. Wine cooler: A must for every dollhouse!

11. Horn of plenty: Use an artificial sweetener bottle cap so shaped, and fill it with fruit made from costume jewelry beads.

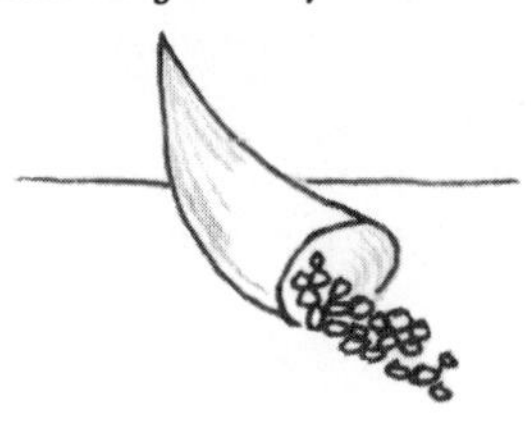

12. Coffee pot: Make a spout, handle, and lid from cardboard. Glue a small tapioca pearl on the lid.

13. Tea kettle: Same as the coffee pot, except make a wire handle.

14. Strainer (or colander): Drill or punch holes in the cap. Add a cardboard or wire handle.

15. Grater: Same as the strainer, except for the bottle cap shape. If possible, drill or punch holes from the inside out.

16. Pitcher: Use a plastic bottle cap, melt the spout to shape, and add a cardboard or thread handle.

17. Cooking pot: Add a cardboard or wire handle.

18. Frying/sauce pan: Add a cardboard handle.

19. Drinking cup/mug: Add a thread handle.

20. Drinking beaker: CBUAI or add a thread handle.

21. Goblet/stemware: Glue a bottle cap on top of a piece of jewelry filigree.

22. Serving tray: Use a shallow can cap or lid.

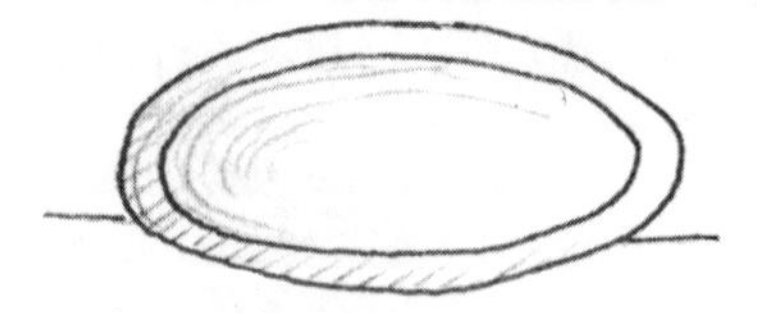

23. Water pail: Add a wire handle.

24. Dipper: Add a dowel handle.

25. Mortar and pestle: Use a costume jewelry bead at the end of a cotton swab stick for the pestle.

26. Scales: Hang two small bottle caps with string to a short dowel (a cotton swab stick). Add a wire loop for hanging, or add a $\frac{1}{4}$-inch diameter dowel to the short dowel going across. Attach a base (from another bottle cap).

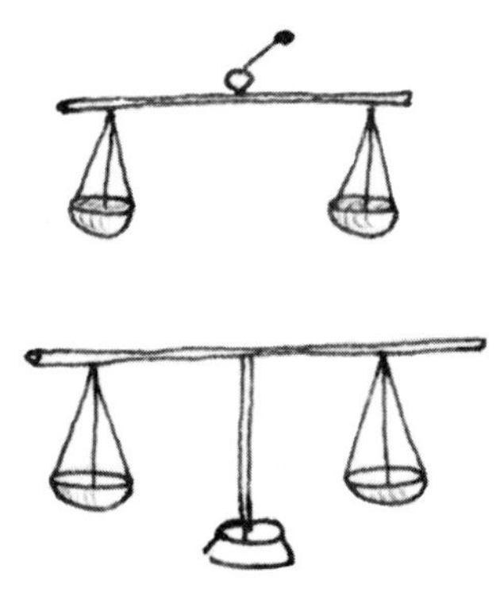

27. Wash tub: Simulate wood with strips of veneer, and add thread handles.

28. Barrel: Make the same as the tub, except use a barrel-shaped bottle cap and leave off the handles. Fill with apples (beads).

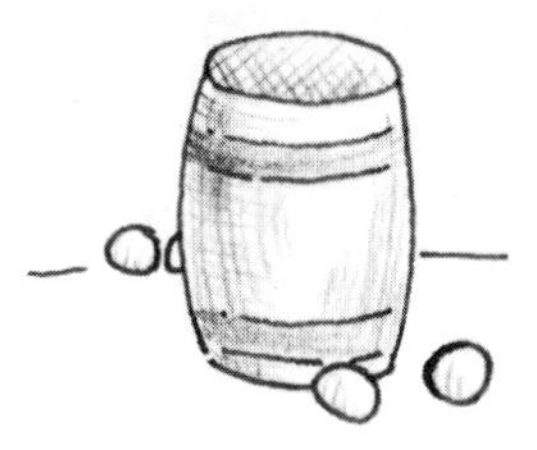

29. Butter churn: Use with a cotton swab stick.

30. Lamp shade: CBUAI or add beads and some filigree for the body.

31. Lamp base: CBUAI (see 30 above).

32. Chandelier body: Use a cone-shaped bottle cap (see the chapter "Chandeliers" on page 155).

33. Wash basin: Use with a water pitcher as a set.

34. Chamber pot: CBUAI or add a thread or cardboard handle.

35. Wastepaper basket: CBUAI.

36. Flower vase/pot: CBUAI.

37. Umbrella stand: CBUAI.

38. Food/flower basket/clothes hamper: Add thread handles and fill with food/flowers/ clothes.

39. Sewing/knitting basket: Use a $\frac{3}{16}$-inch disc or small shallow bottle cap for the base, a cotton swab stick for the stem, and a larger, deep cap for the basket. Wrap yarn in tiny balls and use round-headed stickpins for the knitting needles.

40. Pet bed: Fill with a tiny blanket cut from a knit fabric.

41. Hat box: CBUAI or tie with pretty ribbons.

42. Cosmetic container: Add a small tapioca pearl on top.

43. Jewelry box: Fill with miniature strings of pearls or inexpensive costume jewelry stones.

44. Dressing table tray: Inside a bottle cap, place the dolls' perfume bottles (made from beads and filigrees).

45. Toy box: Fill with miniature cake decorations, charms, or prize "toys."

46. Powder horn: See 11 above. Hang on a wall with thread or yarn.

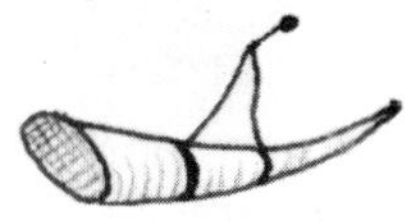

47. Magazine rack: Fill with tiny newspapers of the period (make the newspapers yourself, too).

48. Banjo: Add a handle and cover it with fine thread for the strings.

49. Coal bucket: Fill with real charcoal from a fish aquarium filter, or paint tiny pebbles black.

50. Inkwell: Fill with a tiny feather or a quill pen.

51. Bedwarmer: Fill with charcoal and glue on a tongue depressor or a cotton swab stick.

52. American drum: Decorate with felt, small tapioca pearls, and string or eye screws.

53. Wall candle box: Fill with birthday candles and hang on a wall with string or eye screws.

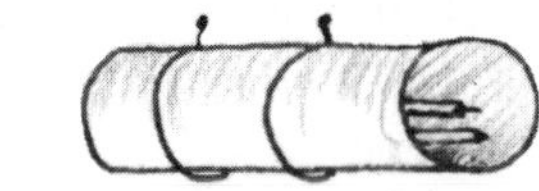

54. Wood carrier: Fill with real wood cut from tree twigs.

55. Plate warmer: Use a plastic bottle or can top and cut it to shape. Add cardboard legs and a wire handle. Fill with plates, and set on a fireplace hearth.

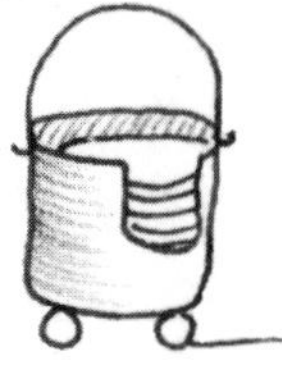

56. Hat base: Add a brim or CBUAI, trimmed with ribbon.

57. Hat rack (or hall tree): Glue on a dowel and bead finial, and add nails for hanging the hats on.

58. Table base: Use with a larger, shallow cap for a table top. Add a dowel or thread spool.

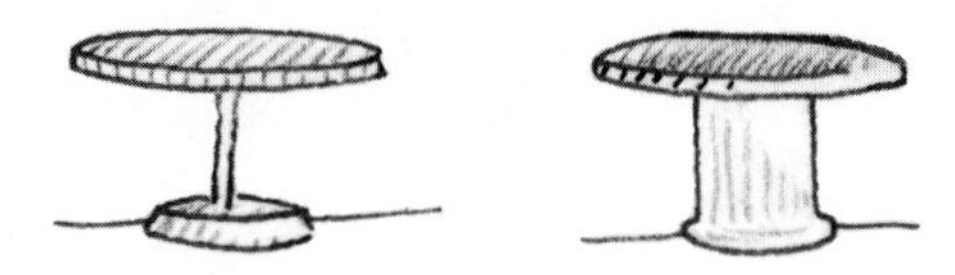

59. Table top: See 58 above.

60. Footstool (ottoman): Upholster like a piece of furniture. Add beads for the feet.

61. Round causeuse (loveseat): Use two large bottle/can caps (with the larger one on the bottom). Upholster everything.

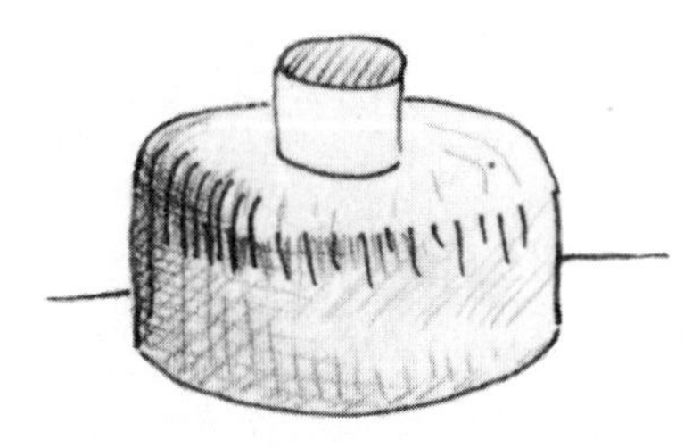

62. Toy table: Use small bottle caps (see 58 and 59 above).

63. Piano stool: Add a thread spool and upholster.

64. Clock: Cut a clock face from a magazine or draw one. Glue it on top of a bottle cap. Add small tapioca pearls for the feet and alarm.

65. Furniture finials: CBUAI or use with beads.

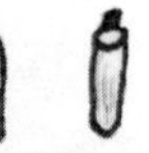

66. Ceiling moulding: Decorate with lace designs for a carved look (or CBUAI if the bottle cap is decorative).

67. Colonnade statue stand: Add a bust, figurine, or other ornament.

68. Firescreen: Glue a cardboard stand behind it for support.

69. Fireplace shovel: Add a cardboard or dowel handle.

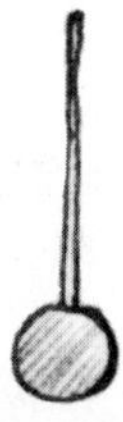

70. Smokestack: Glue together a stack of bottle caps (all the same size) for a Franklin stove or a pot-bellied stove.

71. Candleholder: Add a thread handle and a birthday candle.

72. Wall sconce: Glue a round boutique mirror inside the bottle cap (optional), and place a $\frac{1}{4}$-inch birthday candle inside the edge.

73. Picture/mirror frame: CBUAI from a very shallow can lid. Glue a picture from a magazine or a photo, paint your own picture, or glue in a mirror.

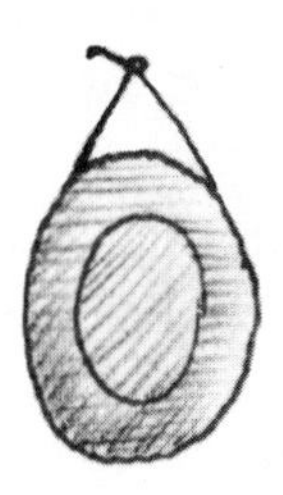

74. Gifts: Wrap with gift paper and tie with ribbon (to put under a Christmas tree or for a birthday party).

75. Umbrella: Use a cone-shaped bottle cap and glue on a pipe cleaner handle.

Patterns and Instructions for the Draperies

Close-up of the draperies in the parlor.

Instructions for the Draperies

For drapery rods, use $\frac{1}{8}$-inch or $\frac{1}{16}$-inch diameter dowels, approximately $6\frac{1}{2}$ inches long. Use miniature eye screws at each end of the top of the windows for the drapery rod to go through. Paint the rods and eye screws gold.

For the draperies, use very light-weight fabrics (to allow the most drape), such as organdy, nylon, or light-weight cotton. If you use cotton, plan on using the same fabric for the chair upholstery or bed coverings, or even wall covering in a particular room. You can also use old nylon slips with lace trimmings for custom-made-look draperies. Simple embroidered trims, such as chain stitches or cross stitches, are also especially nice for the solid-colored draperies. (See page 151 in the chapter "Needlecrafts" for embroidery trim ideas.)

For either style of swag (see the patterns), cut two pieces from fabric to match or contrast the draperies. Sew them together on the wrong side, leaving one side open. Turn them right-side-out through this opening. Finish off by hand.

Patterns for the Draperies

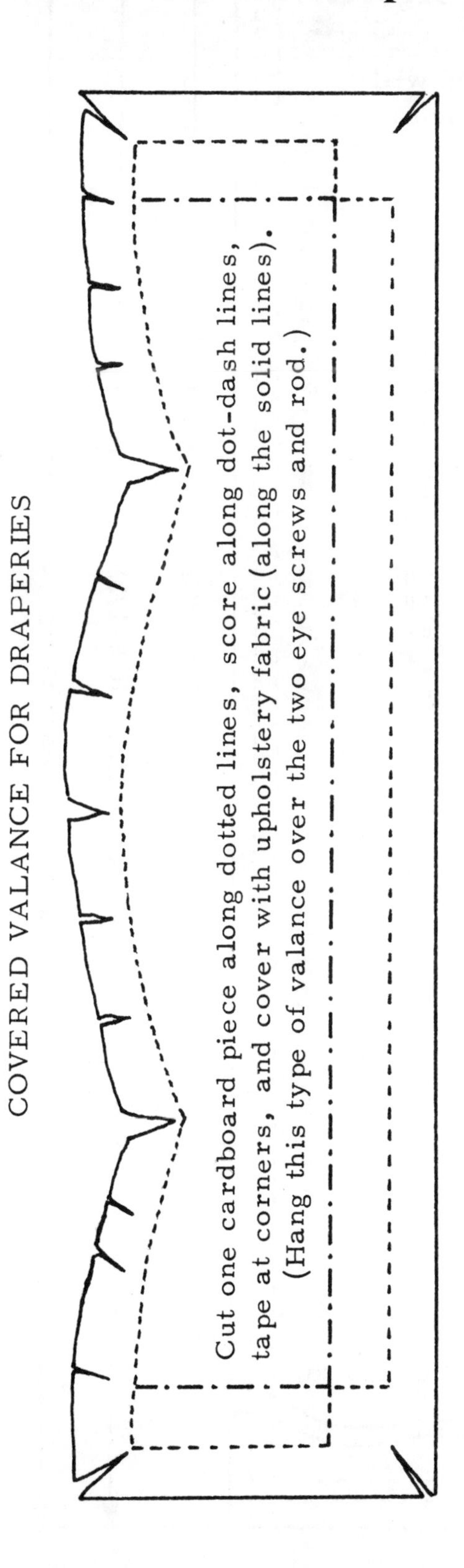

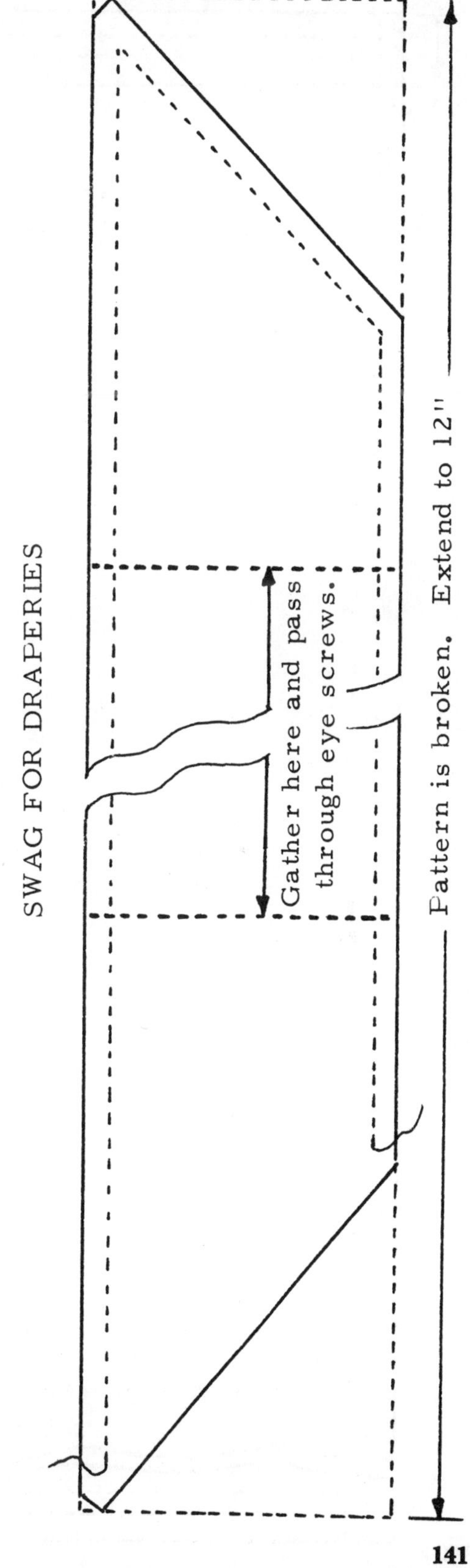

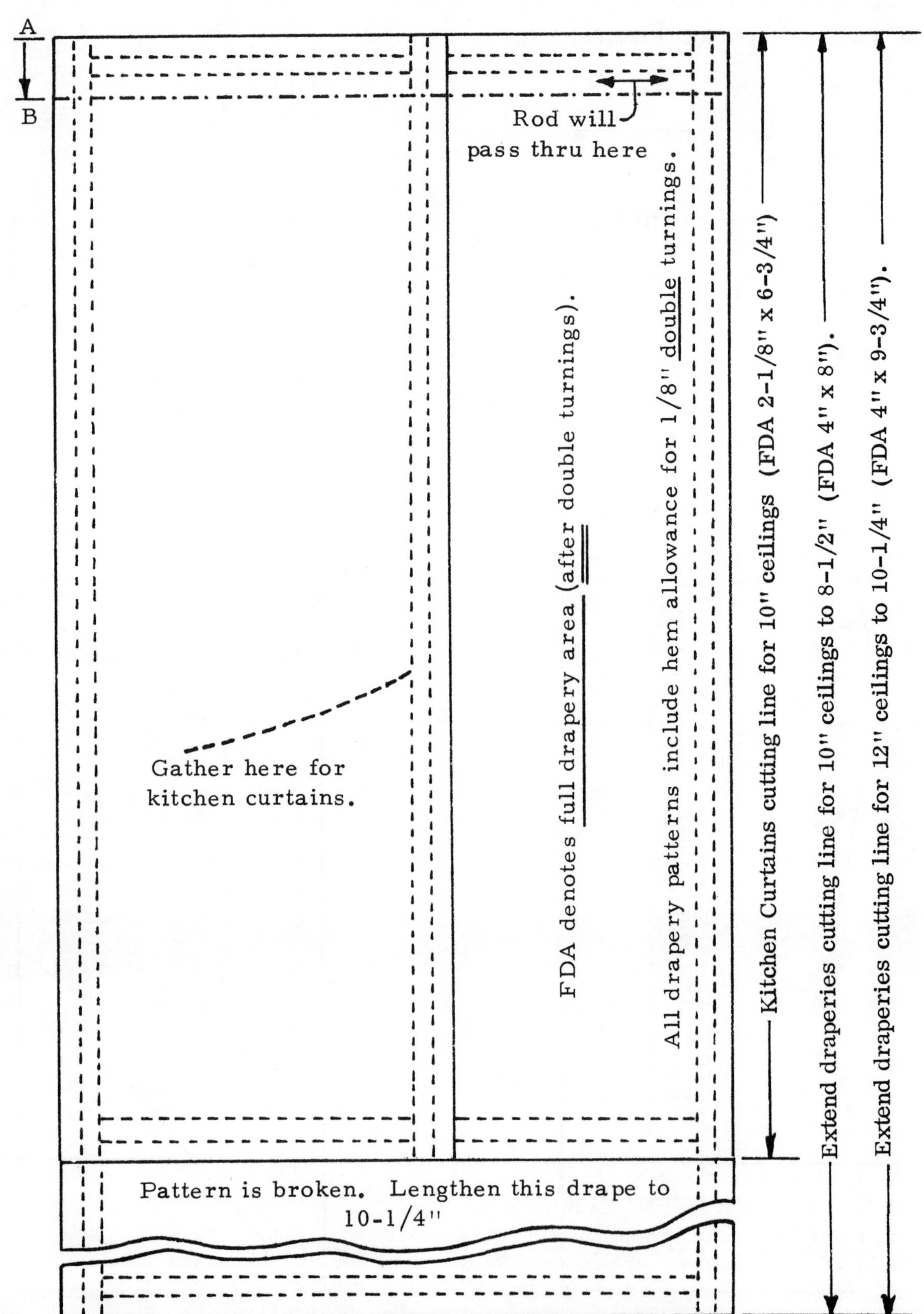
A
B
Rod will
pass thru here
FDA denotes full drapery area (after double turnings).
All drapery patterns include hem allowance for 1/8" double turnings.
Kitchen Curtains cutting line for 10" ceilings (FDA 2-1/8" x 6-3/4")
Extend draperies cutting line for 10" ceilings to 8-1/2" (FDA 4" x 8").
Extend draperies cutting line for 12" ceilings to 10-1/4" (FDA 4" x 9-3/4").
Gather here for
kitchen curtains.
Pattern is broken. Lengthen this drape to
10-1/4"

Patterns and Instructions for the Linens

Instructions for the Bed Linens

Coverette

Cut one piece along the solid lines in the pattern ($6\frac{1}{2} \times 9$ inches overall dimensions) and hem $\frac{1}{4}$ inch all around. Seersucker fabric is good for this because it is light-weight, yet it looks like miniature quilting.

Hanging Canopy

Cut two pieces along the solid lines in the pattern (5×7 inches without the notched corners). With the wrong sides out, sew three edges together. Turn the right sides out, and finish the last edge by hand. Add 1- to $1\frac{1}{2}$-inch wide lace, ruffle, or fringe to hang down.

Mattress

Cut two pieces, one from cardboard and one from fluffy fleece fabric (or $\frac{1}{8}$-inch foam rubber) along the dotted (and dot-dash) pattern lines ($4\frac{1}{2} \times 6\frac{1}{8}$ inches with the two bottom notched corners). Cut one piece around the solid lines from cotton (or muslin) ($4\frac{3}{4}$ inches $\times$ $6\frac{5}{8}$ inches). With the wrong sides out, sew the two larger (cotton) pieces together along three edges. Turn right-side-out and insert the cardboard and the fleecy fabric. Finish the last edge by hand.

Dust Ruffle

Sew 1- to $1\frac{1}{2}$-inch wide lace, ruffle, or fringe to the three edges along only the dot-dash edges of the mattress. (Do not continue the trim in the corners.)

Consider adding embroidered trims and monograms to your bed linens (see the chapter "Needlecrafts" on page 151).

Comforter or Baby's Blanket

Cut two pieces ($5 \times 7\frac{1}{4}$ inches) from cotton. With the wrong sides out, sew three edges together (with a $\frac{1}{4}$-inch seam allowance). Turn right-side-out, and insert one piece of $4\frac{1}{2} \times 6\frac{3}{4}$ inch fluffy fleece fabric. Finish the last edge by hand. Quilt around print designs in a basting stitch (or create quilt designs; see the chapter "Needlecrafts" on page 151).

To make a baby's blanket, knit a $3 \times 4\frac{1}{2}$ inch blanket, or cut a piece that size from a knit fabric.

Pillows and Accessories

To make a pillow, cut two pieces from cotton or muslin (each $1\frac{1}{4} \times 1\frac{3}{4}$ inches), allowing $\frac{1}{8}$ inch for seams. Stuff with cotton batting.

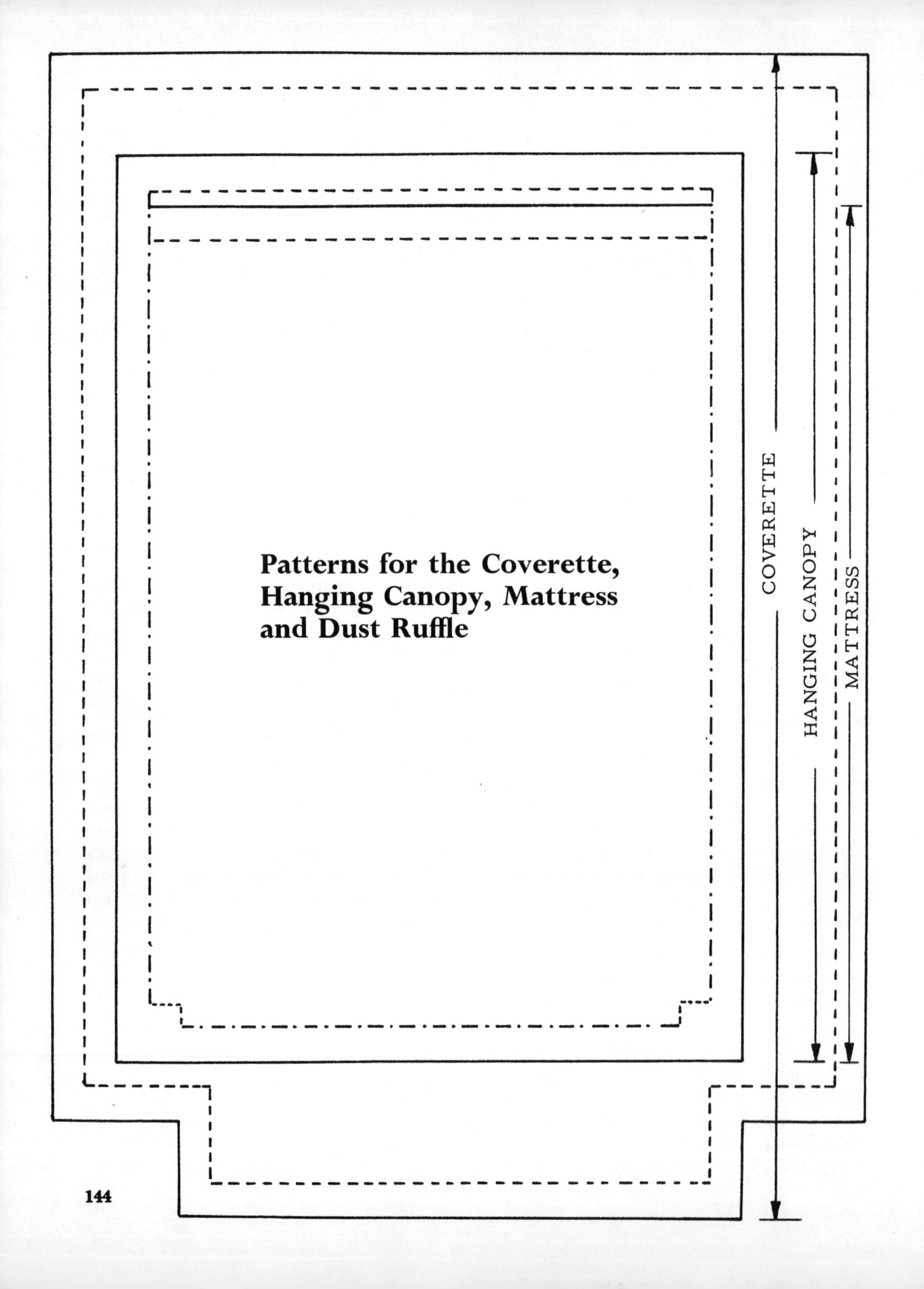

Patterns for the Coverette, Hanging Canopy, Mattress and Dust Ruffle

To make a pillow sham, cut two pieces of fabric to match the coverette (each $1\frac{1}{4} \times 2\frac{1}{4}$ inches), allowing $\frac{1}{8}$ inch for the seams. Stuff with cotton batting. Add lace (to match the dust ruffle and hanging canopy lace) to the top 2-inch edge of the sham.

To make pillowcases, cut two pieces from cotton or muslin (each $1\frac{1}{2} \times 2$ inches), allowing $\frac{1}{8}$ inch for seams. Leave one side open for inserting the pillow.

Table Linens

Doilies make excellent tablecloths. Some doilies are so fine that they actually look like custom-made miniature lace tablecloths for dollhouse tables. These are the most valuable items in any dollhouse. However, if doilies for tablecloths are not readily available, it is very simple to make elegant ones from fabric. Use a light-weight fabric such as cotton, organdy, nylon, or silk. You can trim these with embroidery, lace, or fringe at the hem, if you want.

Kitchen/Dining Room Tablecloth

For either of these, cut one piece $6 \times 7\frac{1}{2}$ inches and hem $\frac{1}{4}$ inch all around. For the kitchen tablecloth, use checkered gingham (to match the curtains).

For napkins, cut $\frac{3}{4} \times \frac{3}{4}$ inch squares from light-weight cotton.

Gate-Leg/Tavern Tablecloth

To make this cloth, cut a $7\frac{1}{4}$-inch diameter circle. Turn up a $\frac{1}{4}$-inch hem. Then trim the bottom edge as you choose.

Cross-Base Tea/Candle Tablecloth

Cut a $6\frac{1}{2}$-inch diameter circle (for the tea table) or an $8\frac{3}{4}$-inch diameter circle (for the candle table). Turn up a $\frac{1}{4}$-inch hem. Trim the bottom edge.

You can leave the cross-base candle table uncovered, as this was the usual practice for this type of table in colonial America.

Miscellaneous Linens

Throw Cushions

You can make throw cushions in various sizes (1×1 inch, $1\frac{1}{4} \times 1\frac{1}{4}$ inches, $1\frac{1}{2} \times 1\frac{1}{2}$ inches) in assorted fabrics and colors, to match or to contrast the bed linens or furniture upholstery. Add $\frac{1}{8}$ inch for a seam allowance before you cut the pillows out. Stuff with cotton batting.

Rug Designs and Ideas

Rugs for the dollhouse are easy to accumulate because their sources are so numerous. Crocheted doilies and potholders, when worked in heavy thread or yarn, make excellent rugs. In the Woodruff Dollhouse, for example, the doilies on the floor of the master bedroom make such perfect, round, "braided" rugs that they could not have been more appropriate had they been custom-crocheted for the 18th century dollhouse. The elegant Oriental rug in the dining room is really a fancy potholder! Other rugs throughout the dollhouse were hand-woven on a mini-loom, embroidered on linen, or worked in Bargello on screen.

Velour wash cloths, especially the fringed ones, also make beautiful miniature rugs. Choose ones appropriate in design and color to the period of your dollhouse. Embroidered linen handkerchiefs are also useful, since embroidered rugs were actually made and used by the colonists. Placemats and napkins, especially fringed ones, are still another possible source for rugs for the dollhouse.

You can cut some solid-colored or appropriately patterned fabrics, such as wool, linen, velour, and velvet, to look like "custom-made" rugs. Pull threads out from the edges to form a fringe, or sew a fringe on.

For round or oval braided rugs, use decorator braid or heavy yarn. Coil it in a round or oval shape, and then sew in place. These types of rugs are very colonial.

If you want to make a copy of a genuine, full-scale 18th century rug, petit point or Bargello on screen are good methods to use. Petit point and Bargello rugs make beautiful dollhouse rugs, yet they are very simple to make.

ORIENTAL RUG

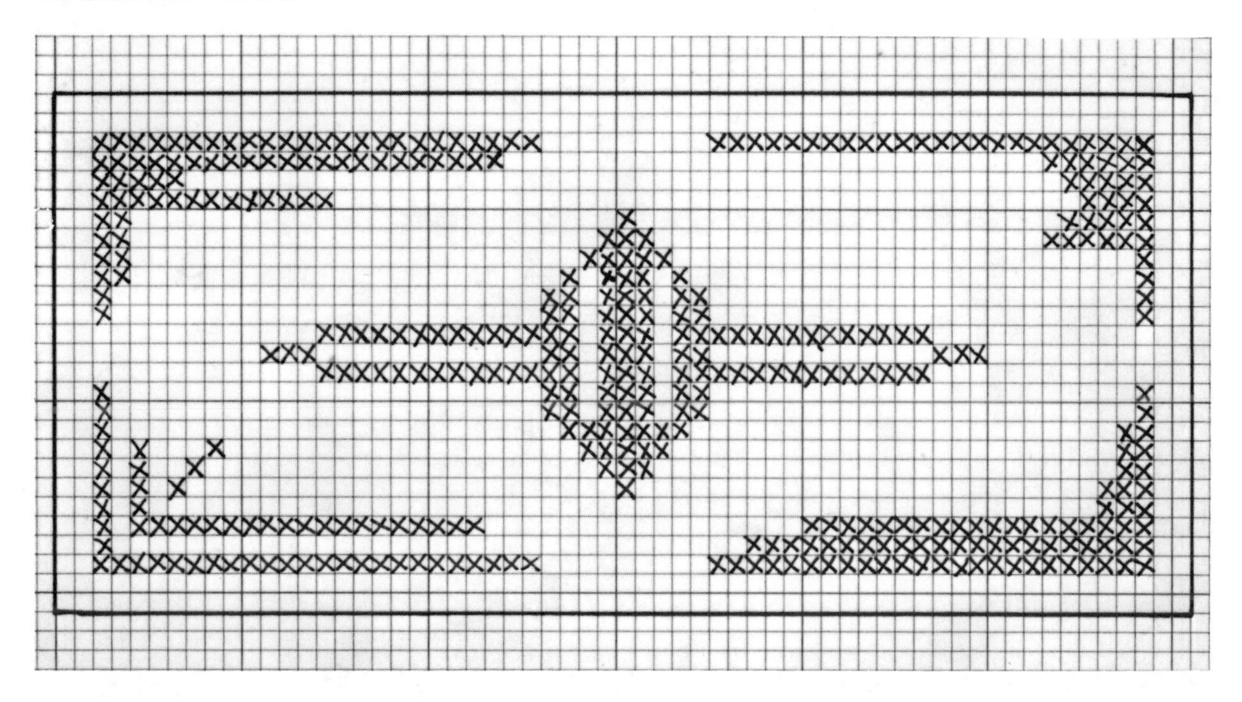

Instructions for an Oriental Rug

Oriental rugs were very popular in 18th century homes. In the Woodruff Dollhouse, there are two: one (a beige linen embroidered placemat) is in the parlor and the other (a potholder) is in the dining room. If you want to make an Oriental rug, you can do it very quickly.

Transfer one of the rug patterns illustrated onto 10 mesh-to-the-inch needlepoint canvas. (You can also use linen to embroider one of these designs.) Work the design in red or maroon, and fill in the rest with royal blue. Add a fringe.

NOTE: Choose only one of the four border designs shown for each rug.

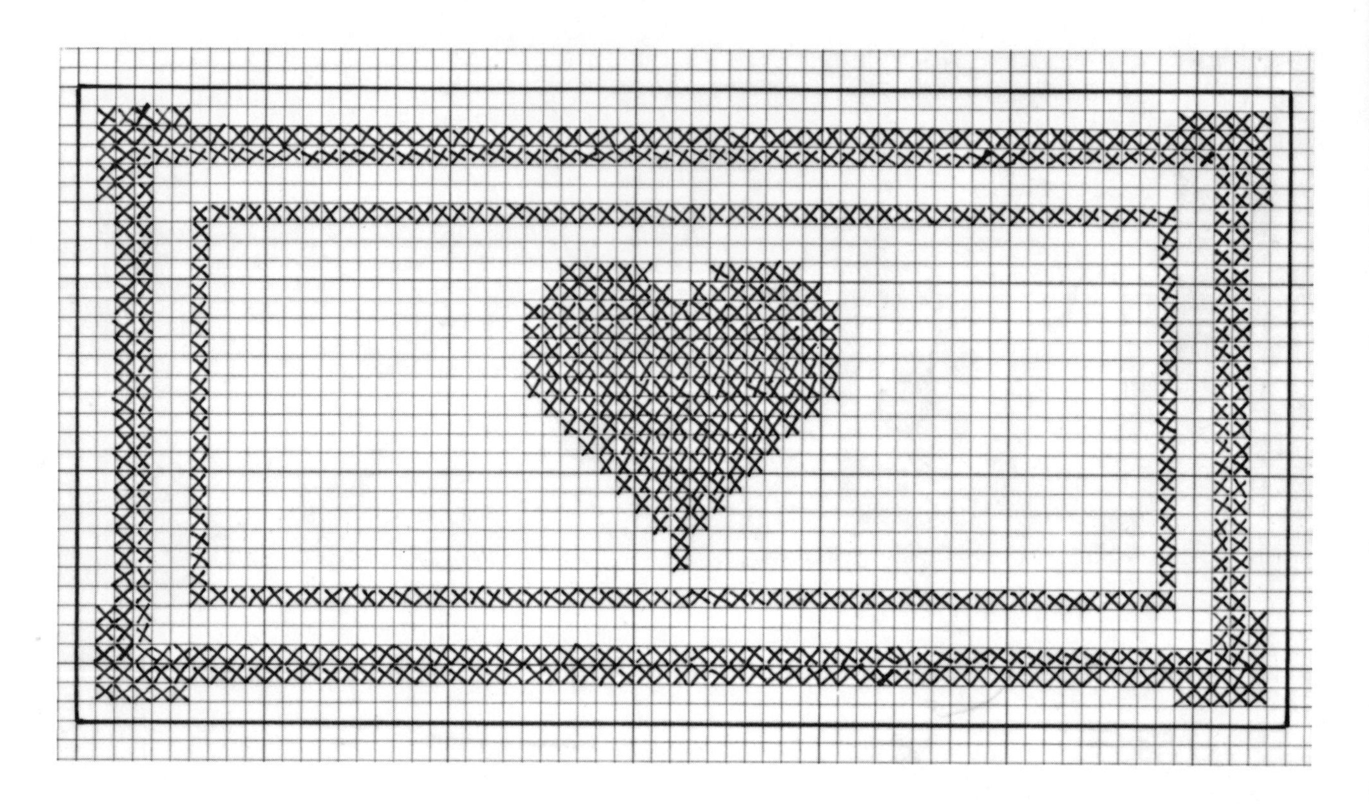

Instructions for a Pennsylvania-German Rug

Although this rug does not appear in the Woodruff Dollhouse, it is a pretty one you can make to use in yours.

Transfer the design shown onto 10 mesh-to-the-inch needlepoint canvas. Work the outside border design in red, the inside border in blue, and the heart in red. Fill in the rest in white.

Instructions for the "Fabled Bird" Rug in the Library

Transfer the design illustrated (adapting it as you wish) to good quality linen, approximately 7 × 8 inches or larger. Use embroidery floss or single-strand Persian wools. Outline the design in the stem stitch and then fill in the rest of the design in appropriate embroidery stitches (see page 151 in the chapter "Needlecrafts" for various embroidery stitches).

Pull threads from the edges for a $\frac{3}{8}$-inch fringe, or sew one on. (You can also use this design on a doll's bedspread.)

This design was inspired by Columbia-Minerva's design, "Fabled Bird," for a full-scale pillow.

"FABLED BIRD"

Close-up of the hand-embroidered "Fabled Bird" rug.

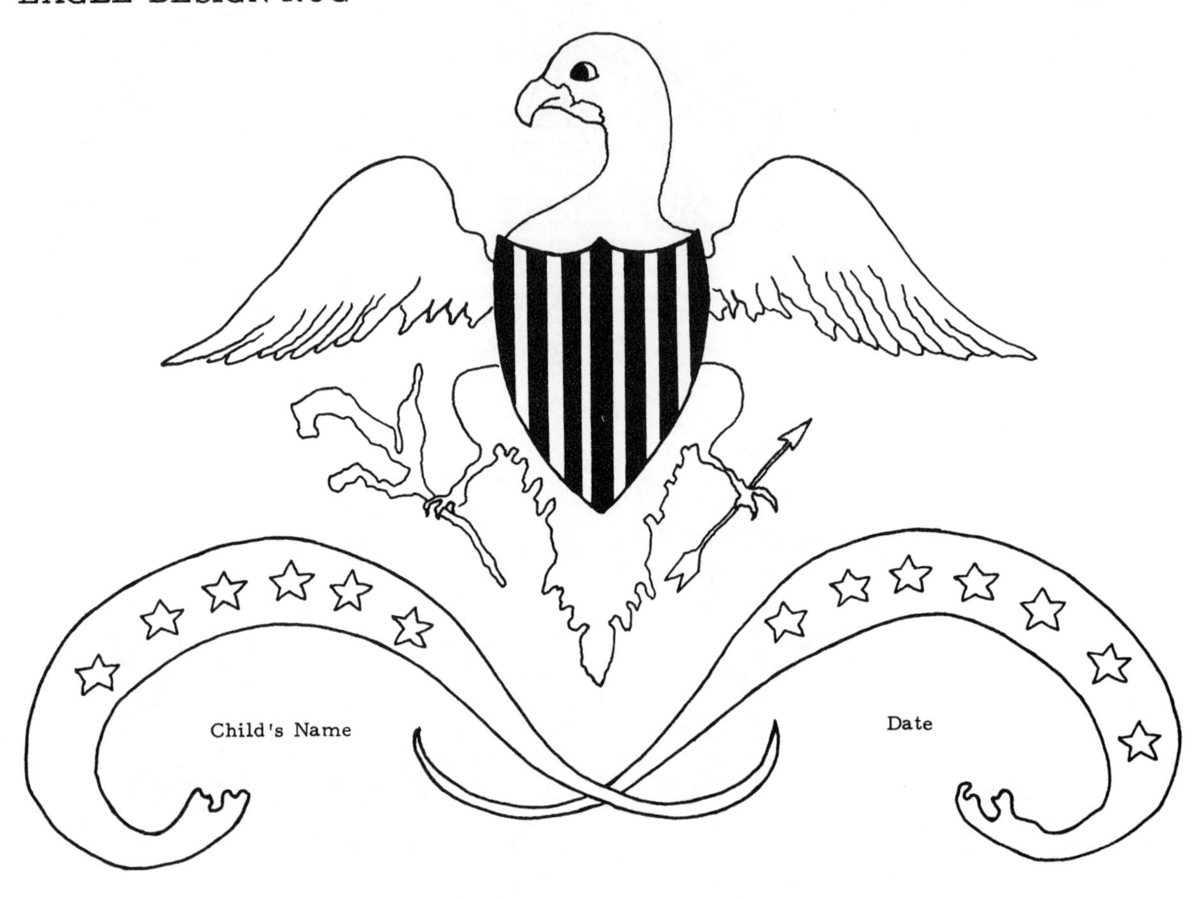

Instructions for an Eagle Design Rug

This is another rug that does not appear in the Woodruff Dollhouse, but it is certainly appropriate for an 18th century home.

Transfer the design shown to a piece of good quality linen, approximately $8\frac{1}{2} \times 11$ inches or larger, if the room needs it. Pull threads from the edges to make a $\frac{3}{8}$-inch fringe, or sew one on.

Use single-thread Persian wools to do the embroidery. Outline everything in the stem stitch. Then work the shield and the stars in the satin stitch. Fill in everything else in the long and short stitch. (See page 151 in the chapter "Needlecrafts" for how to do the stitches.)

Needlecrafts

Embroidery Stitch Chart

Basting Stitch

Cross Stitch

French Knot

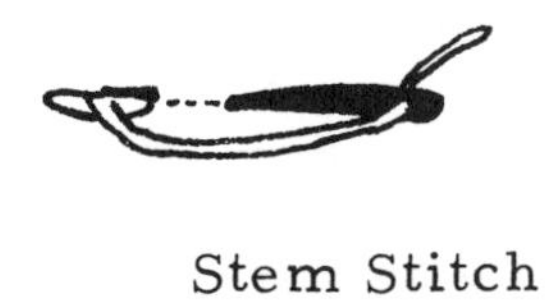
Stem Stitch

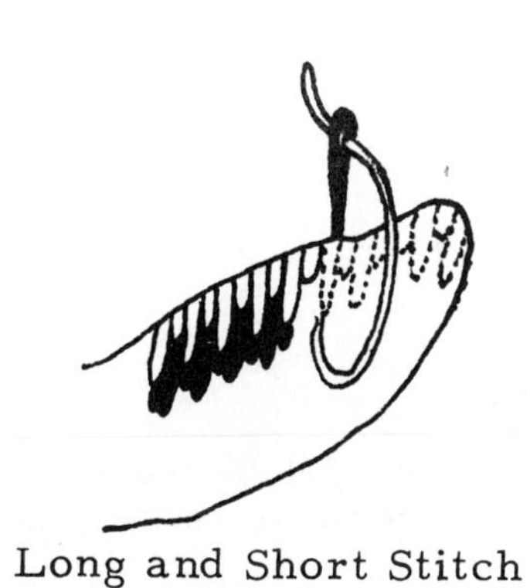
Long and Short Stitch

Buttonhole Stitch

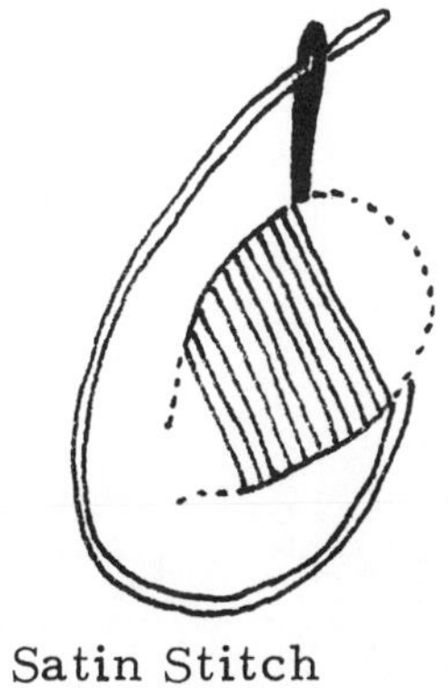
Satin Stitch

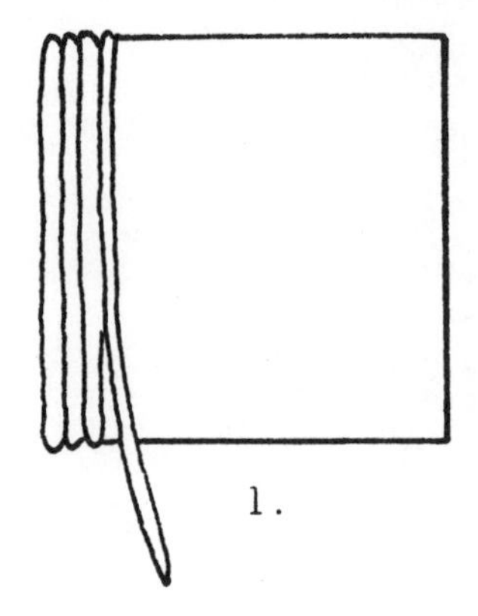

1.

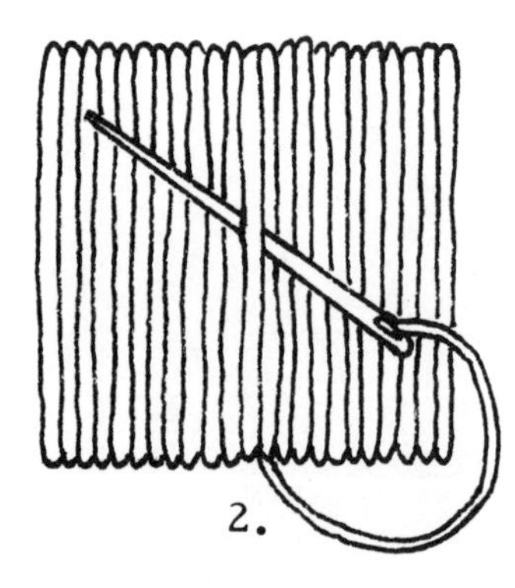

2.

3.

4.

Rush Seat (Woven Fibre) Design

Use the method described below to upholster any chair:

1. Cut a piece of cardboard to fit the desired seat area.
2. Wrap Persian wool (single-strand) vertically around the cardboard, as shown. You must have an odd number of rows of thread when you are finished.
3. Wrap wool (you can use a different color) around the covered rows, but going horizontally. Go under the middle thread.
4. Continue by picking up three threads, then five, then seven, and so on, to the edge. Do the same for the other half.

Bargello Flame Stitch

Use this stitch to upholster the Queen Anne daybed in the library:

1. Transfer the design shown to 14 mesh-to-the-inch needlepoint canvas to cover the seat ($1\frac{5}{8} \times 5\frac{5}{8}$ inches *finished* area).
2. Choose four different colors of single-strand Persian wools (in the Woodruff Dollhouse, rust, salmon, old gold, and yellow were used).
3. Work the Bargello stitch, up and down, from bottom to top, as shown in the pattern.

Bargello Medallion Stitch

Use this design to upholster the Chippendale "French" chairs:

1. Use 14 mesh-to-the-inch needlepoint canvas to cover:

a. one seat ($1\frac{5}{8} \times 2\frac{1}{8}$ inches finished area); you can also use this for an ottoman;
b. one back ($1\frac{5}{8} \times 4\frac{7}{8}$ inches finished area to cover the outside back to the inside back in one continuous strip).

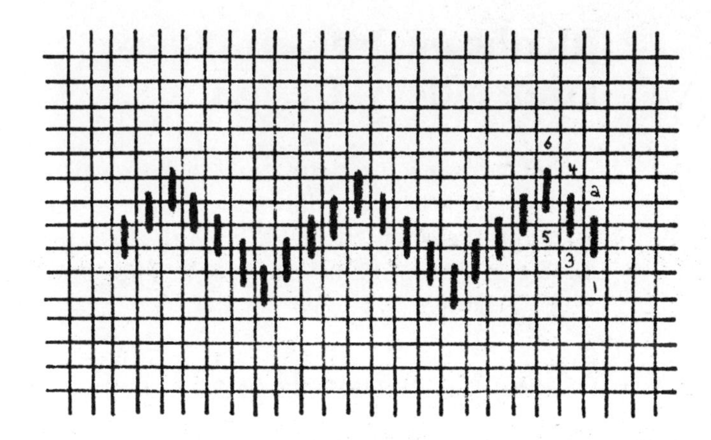

Bargello Flame Stitch

2. Choose about four different colors of single-strand Persian wools (in the Woodruff Dollhouse, the background is pale yellow, and the medallion is brown, salmon, beige, and pale yellow).

3. Work the Bargello stitch (up and down, from bottom to top). The bottom tip of each medallion should be approximately $\frac{1}{4}$ inch from the bottom of each end of the piece.

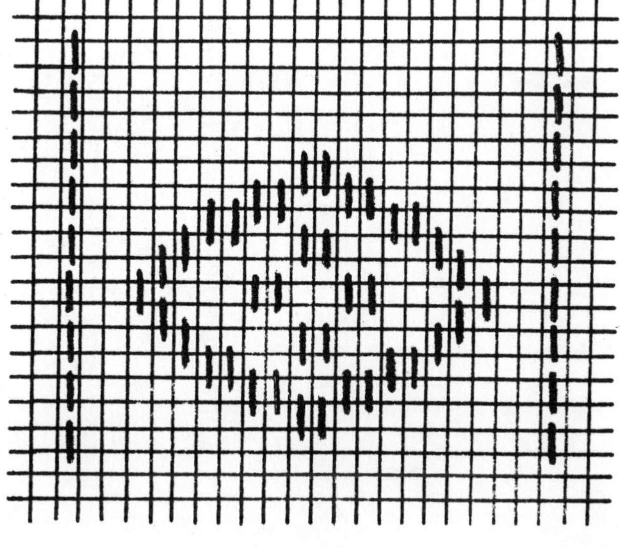

Bargello Medallion Stitch

Jacobean Crewel Embroidery Design

Kitchen Sampler

Transfer the design shown to good quality linen. Use embroidery floss to work the stitches.

Jacobean Crewel Embroidery Design

You can work this design to upholster a pair of chairs or a pair of pillow cases. Outline the shapes in the stem stitch. Fill in with the satin stitch and French knots (see page 151 for how to do the stitches).

Miscellaneous Items

To make doilies, cut out, from scraps of lace, any appropriate designs (such as flowers) for miniature doilies.

For needlecrafted bedspreads, draperies, rugs, upholstery and clothing, use such items as embroidered handkerchiefs and fabrics that look like handcrafted work.

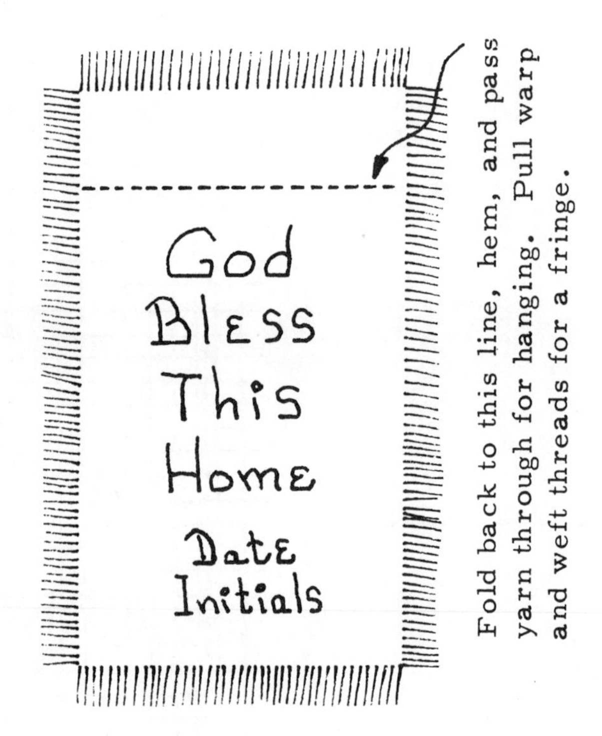

Chandeliers

Following are the instructions for the chandeliers in the Woodruff Dollhouse:

1 and 2. Use a can lid and some jewelry chain. For the kitchen, spray the chandelier black; for other rooms, leave it in its natural state for either a pewter or brass look. Add $\frac{1}{2}$-inch birthday candles.

3 and 4. Use half a plastic foam ball (about 1 inch in diameter). Drape a miniature string of pearls and/or tear-drops (you can buy these in crafts shops or use old jewelry) around the plastic foam ball, holding it in place with decorator push pins. Use a tear-drop for the middle drop. Decorate by draping jewelry chain and beads around the ball. Add glitter, if you want.

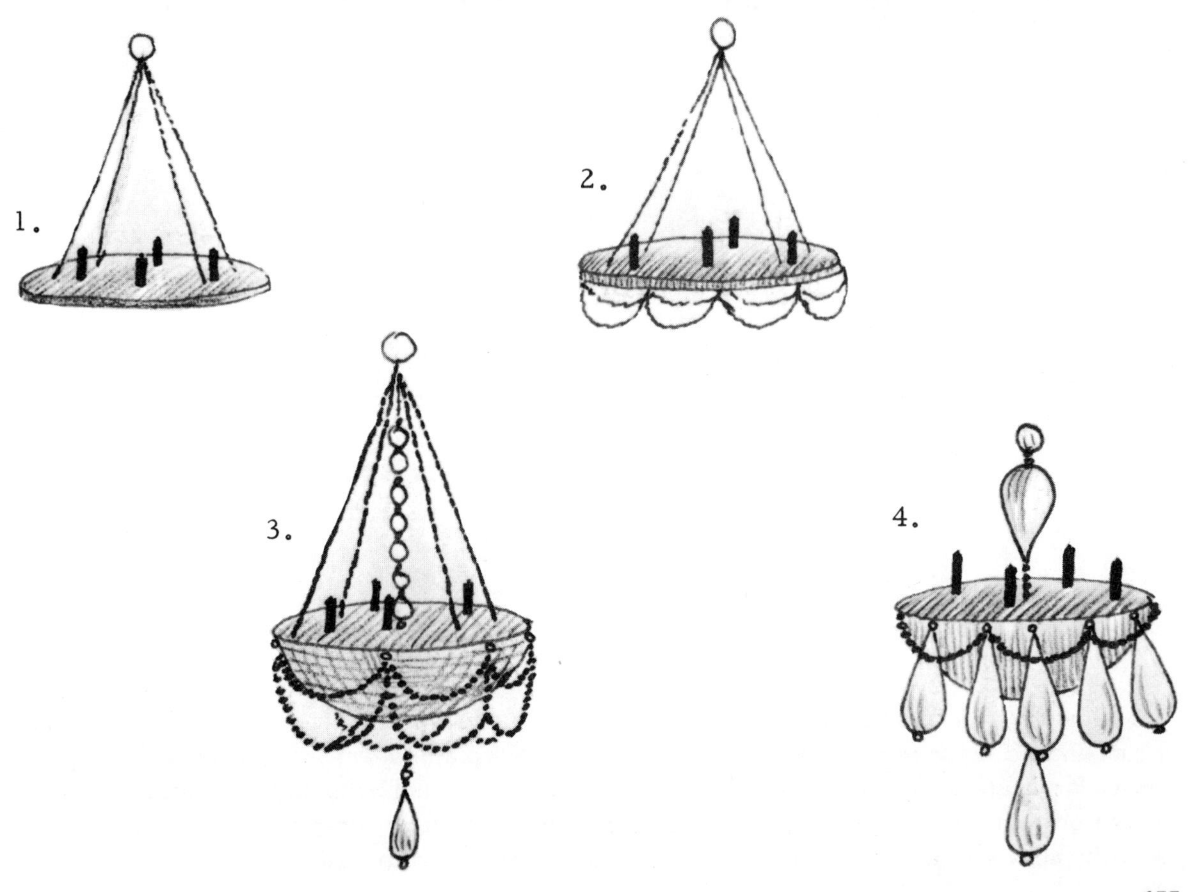

5. This is the same as 3 and 4, except you add hairpins, sprayed gold, with beads glued to the ends, to a brass-sprayed plastic foam ball to give the chandelier a wide, brass-armed look. Drape another string of miniature pearls from hairpins for a really elaborate chandelier. Decorate by draping brass chain or beads around the ball. Add birthday candles.

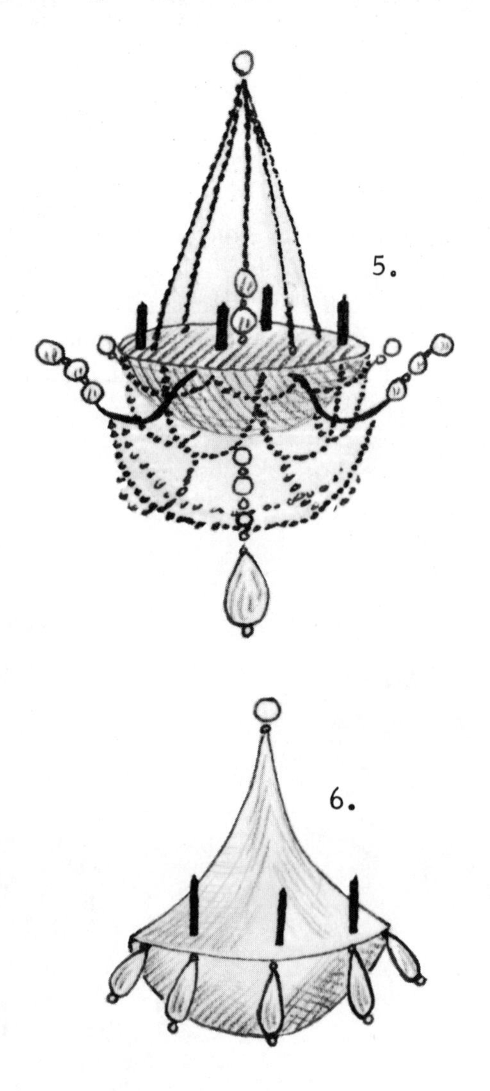

6. Glue together half a plastic foam ball and a cone-shaped bottle cap. Spray any color you want. Pin tear-drop beads to the ball with decorator push pins. Decorate by draping with gold thread. Add birthday candles.

7. Glue together half a plastic foam ball and the bottom part of a dishwashing soap dispenser, as shown. Wrap a rhinestone necklace (or pretty ribbon) around the middle. Decorate by draping beads around the ball. Add birthday candles.

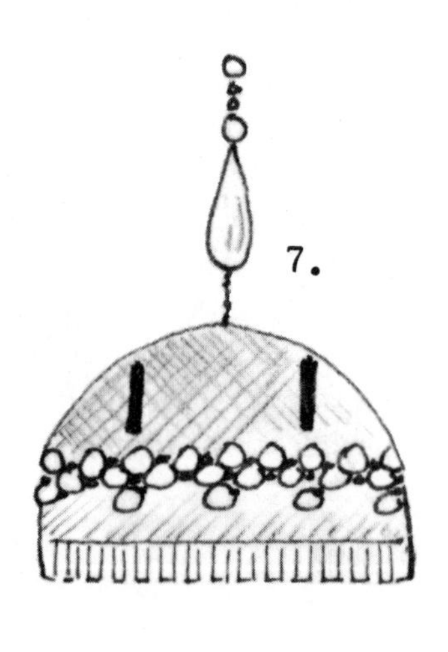

8. Glue together a decorative bottle cap and half a plastic foam ball, as shown. Add pretty ribbon around the ball. Use beads for the drop, and decorate by draping beads around the ball or with matching ribbon.

The Doll Family and Their Costumes

Having a family to inhabit your dollhouse adds the final warmth and authenticity to the project. It is especially fun to make a family of period dolls to live in the dollhouse.

Six-inch-tall dolls were chosen for the adults in the Woodruff Dollhouse and 4-inch child dolls were used for the children. All the dolls' bodies chosen are streamlined in scale to the dollhouse and its furnishings. There are several varieties of dollhouse dolls available on the market. The patterns in this book are for any 5½- to 6-inch adult dolls and 4-inch child dollhouse dolls. Do not confuse the popular 8-inch crafts dolls (which are not properly streamlined in scale to the dollhouse) with *dollhouse* dolls, which are proportioned to fit the one-inch to one-foot scale dollhouses.

The doll family in the Woodruff Dollhouse represents the owner's ancestors, but not necessarily of the 18th century.

The fabrics and laces used for the ladies' ensembles represent mid- to late 18th century styles. All the dresses are made from basically two pattern pieces that are varied by changing the neckline, lace and accessory arrangements, or adding a fichu (a three-cornered cape), apron, or hat. Remnants of laces and trims, old lace-bordered slips, colored mesh hosiery, commercially available miniature buttons and accessories for dolls, and miniature beads (for buttons) were the basic materials used to fashion the doll family's 18th century wardrobe. An entire doll's ensemble, after some practical experience, can be made leisurely in two hours' time—even while watching television.

The costumes for the men are a little more difficult because the coats have to be lined, since the facings of them show. Therefore, felt fabric was used exclusively for the coats, waistcoats, and hats because felt can be cut without ravelling and without being hemmed. Simplicity in designing the patterns for the men's clothes is important. Miniature buttons on most of the coats are sewn on and do not button. The waistcoats, however, all actually button up. Three of the men dolls are wearing military costumes, out of respect for three generations of Woodruff family members having had military careers. The other men's clothes in mid- to late 18th century styles are for civilians.

Appropriate 18th century hair-style wigs were made from embroidery floss for most of the ladies, all the gentlemen, and one child. Masculine features, such as heavy eyebrows, were oil-painted on the men's faces.

The dolls do indeed make the dollhouse a home! In their period costumes, the dolls make the house so alive with activity that 18th century American history can actually be re-lived in miniature.

A gorgeous Watteau gown, military attire for the gentlemen, and two lovely children's dresses make Christmas in the parlor of the Woodruff Dollhouse a truly festive occasion.

The Christmas Celebration

This scene in the parlor depicts three military costumes, a Watteau gown, and two little girls' dresses. The lady's elegant Watteau ensemble is made of beige brocade, trimmed with white lace at the neckline, hemline, and sleeves, overlaid with a beige organdy overskirt which opens in front to show the beautiful petticoat, and completed with a lace-trimmed, beige organdy train. Her string of pearls was made from miniature imitation pearls.

The little girl on the left wears a blue-grey-white-mauve sleeveless cotton plaid dress, trimmed with mauve rick-rack, and hemmed with white lace. The little girl on the right wears a red and white polka-dotted, peasant-style dress, lavishly trimmed with white eyelet lace at the hem. Her mob cap is white cotton.

To illustrate military costumes, the soldier at the left wears an army uniform; the general in the middle wears a George Washington army uniform; and the captain at the right wears a navy uniform. All the men's coats are felt, "faced" in a contrasting color, also felt. The buttons are beads, and on the felt waistcoats, they actually button. The buttonholes on the coats are embroidered. The general and soldier wear cotton breeches and felt top boots. The captain wears long, "silk" stockings over cotton breeches, and felt buckled shoes. The soldier wears a felt, tasseled hat, and the captain a felt, braid-trimmed tricorne. The general's and captain's epaulettes are made from embroidery floss. All three men carry swords, which are cocktail stirrers.

With the exception of the plaid-dressed little girl who has rooted human hair, all the dolls in this scene wear wigs made from embroidery floss.

The Christmas tree is a plastic foam cone studded with artificial pine needle clusters, beads, and curling ribbon. The "Mr. and Mrs. Santa Claus treetop" is made from two cake decorations. The miniature wreath and angel over the mantel, and the Santa Claus in the middle back are from the Woodruff family's collection of Christmas tree ornaments. The miniature, potted Christmas trees are cake decorations; the holly in the ceiling is a gift decoration. All the gifts were hand-crafted from cardboard, wrapped with real gift wrapping paper and tied with ribbon.

The New Year's Ball

Men's civilian clothes and the women's famous polonaise dresses with opened, panniered (framed) overskirts are shown in this New Year's ball scene in the drawing room of the Woodruffs' International Christmas Castle (see page 4).

Imagine the magnificence of the ballroom on New Year's eve when it is filled with many more beautiful gowns such as these, as well as lots of handsome men in civilian outfits like the ones shown here.

The two gentlemen on the ends wear felt greatcoats with real miniature buttons (from dolls' clothes); the gentleman in the middle wears a felt Cossack-style riding coat, trimmed with gold cord. All the men's waistcoats are made from felt and really button with tiny beads. The buttonholes are embroidered on their coats. Their tricorne hats are also made from felt, and trimmed with self-adhesive braid; their cravats and "shirt" cuffs are lace; their breeches are cotton. The two gentlemen on the ends wear top boots; the one in the middle wears long, "silk" stockings and felt buckled shoes.

The lady on the left wears an elegant ensemble of yellow nylon and rows of lace. A panniered, organdy overskirt opens in front to reveal a matching petticoat, trimmed with six rows of ruffled lace (that was the hem of an old slip). The same lace trims the neckline, bodice, sleeves, and overskirt.

The lady on the right wears an outfit of blue, trimmed with rosebud lace. A white, sheer, panniered overskirt is trimmed diagonally with white rosebuds, and opens to show a blue, ribbed cotton petticoat. More rosebuds trim the ribbed bodice, sleeves, neckline, and hemline.

All the dolls wear wigs fashioned from embroidery floss.

The festive decorations are miniature Christmas tree baubles, beads, wire, pipe cleaners, and curling ribbon, all arranged over a baroque chandelier that really lights.

The Easter Parade

The ladies take good advantage of an opportunity that calls for "Sunday best" dress in this scene that illustrates women's fashions, including outdoor apparel. The setting is in the sitting room of the Woodruff Dollhouse. The time is Easter Sunday.

The lady on the left wears a yellow cotton print ensemble with a white, blue-bordered apron. Her fichu and hat are merely eyelet lace strips. Her basket is from The Last Straw, in Solvang, California (see page 175 for the address).

Next is a lady in pink who wears a "milkmaid" costume of pink-checkered cotton, flocked with bouquets of flowers in bas-relief. Her apron is white eyelet. The mob cap and handbag match the dress.

The next lady in the parade wears a red and navy cotton petticoat, overlaid with a red knit overskirt. The short apron matches the petticoat. Her fichu is also made from eyelet lace, and the matching satchel has a good luck penny in it. The Gainsborough hat is made of red felt, trimmed with a feather and curling ribbon.

The last lady is dressed in green and carries a bouquet of flowers. She is wearing a green-checkered gingham overskirt that opens in front to show a pink and white polka-dotted, polished cotton petticoat, trimmed with green gingham ruffles at the hem and sleeves. A fringed fichu matches the overskirt; the hat matches the petticoat and is trimmed in green Persian wool.

Lots of freshly "starched" cotton dominates this sprightly Easter Parade in the sitting room of the Woodruff Dollhouse.

The little girl on the staircase wears a cotton, peasant-style dress, trimmed with white rick-rack scallops at the hem. The other little girl wears a pink sateen dress, trimmed with fine, white lace. Her green fichu is a piece of ribbon tied with very narrow blue rick-rack.

The ladies in the pink and green ensembles and the little girl in the print dress wear wigs of embroidery floss. The other dolls have rooted human hair.

The Easter bunnies are cake decorations, and the eggs are beads. The baskets are from The Last Straw, in Solvang, California (see page 175 for the address).

A Champagne Party for Two

This scene emphasizes the drastic, new trend in clothing fashion towards simplicity, classic elegance, and comfort that ensued as a result of the political upheaval in France and socio-economic changes and improvements in England in the late 18th century. The romantic party with champagne and caviar is in the drawing room of the owner's International Christmas Castle (see page 4).

A cozy evening lies ahead for this elegant couple. Simplicity characterizes their clothes at this intimate champagne party for two.

The graceful lady wears a crocheted gown (that was once a leg of a knit pantyhose), trimmed with pink-embroidered lace at the neckline, to look like a small cape, and at the hemline.

The gentleman wears the "new look," which consists of a red felt cutaway coat with a short, white felt waistcoat, white knit breeches, and red commercially available top boots. Both the coat and waistcoat actually button. His cravat and "shirt" cuffs are white lace.

Both dolls are wearing wigs made of embroidery floss.

The party decorations were described for the New Year's Eve party on page 160.

Patterns and Instructions for the Costumes, Accessories and Wigs

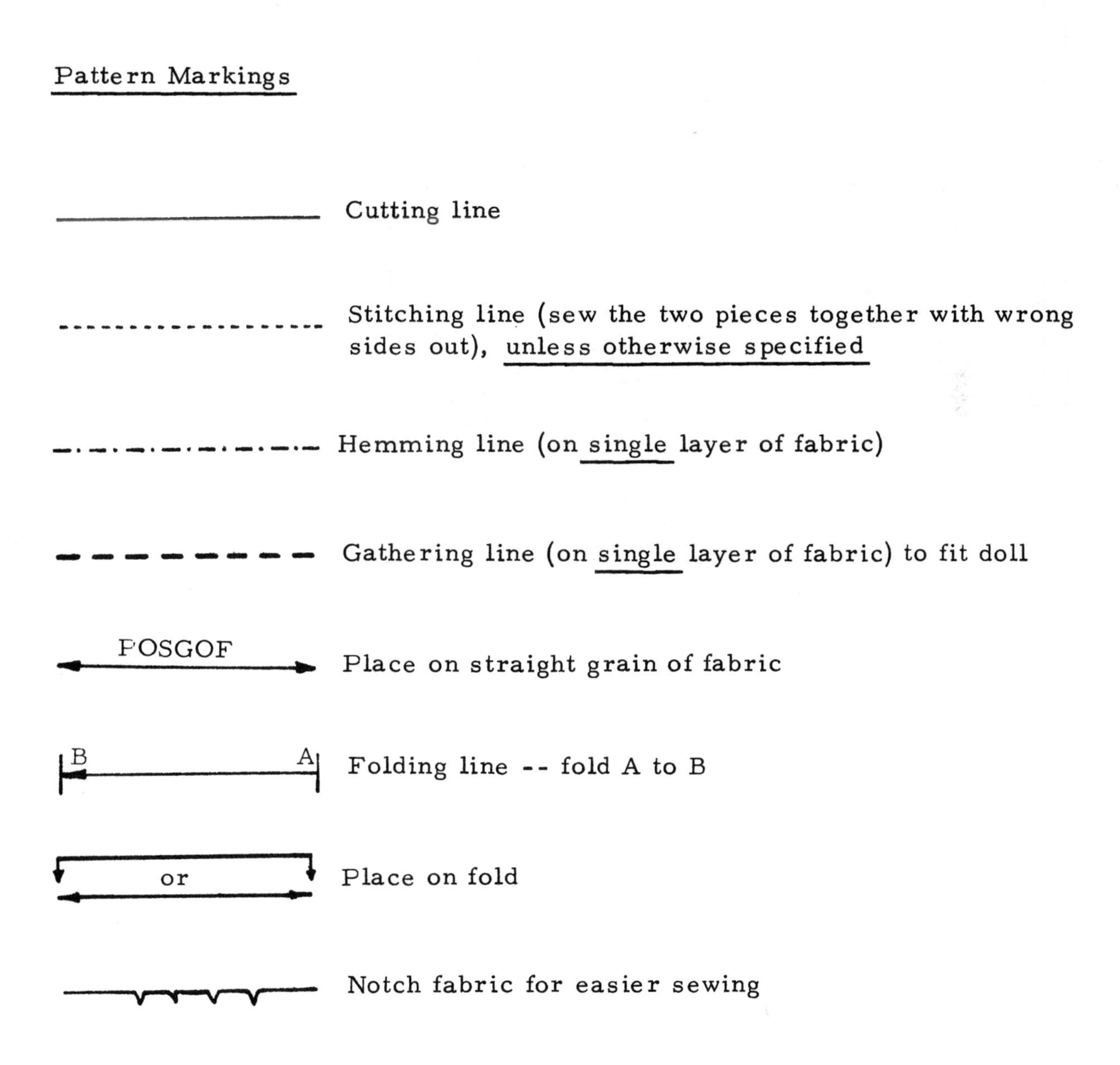

Patterns for the Little Girls' Dresses

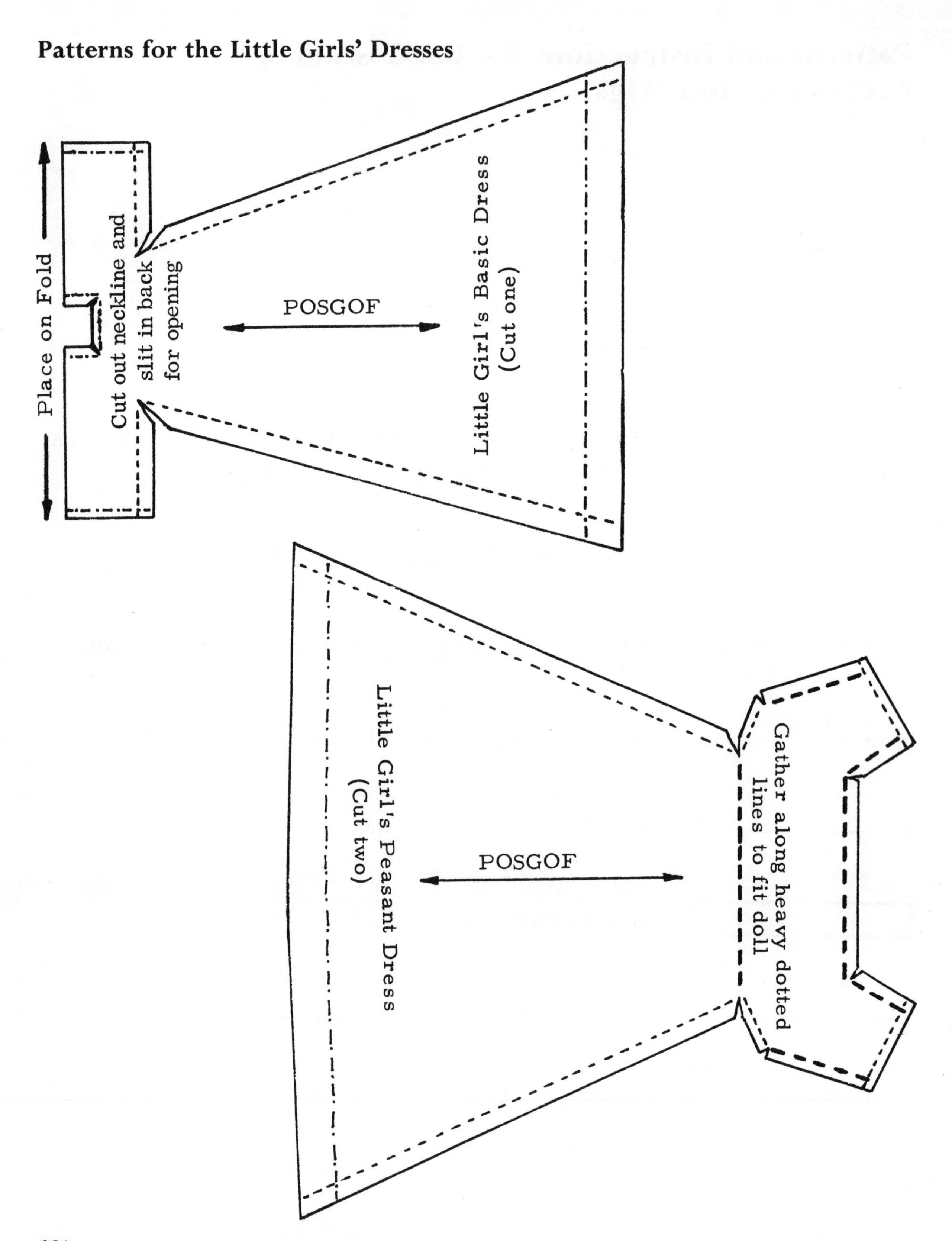

Instructions for the Little Girls' Dresses

All the little girls' dresses are designed to tie with ribbon at the waist. Add pretty ribbon, ruffle, rick-rack, lace, or braid around the hemline to finish off the dresses.

You can make the little girl's peasant dress and the sleeveless dress into a woman's dress by lengthening the skirt to fit an adult doll.

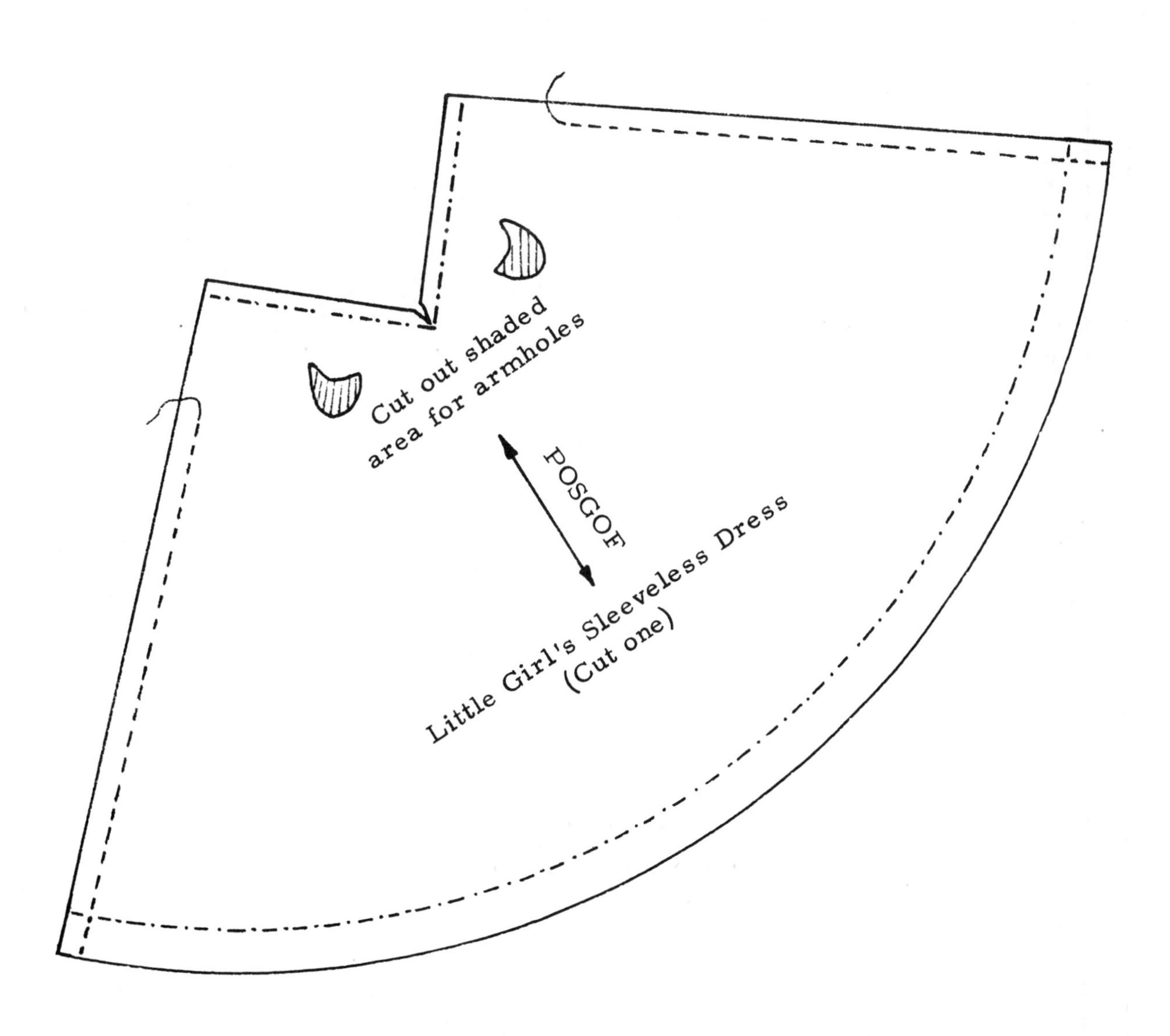

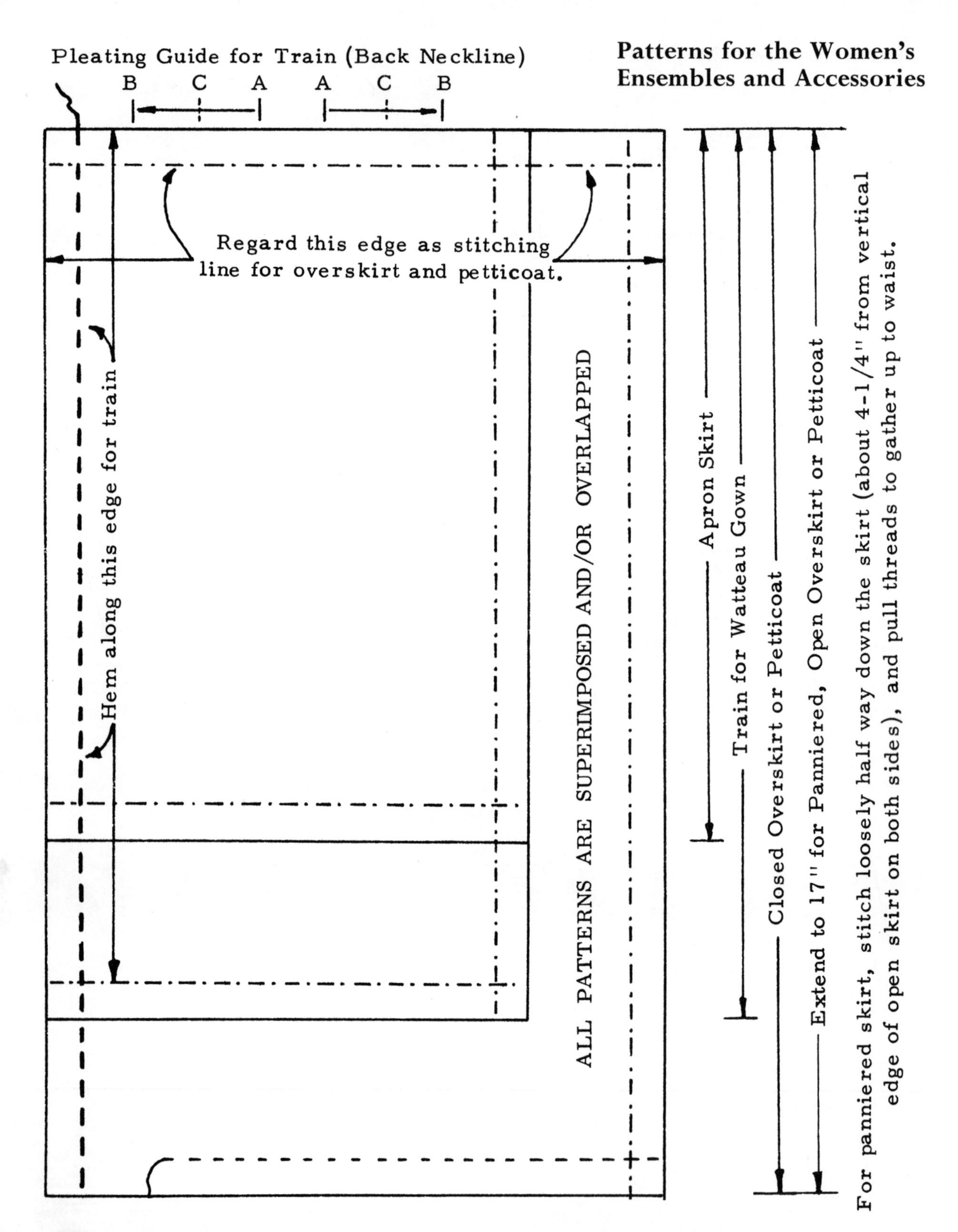
Pleating Guide for Train (Back Neckline)
B C A A C B
Regard this edge as stitching line for overskirt and petticoat.
Hem along this edge for train
ALL PATTERNS ARE SUPERIMPOSED AND/OR OVERLAPPED
Apron Skirt
Train for Watteau Gown
Closed Overskirt or Petticoat
Extend to 17" for Panniered, Open Overskirt or Petticoat
For panniered skirt, stitch loosely half way down the skirt (about 4-1/4" from vertical edge of open skirt on both sides), and pull threads to gather up to waist.

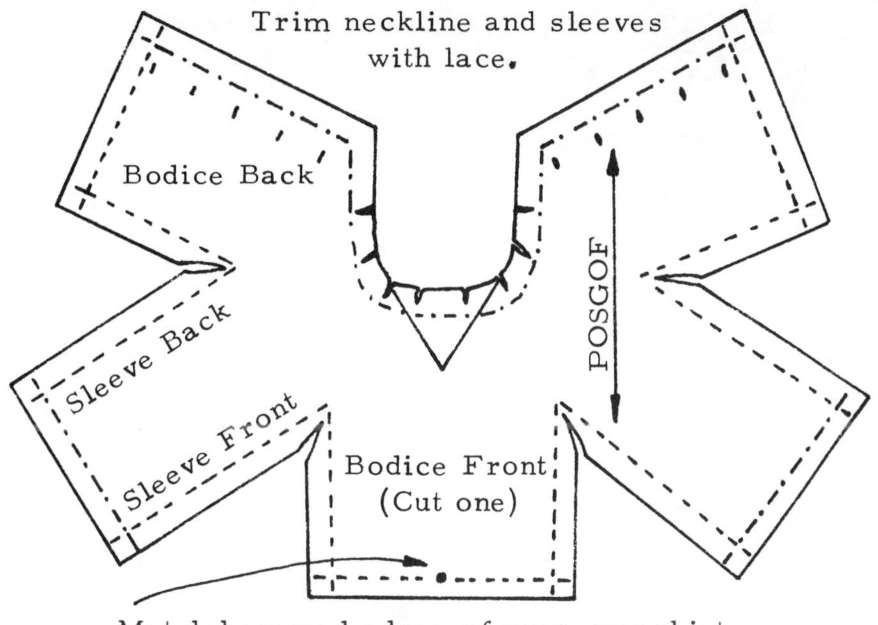

Instructions for the Women's Accessories

Use small beads for buttons; poke buttonholes with a knitting needle to fit the beads. Trim the neckline and sleeves with lace. For variation, you can use the back for a buttoned front, or you can use the pattern for a short jacket.

For the "milkmaid" dress, sew the apron skirt into the waistline with the other skirt(s). Add ties on top to go around the neck.

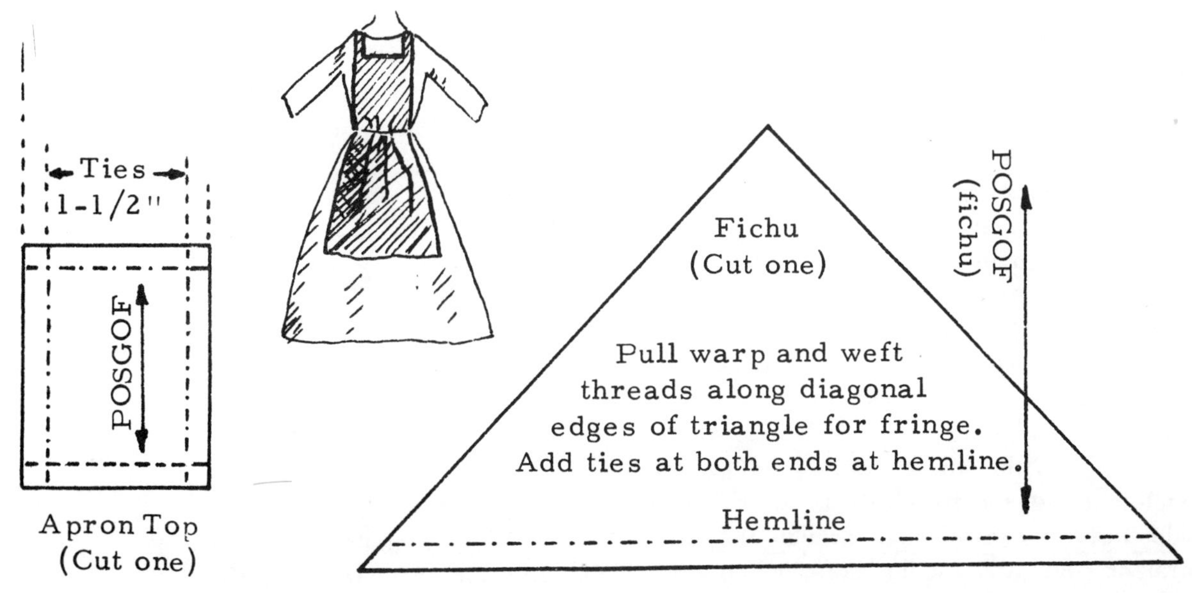

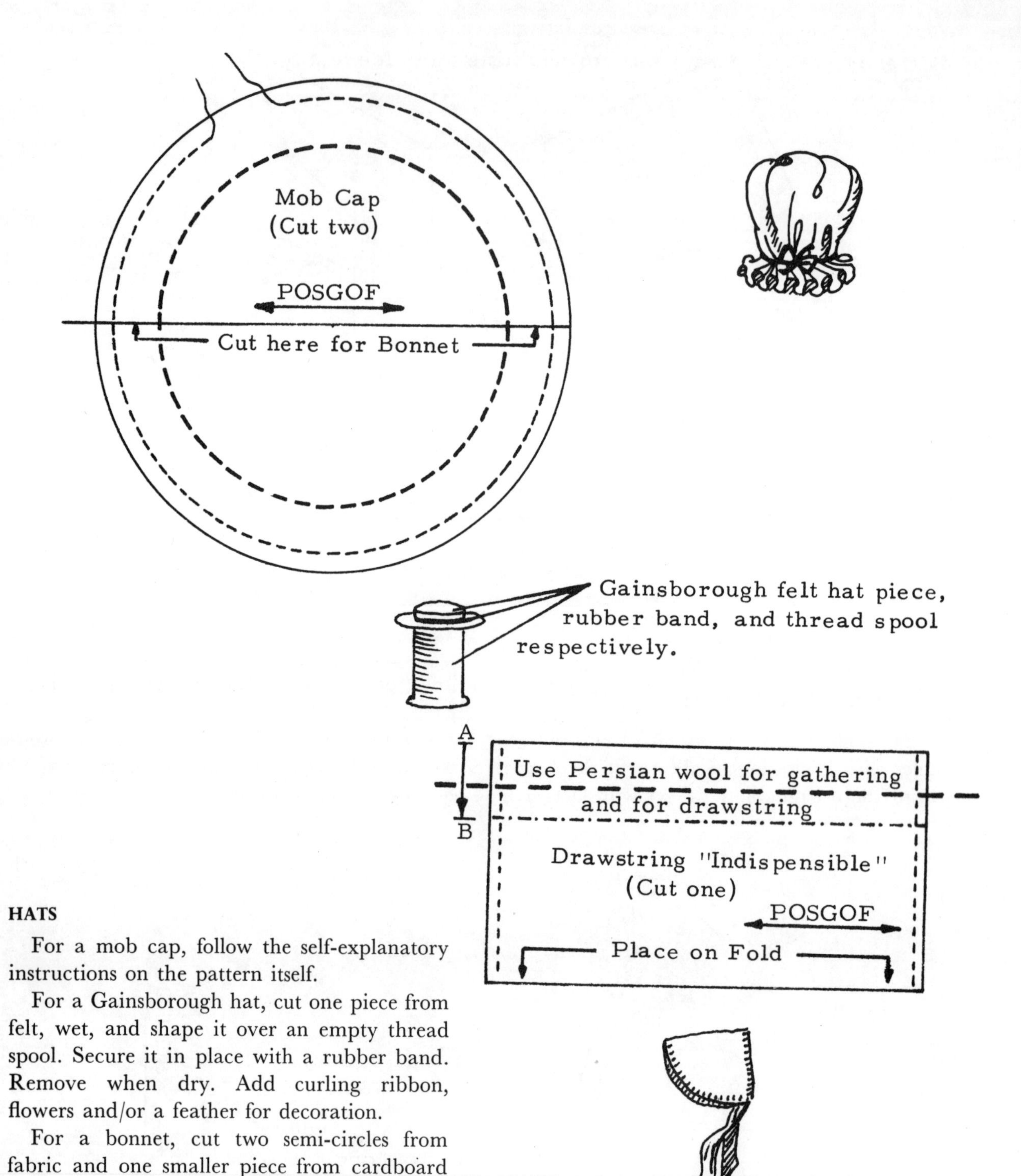

HATS

For a mob cap, follow the self-explanatory instructions on the pattern itself.

For a Gainsborough hat, cut one piece from felt, wet, and shape it over an empty thread spool. Secure it in place with a rubber band. Remove when dry. Add curling ribbon, flowers and/or a feather for decoration.

For a bonnet, cut two semi-circles from fabric and one smaller piece from cardboard (along the dotted lines). Sew both fabric pieces together with the wrong sides out (along the semi-circle edge only). Reverse to the right side, insert the cardboard through the open straight edge, and use Persian wool to trim, using the buttonhole stitch (see page 151) or self-adhesive trim. Add wool ties.

Patterns for the Men's Fashions and Accessories

NOTE: All patterns (except the cravat and breeches) are designed to eliminate hemming and lining, and to limit the need to sew seams to an absolute minimum. Therefore, use *felt* for all the men's fashions, unless otherwise noted.

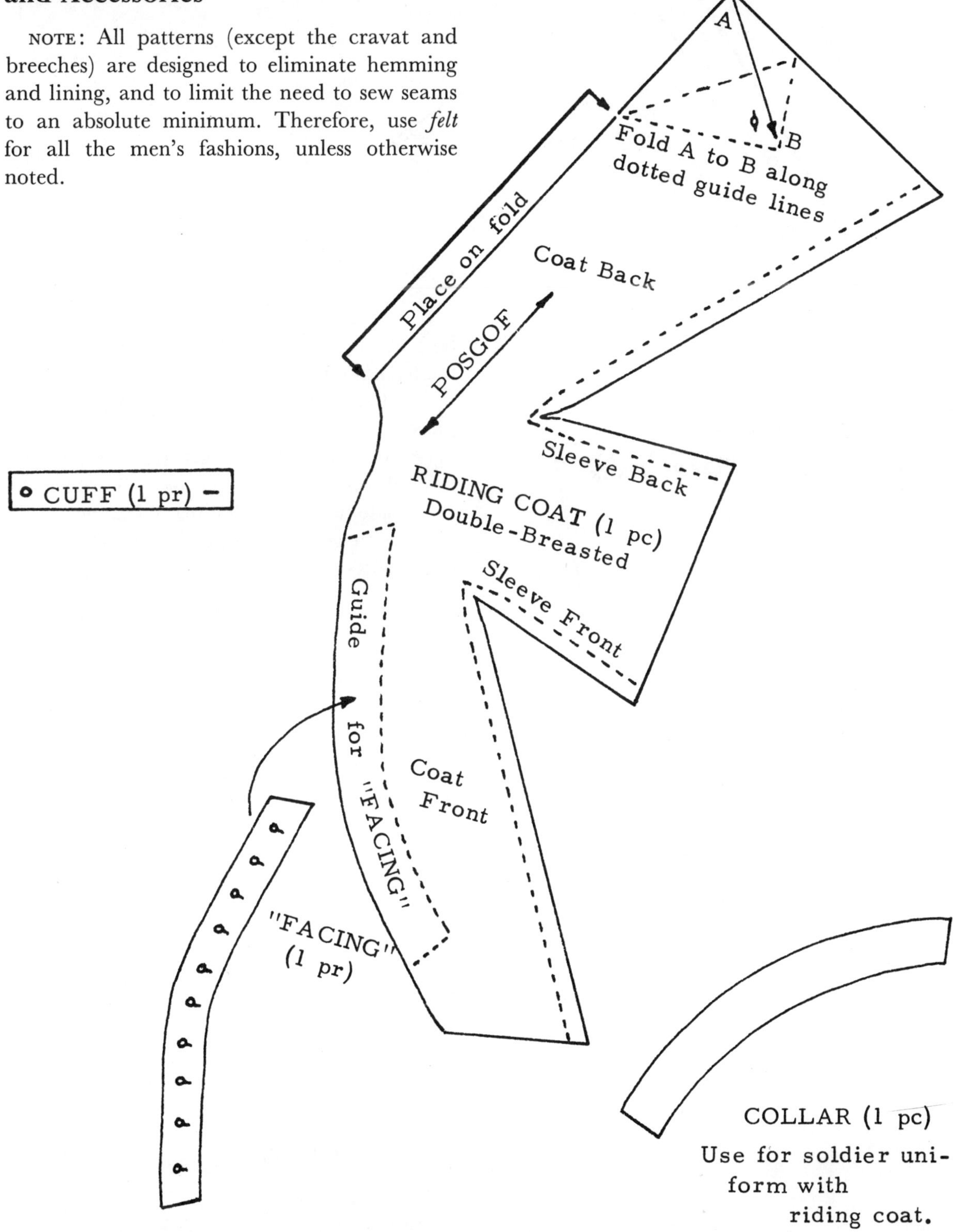

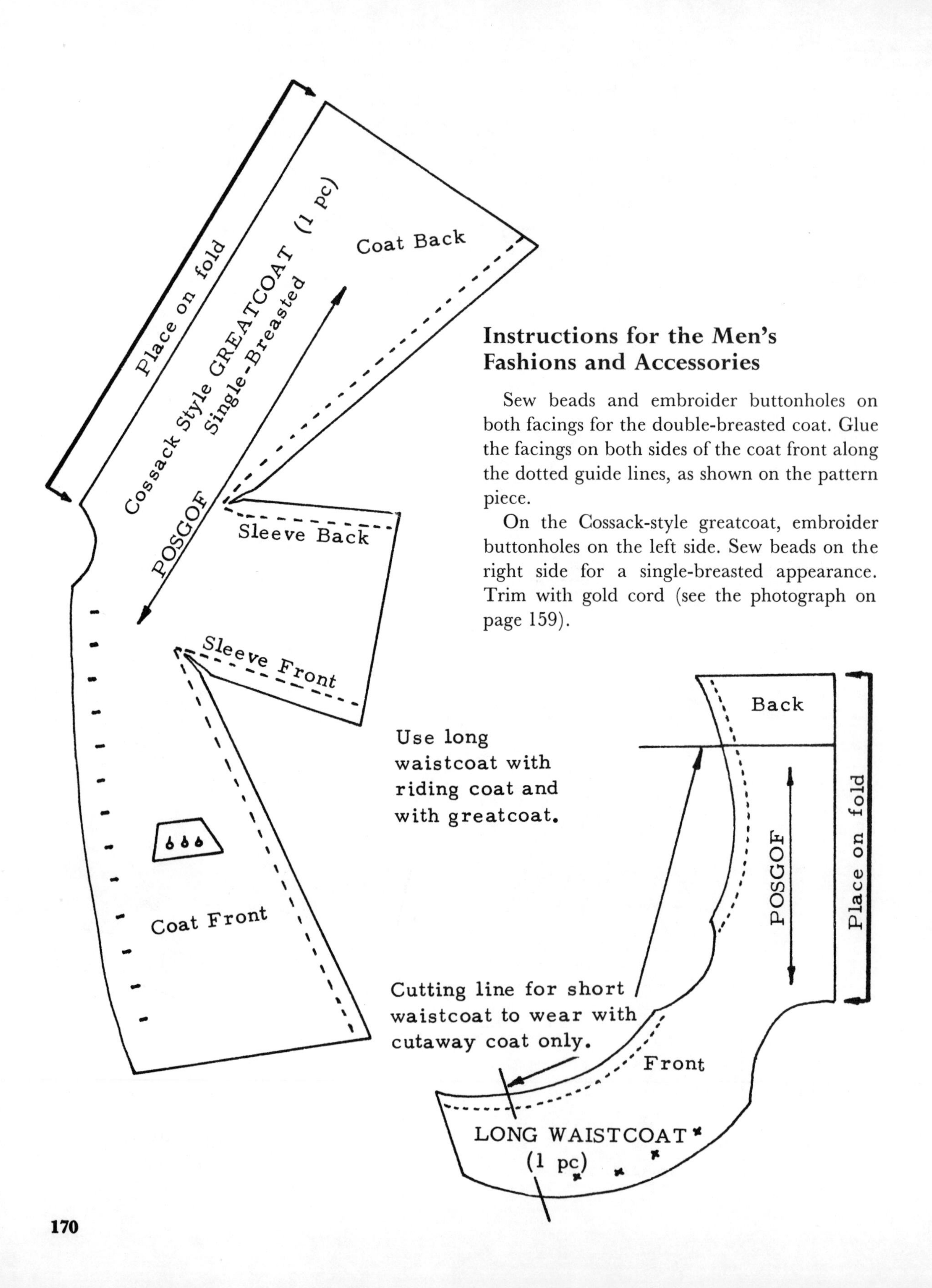

Instructions for the Men's Fashions and Accessories

Sew beads and embroider buttonholes on both facings for the double-breasted coat. Glue the facings on both sides of the coat front along the dotted guide lines, as shown on the pattern piece.

On the Cossack-style greatcoat, embroider buttonholes on the left side. Sew beads on the right side for a single-breasted appearance. Trim with gold cord (see the photograph on page 159).

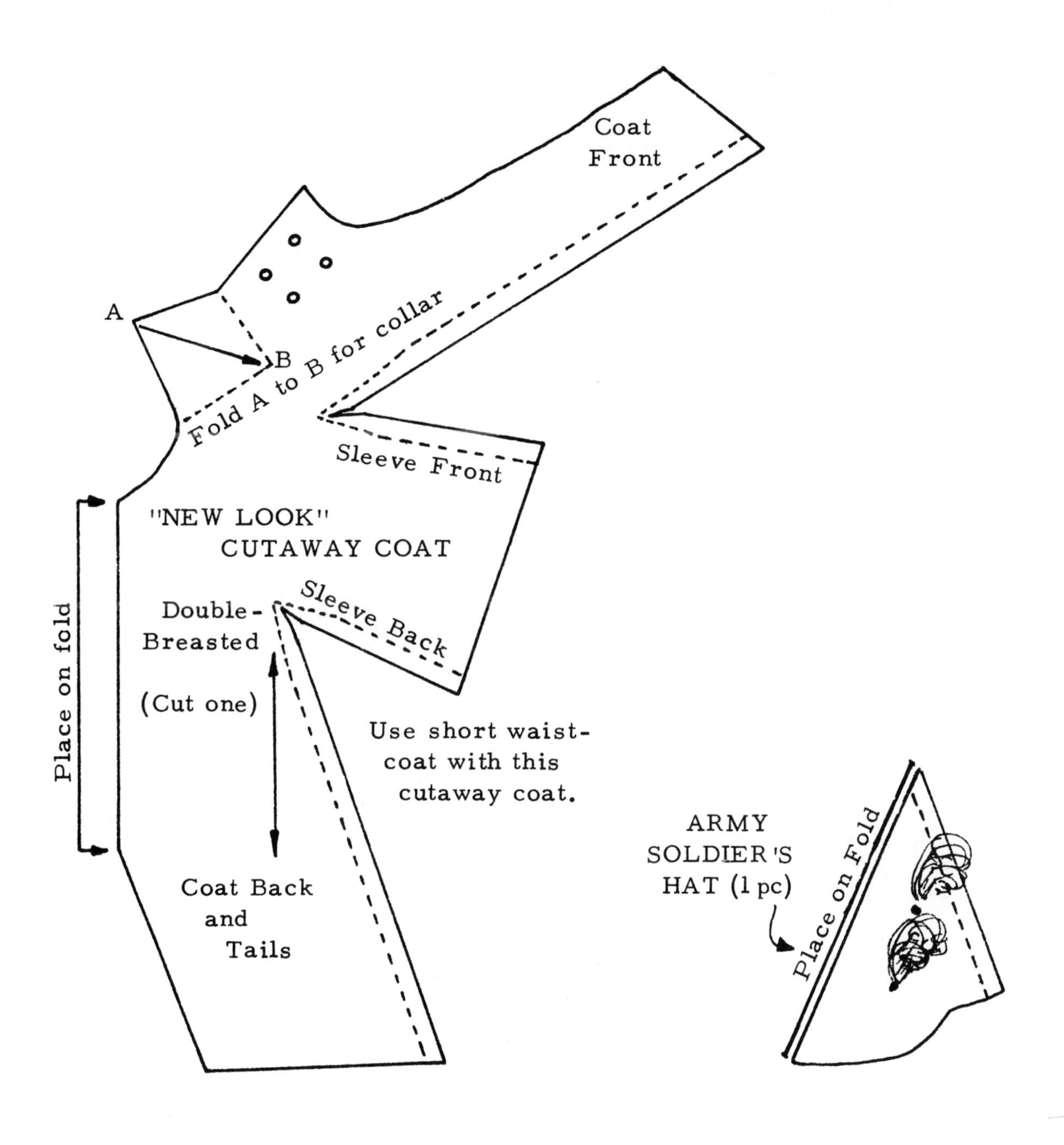

CRAVAT & "SHIRT" CUFFS

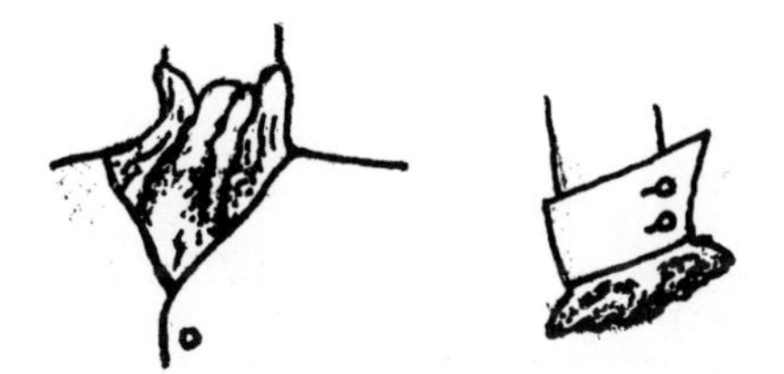

For a cravat, use 3 inches of 1-inch-wide lace. Tie it around the neck.

For "shirt" cuffs, ruffle 1-inch-wide lace (to match the cravat) around the wrist. Tuck it under the coat cuffs.

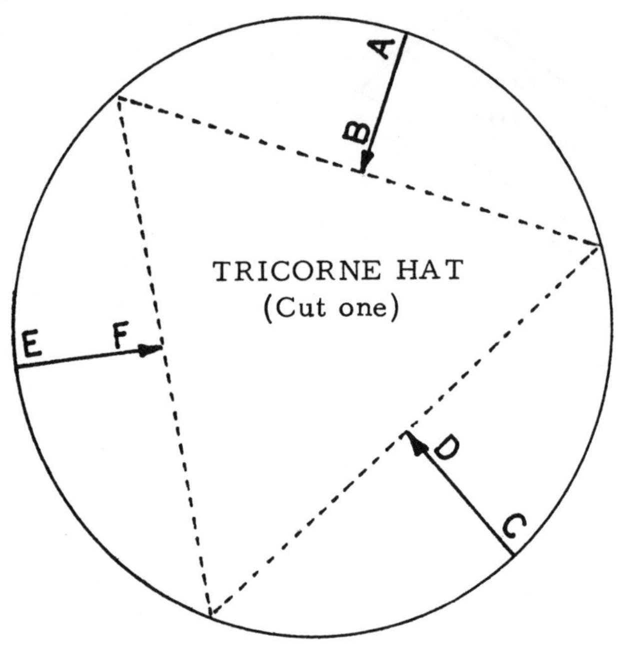

For a tricorne hat, follow the directions and illustration for the Gainsborough hat on page 168. In addition, tie three corners of the hat (while wet) as shown. Remove when dry and trim with braid.

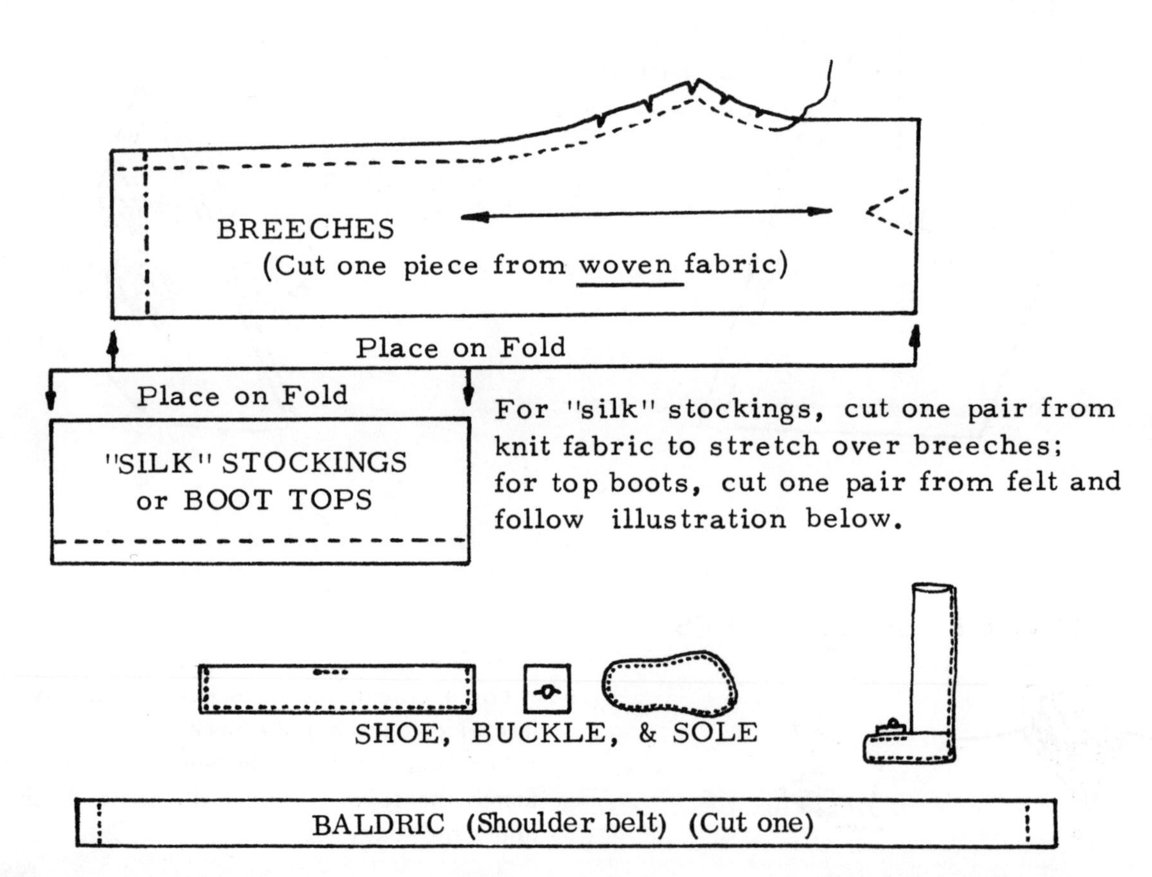

For "silk" stockings, cut one pair from knit fabric to stretch over breeches; for top boots, cut one pair from felt and follow illustration below.

The Dolls' Wigs

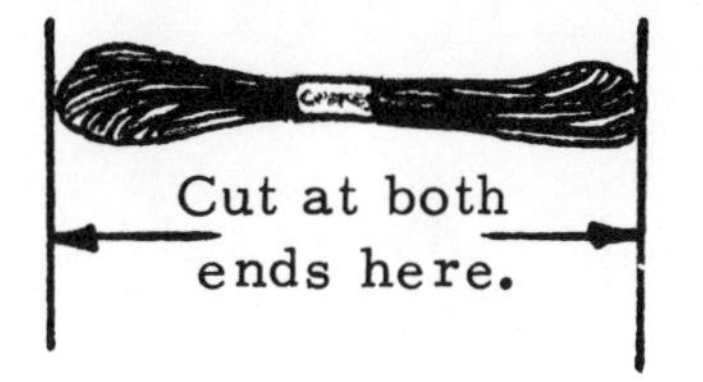

How to sew floss to strip of fabric.

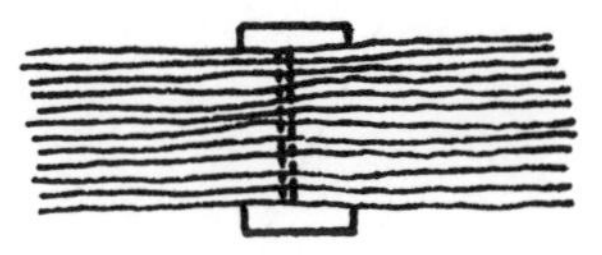

Most of today's four- to six-inch dress-me dolls come with long, straight artificial hair that is too difficult to curl on dolls so miniature. Therefore, you have to make colonial-style wigs for all the men (cadogans) and for most of the women (pompadours).

In addition, since manufacturers just do not make male dress-me dolls in the 4-to-6-inch size, you have to use female dolls and oil paint masculine features on their faces. You "paint off" the eye make-up and "paint on" heavy eyebrows. And, if the faces still look feminine, that's all right, too—18th century men used make-up, and perfume, just as much as the women did. And both sexes wore wigs!

For the women's wigs, use a skein of embroidery floss (nine yards of six-strand floss) and cut at both ends. Cut a strip of cloth (the same color as the floss) about $1\frac{1}{2} \times 1\frac{1}{2}$ inches. Spread the floss to about 1 inch across and sew it to the cloth. Trim away the excess cloth. Curl the ends of the floss with scissors by placing floss between the blade edge of the scissors and your thumb, and scraping the floss across the blade until the floss curls (see the illustration). Glue the wig on the doll's head. Fashion the floss to stand high on the doll's head for a pompadour look (see the photographs of the women). The floss is very malleable and you can fashion it into any desired hair style.

For the men's cadogans, make a shorter version of the women's wig. For variation, you can leave some longer strands in the back for tying into a pigtail.

Illustration showing how to curl embroidery floss wig.

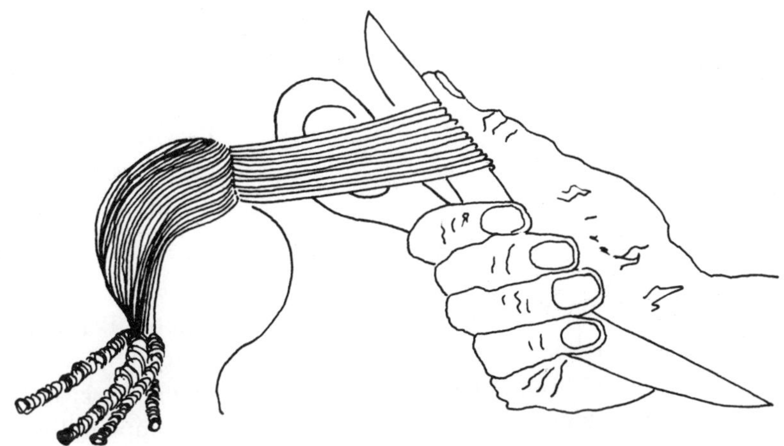

Suppliers

In addition to the suppliers listed here, local crafts, hobby, stationery, hardware and variety shops, as well as local fairs and department stores, are excellent sources for materials. Also, do not forget to search through your discards for useful items!

Avon Products Inc.
2940 E. Foothill Boulevard
Pasadena, California 91107
Headquarters: 9 West 57th Street
New York, N.Y. 10019
Sample lipstick tubes for drinking beakers.

Bandwagon, Inc.
401 Summer Street
Boston, Massachusetts 02210
Weave Easy Hand Loom® for hand-looming rugs. Includes easy-to-follow instructions on how to loom.

Colonial Craftsmen
Division of Cape May Country Store
Cape May, New Jersey 08204
Pewter dresser set.

Cunningham Art Products, Inc.
1555 Roadhaven Drive
Stone Mountain, Georgia 30083
Miniature door hinges.

The Flea Market
Tijuana, Mexico
Just below the California-Mexico border, there are numerous artisans who craft their own earthenware and glass-blown pots, dishes, cups, and figurines in perfect scale for dollhouses. You can find similar items in crafts, hobby and variety shops anywhere.

Grey Iron Casting Company
P.O. Box 40
Wrightsville, Pennsylvania 17368
Black cast iron pots and pans.

Gries Reproducer Co.
Division of Coats & Clark Inc.
Beechwood Avenue
New Rochelle, New York 10802
Miniature combination lock.

Knott's Berry Farm
Beach Boulevard (Highway #39)
Buena Park, California 90620
Complete line of dollhouse miniatures.

The Last Straw
446 Alisal Road
Solvang, California 93463
Miniature straw baskets.

Lesney Products
141 W. Commercial Avenue
Moonachie, New Jersey 07074
Four-inch Matchbox® dolls for dollhouse child dolls.

Lovelia Enterprises Inc.
2 Tudor City Place
New York, New York 10017
Beautiful prints of 18th century American and Oriental scenes to cut out from Lovelia's tapestries catalog. Send 50¢ and self-addressed, stamped envelope for a catalog of tapestries.

Mini Mundus Lumberyard and Shop
1030 Lexington Avenue
New York, New York 10021
Materials, supplies and furnishings for dollhouses.

Moskatel's
717 South San Julian St.
Los Angeles, California 90014
All decoration and crafts supplies, including gold leaf supplies; cake decorations and party favors to use as miniature bric-a-brac; plastic doilies for rosette ceiling moulding and for decorated plaster ceiling.

Natalie's Doll Shop
463-B Alisal Road
Solvang, California 93463
Dollhouse miniatures, including German handcrafted Spielwaren miniatures.

Nevco Products Inc.
500 Nepperhan Avenue
Yonkers, New York 10701
Decorative picture hooks in the shape of eagles to use as adornment on furniture and mirrors.

Santa Claus Lane Novelty Shop
Hwy. #101
Santa Claus, California 93013
Tea sets.

B. Shackman & Co. Inc.
85 Fifth Avenue
New York, New York 10003
Wooden kitchen utensils (made in Mexico); complete line of dollhouse dolls and miniatures.

Tiny Line
J. Hermes
P.O. Box 4023
El Monte, California 91731
Dollhouse wallpaper.

Lillian Vernon
510 South Fulton Avenue
Mt. Vernon, New York 10550
Mini-sized rose-studded picture frames; will engrave name-plate on these frames.

William E. Wright & Sons Co.
South Street
West Warren, Massachusetts 01092
Laces and trims.

Wyeth Laboratories Inc.
King of Prussia Road & Lancaster Avenue
Radnor, Pennsylvania 19088
Eyewash cup for kitchen coal bucket.

Index

Italics indicate Patterns and/or Instructions.